CHAUCER STUDIES XXXVIII

MEN AND MASCULINITIES IN CHAUCER'S *TROILUS AND CRISEYDE*

CHAUCER STUDIES

ISSN 0261-9822

Previously published volumes in this series
are listed at the back of this book

MEN AND MASCULINITIES IN
CHAUCER'S *TROILUS AND CRISEYDE*

Edited by
TISON PUGH
MARCIA SMITH MARZEC

D. S. BREWER

First published 2008
D. S. Brewer, Cambridge

Transferred to digital printing

ISBN 978–1–84384–160–9
ISSN 0261–9822

D. S. Brewer is an imprint of Boydell & Brewer Ltd
PO Box 9, Woodbridge, Suffolk IP12 3DF, UK
and of Boydell & Brewer Inc.
668 Mt Hope Avenue, Rochester, NY 14620, USA
website: www.boydellandbrewer.com

A CiP catalogue record for this book is available
from the British Library

This publication is printed on acid-free paper

Contents

Contributors

John M. Bowers, a Guggenheim and National Endowment for the Humanities Fellow, is Professor of English at the University of Nevada, Las Vegas. He is the author of several books including *Chaucer and Langland: The Antagonistic Tradition* and *The Politics of* Pearl: *Court Poetry in the Age of Richard II*, as well as numerous articles.

Michael Calabrese, Professor of English at California State University, Los Angeles, is the author of *Chaucer's Ovidian Arts of Love* and many articles on medieval literature, including studies of *Cleanness*, Marco Polo, Abelard and Heloïse, Boccaccio, and Chaucer in such journals as *Philological Quarterly, Medievalia et Humanistica*, and *Studies in the Age of Chaucer*. He is an editor of the Piers Plowman Electronic Archive.

Holly A. Crocker is Assistant Professor of English at the University of South Carolina. She is author of *Chaucer's Visions of Manhood* and editor of *Comic Provocations: Exposing the Corpus of Old French Fabliaux*. She has published many articles on premodern masculinities, including essays in *Chaucer Review, Shakespeare Quarterly*, and *Studies in the Age of Chaucer*.

Kate Koppelman is Assistant Professor of English at Seattle University, where she teaches classes in medieval and early modern literature, critical theory, and composition. She has published essays on devotional literature, *Beowulf*, the Old English *Judith*, and detective fiction. She is currently working on a project investigating the signifying history of the Virgin Mary in late medieval England.

Molly A. Martin is Assistant Professor at McNeese State University in Lake Charles, Louisiana. She recently completed her PhD in medieval English literature at Purdue University. Her current project investigates gender and vision in Malory's *Morte D'Arthur*.

Marcia Smith Marzec is Professor of English at the University of St. Francis, where she coordinates a national symposium showcasing undergraduate research in English. She also directs the university's sophomore core program. She has published articles on medieval literature and textual studies, as well as pedagogical articles in the MLA *Approaches* series and *Studies in Medieval and Renaissance Teaching*. With Cindy Vitto, she edited *New Perspectives on Criseyde*.

Gretchen Mieszkowski is Professor of Literature at the University of Houston, Clear Lake. She is the author of *Medieval Go-Betweens and Chaucer's Pandarus* and *The Reputation of Criseyde: 1155–1500*. She has been a Fellow of the American Council of Learned Societies and the Radcliffe Institute of Advanced

Study. Mieszkowski has taught at the University of Chicago, Yale University, and Queen's University, Canada. Her PhD, in English, is from Yale University.

James J. Paxson teaches medieval literature and literary theory at the University of Florida. He is author of *The Poetics of Personification* and has co-edited *Desiring Discourse: The Literature of Love, Ovid through Chaucer* and *The Performance of Middle English Culture: Essays on Chaucer and the Drama in Honor of Martin Stevens*. He is an editor of *Exemplaria: A Journal of Theory in Medieval and Renaissance Studies*.

Tison Pugh is Associate Professor of English at the University of Central Florida. He is the author of *Queering Medieval Genres* and *Sexuality and Its Queer Discontents in Middle English Literature*. With Angela Jane Weisl of Seton Hall University, he edited *Approaches to Teaching Chaucer's* Troilus and Criseyde *and the Shorter Poems*; with Lynn Ramey of Vanderbilt University, he edited *Race, Class, and Gender in "Medieval" Cinema*.

R. Allen Shoaf, a former Marshall Scholar and Danforth Fellow and recipient of two Fellowships of the National Endowment for the Humanities, is the author of eleven books, including *Chaucer's Body, Shakespeare's Theater of Likeness*, and *Milton, Poet of Duality*. Over the past twenty years at the University of Florida, he has won six teaching awards as well as the Alumni Professorship in the Department of English. With the late Julian N. Wasserman, he founded the prize-winning journal *Exemplaria*.

Robert S. Sturges has taught at MIT, Wesleyan University, and the University of New Orleans; he is now Professor of English at Arizona State University. He has published numerous essays on medieval literature and is the author of three books: *Medieval Interpretation* (1991), *Chaucer's Pardoner and Gender Theory* (2000), and *Dialogue and Deviance* (2005). He is now working on a new edition and translation of *Aucassin et Nicolette*.

Angela Jane Weisl is Associate Professor of English at Seton Hall University. She is the author of *Conquering the Reign of Femeny: Gender and Genre in Chaucer's Romance* and *The Persistence of Medievalism: Narrative Adventures in Contemporary Culture*. With Cindy L. Carlson she edited *Constructions of Widowhood and Virginity in the Middle Ages*, and with Tison Pugh, *Approaches to Teaching Chaucer's* Troilus and Criseyde *and the Shorter Poems*.

Richard Zeikowitz is Associate Professor of English at John Jay College, the City University of New York. He is the author of *Homoeroticism and Chivalry: Discourses of Male Same-Sex Desire in the Fourteenth Century*. His articles, which apply queer theories to the reading of medieval and modern texts, have appeared in *College English, Dalhousie Review, College Literature*, and the *Journal of Modern Literature*.

Abbreviations

BMMA	Jeffrey Jerome Cohen and Bonnie Wheeler, eds., *Becoming Male in the Middle Ages* (New York: Garland, 1997)
ChauR	*Chaucer Review*
CIMM	Jacqueline Murray, ed., *Conflicted Identities and Multiple Masculinities: Men in the Medieval West* (New York: Garland, 1999)
CTC	R. A. Shoaf, ed., *Chaucer's* Troilus and Criseyde*: "Subjit to alle poesy": Essays in Criticism* (Binghamton, NY: Medieval & Renaissance Texts & Studies, 1992)
CTEC	Stephen Barney, ed., *Chaucer's Troilus: Essays in Criticism* (Hamden, CT: Archon, 1980)
EETS	Early English Text Society
ELH	*English Literary History*
ETC	Mary Salu, ed., *Essays on Troilus and Criseyde* (Cambridge: D. S. Brewer, 1979)
JEGP	*Journal of English and Germanic Philology*
JMEMS	*Journal of Medieval and Early Modern Studies*
MC	Peter Beidler, ed., *Masculinities in Chaucer: Approaches to Maleness in the* Canterbury Tales *and* Troilus and Criseyde (Cambridge: D. S. Brewer, 1998)
MED	*Middle English Dictionary*
MH	*Medievalia et Humanistica*
MM	Clare Lees, ed., *Medieval Masculinities: Regarding Men in the Middle Ages* (Minneapolis: University of Minnesota Press, 1994)
MME	D. M. Hadley, ed., *Masculinity in Medieval Europe* (London: Longman, 1999)
MP	*Modern Philology*
NPC	Cindy Vitto and Marcia Smith Marzec, eds., *New Perspectives on Criseyde* (Asheville, NC: Pegasus, 2004)
PLL	*Papers on Language and Literature*
PMLA	*Publications of the Modern Language Association*
PQ	*Philological Quarterly*
SAC	*Studies in the Age of Chaucer*
SP	*Studies in Philology*
YLS	*Yearbook of Langland Studies*

All quotations of Chaucer are taken from *The Riverside Chaucer*, ed. Larry Benson, 3rd edn. (Boston: Houghton Mifflin, 1987). In quotations of medieval literature, we have used modern equivalents for medieval letters.

Introduction:
The Myths of Masculinity in Chaucer's
Troilus and Criseyde

TISON PUGH, MICHAEL CALABRESE and MARCIA SMITH MARZEC

What is a man? What groups together approximately half of the humans on this planet, in contrast to the other half? Jacqueline Murray states it bluntly, noting that the male genitals are "inextricably linked to a man's sense of self and his masculine identity."[1] Although this formulation may appear somewhat stark, it is not to be left aside, for the physical form upon which masculinity is enacted and thus reproduced must be taken into account in analyzing the intersections between masculinities (the cultural constructions of gender in relation to male bodies) and men. Beyond the physical presence of genitals on male bodies, men are also expected to perform sexually in the enactment of masculinity.[2] Confronting these bald facts helps us to achieve the goals of masculinity studies, one of which is, as Murray states, to "reinsert men into the picture, men *qua* men, men in their historical and cultural specificity."[3] Thus, we see that penises – those floppy appendages, subject to irrepressibly awkward and sometimes invited tumescence – matter; they make men, and although we need not dip too deeply into psychoanalysis in this brief introduction, they also highlight fundamental biological differences between men and women that influence other factors of personal identity. In offering this volume of essays, *Men and Masculinities in Chaucer's* Troilus and Criseyde, we hope to continue the ongoing process of understanding the ways in which gender and sexuality underpin (and at times undermine) human relationships.

Men and Masculinities in Chaucer's Troilus and Criseyde explores issues relating to the male characters and the construction of masculinities within Chaucer's masterpiece of love gained and love lost. The volume addresses the questions of what it means to be a man in the Middle Ages, what constitutes

---

1 Jacqueline Murray, "Introduction," *CIMM*, p. xv.
2 The history of performance anxiety is worthy of its own study. To look at one brief example, Shannon McSheffrey explores the "importance of virility and sexual prowess in male reputation" from a case in London in 1515 in which "Robert Harding testifies that he had bedded the 'whore' Katherine Worsley simply to prove that he could, because otherwise Katherine might tell women in the parish that he was impotent and scuttle his courtship of a wealthy widow" ("Men and Masculinity in Late Medieval London Civic Culture: Governance, Patriarchy, and Reputation," *CIMM*, 243–78, at p. 265).
3 Jacqueline Murray, "Introduction," p. x.

masculinity in this era, how masculinities are culturally constructed (despite their cultural contradictions), and how gaps between historical men and literary representations of men enable fantasies of male identity to flourish; it seeks to advance scholarly understanding of the themes, characters, and actions of *Troilus and Criseyde* through the hermeneutics of medieval and modern conceptions of masculinity. For example, Troilus is subject to multiple and conflicting interpretations, especially in regard to the intersections of his masculinity with his sexual performance, his masochistic suffering, and his embodiment of a heroic ethos second only to his brother Hector's. Likewise, Pandarus plays on the borders of normative male identities, especially in regard to the latent homoeroticism in his relationship with Troilus. Minor characters such as Hector and Diomede give Chaucer room to consider further the range of masculine behavior and to establish comparative touchstones through which to analyze the masculine behavior of his protagonist. Even Criseyde has a place in this collection, for if gender is socially constructed, we can examine her masculinity in terms of how she oscillates between gendered positions ostensibly suggestive of feminine and masculine behaviors; we can also use her relationships with the male characters as a lens for examining the creation and maintenance of masculine identity. In sum, the circulating masculinities of *Troilus and Criseyde* structure much of the meaning of this enigmatic text; this collection of essays expands critical discussions of the ways in which Chaucer depicts contradictory models of masculinity within his re-creation of the Trojan world.

Since Clare Lees's *Medieval Masculinities: Regarding Men in the Middle Ages*, numerous important studies of medieval men have appeared that query the cultural meanings of maleness in the Middle Ages, including Jeffrey Jerome Cohen and Bonnie Wheeler's *Becoming Male in the Middle Ages*, D. M. Hadley's *Masculinity in Medieval Europe*, Jacqueline Murray's *Conflicted Identities and Multiple Masculinities: Men in the Medieval West*, Ruth Mazo Karras's *From Boys to Men: Formations of Masculinity in Late Medieval Europe*, and William Burgwinkle's *Sodomy, Masculinity, and Law in Medieval Literature*.[4] These studies analyze men from a variety of perspectives, but they unite in underscoring the necessity of looking for various masculinities and the diversity of their embodiments rather than at an overarching sense of masculinity. Refuting decades of scholarship that viewed maleness as an unproblematic reflection of the ruling half of the aristocracy, scholars now demand a new perspective by "revis[ing] the emphasis on 'hegemonic' males – the kings, princes, lawmakers, and so forth – that can obscure the rich and varied evidence for men's history in ways similar to the better-known silencing of women's history."[5] As is well understood, a scholarly emphasis on hegemonic masculinity marginalizes women, and this

---

[4]   Citational information for the essay collections of Lees, Cohen and Wheeler, Hadly, and Murray are available in the "Abbreviations" section, p. ix. See also Ruth Mazo Karras, *From Boys to Men: Formations of Masculinity in Late Medieval Europe* (Philadelphia: University of Pennsylvania Press, 2003) and William Burgwinkle, *Sodomy, Masculinity, and Law in Medieval Literature: France and England, 1050–1230* (Cambridge: Cambridge University Press, 2004).

[5]   Clare Lees, "Introduction: Men's Studies, Women's Studies, Medieval Studies," *MM*, xv–xxv, at p. xv.

dynamic must be investigated and exposed if we are to understand the ways in which women's experience has been obscured from the historical record; similarly, nonhegemonic men often suffer under cultural constructions of dominant masculinity in which they cannot participate, and so too must these dynamics be explored in all of their sociohistoric complexity if we are to comprehend who benefits and who loses from ideological constructions of gender.

As the most significant effort to date in Chaucerian masculinities studies, Peter Beidler's *Masculinities in Chaucer: Approaches to Maleness in the* Canterbury Tales *and* Troilus and Criseyde includes many remarkable essays and has greatly advanced gender criticism of Chaucer's works. Masculinity studies tend to proceed with caution because some scholars feel that feminist readers will see the study of men as somehow antithetical or hostile to feminist projects. Consider, therefore, Beidler's prefatory apologia: "It goes without saying – but let me say it anyhow – that it is not part of our project to 'erase' women by spending all these pages on masculinities."[6] One sees eight years later a similar disclaimer by Ruth Mazo Karras: "It should go without saying – but perhaps does not – that a feminist scholar's writing a book on men and masculinity does not represent a recantation of feminist views."[7] In this climate of politicized caution, it is apparent that masculinities studies must acknowledge the need for continued focus on feminist studies. Studying men is not an attempt to turn the tide back against women but to advance the study of both genders – as well as the contested cultural space between them – and their role in building men and women.

As masculinities studies emerges not simply as another critical approach that manufactures politicized readings according to canned rhetorical models but as a valid historical inquiry into human lives not studied or understood during or before feminism, one hopes that these *apologiae* will no longer be necessary. Additionally, like many masculinities, feminist, and gender studies in the 1980s and 1990s, Beidler's volume relies on the assertion that "Chaucerian masculinity is more a matter of gender than of sex. That is, masculinity has little to do with one's biology but much with one's reaction to and relations with others."[8] Hadley avers that "it has come to be accepted that gender is socially constructed,"[9] and Karras likewise declares "'[m]asculinity' does not refer to the male body, whose biological and anatomical features remain relatively constant among different men and over time, but rather to the meanings that society puts on a person with a male body, which do change over time."[10] As is apparent from these citations, Judith Butler's theories of gender as a performative system of meaning informs much literary analysis, as she trenchantly observes that gender creates a double bind of identity enacted both consciously and unconsciously:

---

6   Peter Beidler, "Introduction," *MC*, 1–5, at p. 3.
7   Ruth Mazo Karras, *From Boys to Men*, pp. 18–19.
8   Peter Beidler, "Introduction," p. 3. This is not true of all the essays in *Masculinities in Chaucer*, but it is asserted by Beidler as one of the "most general theses" of the volume (p. 3).
9   D. M. Hadley, "Introduction: Medieval Masculinities," *MME*, p. 1.
10 Ruth Mazo Karras, *From Boys to Men*, p. 3.

> If gender is a kind of doing, an incessant activity performed, in part, without one's knowing and without one's willing, it is not for that reason automatic or mechanical. On the contrary, it is a practice of improvisation within a scene of constraint. Moreover, one does not "do" one's gender alone. One is always "doing" with or for another, even if the other is only imaginary.[11]

The ideological forces that create and regulate identities require people – in both their consciousnesses and their bodies – to enact genders, but this does not therefore construe gender as a "natural" and "true" representation of reality. Gender can be understood as a biologically inflected mythology of identity, one grounded in a body that nonetheless reveals the at times arbitrary connections between bodies and genders.

The distinction between nature and nurture is critical to understanding the ways in which gender roles conscript and coerce "appropriate" behaviors, but this distinction potentially excludes the realities of the body, which has, for its part, also been one of the major concerns of medieval studies in the past twenty years.[12] We seem to have a sense that gender is constructed solely to preserve oppression and patriarchy: as the evolutionary psychologist Anne Campbell puts it, "the prevailing dogma is that the distinction between men and women is a collective and tyrannical fiction."[13] Social roles make demands of both men and women, but the roles may, far from being entirely arbitrary or perniciously designed to oppress women, be rooted to some degree in biology, physical strength, sex drives, and the different roles in procreation and competition, as has been studied widely in the scientific community. Campbell addresses both the naiveté and the political opportunism of those who belittle biology in favor of social construction and relativistic arguments about sexual roles and behavior.[14]

Performative and citational analyses of gender should not thus be discarded but further investigated, and the same holds true for studies of sexuality. The dominant models of sexuality in the twenty-first century – heterosexuality and homosexuality – ask us to see a great divide between desires, culturally lionizing the former and typically casting the latter with suspicion, if not outright

---

[11] Judith Butler, *Undoing Gender* (New York: Routledge, 2004), p. 1. See also her *Gender Trouble: Feminism and the Subversion of Identity* (New York: Routledge, 1990) and *Bodies That Matter: On the Discursive Limits of "Sex"* (New York: Routledge, 1993).

[12] Recent studies of the body in the Middle Ages include Manuele Gragnolati, *Experiencing the Afterlife: Soul and Body in Dante and Medieval Culture* (Notre Dame, IN: Notre Dame University Press, 2005); Liz Herbert McAvoy, *Authority and the Female Body in the Writings of Julian of Norwich and Margery Kempe* (Cambridge: D. S. Brewer, 2004); Sergio Bertelli, *The King's Body: Sacred Rituals of Power in Medieval and Early Modern Europe*, trans. Burr Litchfield (University Park: Pennsylvania State University Press, 2001); Bruce Holsinger, *Music, Body, and Desire in Medieval Culture* (Stanford, CA: Stanford University Press, 2001); and Darryll Grantley and Nina Taunton, eds., *The Body in Late Medieval and Early Modern Culture* (Aldershot, England: Ashgate, 2000).

[13] Anne Campbell, *A Mind of Her Own: The Evolutionary Psychology of Women* (Oxford: Oxford University Press, 2002), p. 1.

[14] See, in particular, her introductory chapter, "Biophobia and the Study of Sex Differences," pp. 1–33, which summarizes the debates about sex typing, social conditioning, and human biology, as well as Simon Baron Cohen, *The Essential Difference: Men, Women, and the Extreme Male Brain* (London: Allen Lane, 2003).

denigration. Transporting modern notions of sexuality back to the Middle Ages carries enormous hermeneutic risks, and scholars such as Karma Lochrie and James Schultz warn that today's sexual models cannot be used to analyze sexualities of the Middle Ages: "it seems reckless, to say the least, for medievalists to continue to use the crude, ham-fisted concept of heteronormativity to describe medieval sexualities and desires," declares Lochrie.[15] Schultz agrees: "The Middle Ages had no notion of sexual orientation."[16] Modern sexual norms cannot be ahistorically transported to the past to make sense of a past that is so different from our present.

But if sexual orientation was not a category of interest to the people of the Middle Ages, sexual activity was, and scores of writings document the ways in which sexual acts and actors were praised and condemned, celebrated and mocked. We must try to recapture the different constructions of sexual normativity in the Middle Ages within their proper social contexts, whether, for example, the "aristophilia" Schultz documents in courtly literature or the continued focus on disruptive sexualities in monasteries.[17] Lochrie and Schultz are correct that heteronormativity, as we understand the term today, did not exist in the Middle Ages, but codes of normativity in relation to sexuality certainly did exist, as penitential manuals, law codes, and the literary record attest. With *Troilus and Criseyde*, the problems of defining normativity – whether the normativity of gender or of sexuality – in relation to any code of conduct becomes increasingly difficult because we must also contextualize which normative codes Chaucer might be employing for his tale: those of the fourteenth-century English court as filtered through centuries of French romances and French courtiers, or those of his re-creation of classical Trojan society as mediated through his sources? Does Chaucer write the masculinities of *Troilus and Criseyde* looking through the lens of fourteenth-century Catholicism, or of English civic culture? The various mythologies of masculinity generated within each of these overlapping yet discrete arenas testify to the complexity of pinpointing masculinity and its effects. With so many competing and, at times, complementary mythologies about the meanings of maleness, it becomes difficult, and possibly counterproductive, to isolate a dominant model of Chaucerian masculinity, as this could obscure the ways in which multiple masculinities function together.

What scholars of medieval gender and sexuality are faced with, then, is the murkiness of the past. Its genders and sexualities are recognizably different from our own, yet, adding another level of complexity to an already rich amalgam, our

[15] Karma Lochrie, *Heterosyncrasies: Female Sexuality When Normal Wasn't* (Minneapolis: University of Minnesota Press, 2005), p. xvii.

[16] James Schultz, *Courtly Love, the Love of Courtliness, and the History of Sexuality* (Chicago, IL: University of Chicago Press, 2006), p. 57.

[17] See James Schultz, "Aristophilia," in *Courtly Love, the Love of Courtliness, and the History of Sexuality*, pp. 79–98. For disruptive sexualities in monasteries, see such studies as Christopher Jones, "Monastic Identity and Sodomitic Danger in the *Occupatio* by Odo of Cluny," *Speculum* 82.1 (2007): 1–53; V. A. Kolve, "Ganymede / *Son of Getron*: Medieval Monasticism and the Drama of Same-Sex Desire," *Speculum* 73 (1998): 1014–67; Mark D. Jordan, *The Invention of Sodomy in Christian Theology* (Chicago, IL: University of Chicago Press, 1997); and John Boswell, *Christianity, Social Tolerance, and Homosexuality* (Chicago, IL: University of Chicago Press, 1980).

own experiences with our genders, bodies, desires, and sexualities necessarily provide another filter through which to view the past. Particularly for readers of literature, such a dual perspective can be more liberating than limiting. We want to understand the Middle Ages on its own terms, but that does not therefore entail the need to experience literature as it was experienced by its original audience. Rather, the perpetual anachronism inherent in any act of reading – in that every time a text is picked up subsequent to its penning, it is a little bit further from its historical circumstances – creates a new space to consider gender and sexuality in the past in relation to gender and sexuality in the present.

To study gender and sexuality, then, is to study a cultural mythology peculiar to its time and place that nonetheless bubbles with meaning in relation to both its past and its future. Mythologies matter: they comprise the spoken and unspoken guidelines of a society, yet they rarely communicate precisely. Roland Barthes claims that "Myth hides nothing and flaunts nothing: it distorts; myth is neither a lie nor a confession: it is an inflexion."[18] Scholars must simultaneously decode and pierce these mythologies to deflate them of their sacrosanct status while nonetheless recognizing the significance of their cultural work. This is the perspective we adopt in this volume: that the mythologies of gender and sexuality in general, and of masculinity and normative sexuality in particular, matter, but these mythologies must be explored if one is to understand other mythologies as well. As Holly Crocker declares, one of the most pervasive mythologies of masculinity limns it as invisible and thus as completely natural: "As *the marker* of the ordinary, masculinity gathers material power by putting on the veil of visible neutrality."[19] Normative masculinity proceeds through the invisibility made possible by mythology, and in this system, the visible are the different, the Other(ed). The marginalized are no less mythic, and the contributors to this volume, despite their kaleidoscopic variety in theoretical approaches, unite in tackling the cultural myths of masculinity in Chaucer's *Troilus and Criseyde*.

The first two essays of *Men and Masculinities in Chaucer's* Troilus and Criseyde look at the meaning of masculinity in relationship to constructions of monarchy and sovereignty. In "'Beautiful as Troilus': Richard II, Chaucer's Troilus, and Figures of (Un)Masculinity," John Bowers examines Chaucer's depictions of masculinity in *Troilus and Criseyde* and certain *Canterbury Tales* as mirroring the suspect masculinities of Richard II's court. Citing Richard Maidstone's *Concordia*, which describes Richard as "beautiful as Troilus," Bowers argues that the elegant but sexually inept young Troilus impugns the masculine performance of Richard in his own marriage. In "The State of Exception and Sovereign Masculinity in *Troilus and Criseyde*," Robert Sturges approaches his subject from the perspective of Giorgio Agamben's political theory, investigating the operation of a specifically sex-linked biopolitics in Chaucer's poem. Sturges concludes that the poem can be seen as both resisting and reinforcing sovereign male power, and he discusses the meaning of this ambiguity in relation to definitions of masculine privilege.

---

[18]   Roland Barthes, *Mythologies*, trans. Annette Lavers (New York: Hill & Wang, 1972), p. 129.
[19]   Holly Crocker, *Chaucer's Visions of Manhood* (New York: Palgrave, 2007), p. 1; her italics.

Troilus's masculinity is frequently questioned, and the next four essays address this character in his somewhat contradictory roles as romance lover and epic hero. Responding to recent criticism that castigates Troilus for his famous swoon and suggests his sexual inadequacy, Gretchen Mieszkowski, in "Revisiting Troilus's Faint," traces the history of the male swoon in romance literature of the Middle Ages to defend Troilus from aspersions against his masculinity. She explains that the faint was geared to show Troilus's sensitivity and spiritual greatness, as well as the magnitude of his love. Examining the allusions to Hector in *Troilus and Criseyde*, as well as the character's actual appearances, and drawing upon the audience's knowledge of the character from other, earlier medieval treatments, Marcia Smith Marzec argues that Chaucer uses the hero Hector as Troilus's foil to illustrate the inverse relationship between martial and sexual prowess. Her essay, "What Makes a Man? Troilus, Hector, and the Masculinities of Courtly Love," shows that sexual involvement outside marriage weakens and feminizes a knight. James Paxson contrasts markedly "male" activity regarding the tracing or realizing of architecture and building (in the architecture of Pandarus's house) with the poem's enshrinement of nonsanctioned activities that define the lover as lover. His essay, "Masculinity and Its Hydraulic Semiotics in Chaucer's *Troilus and Criseyde*," reveals that the semiotically charged moment of the lover Troilus's spilling of ink and tears onto his initial letter to Criseyde, collated with his correspondent male and dominant action upon his desires, programs the poem's opposition to the biophysical paradigm of potential masculinity through biblical allegory. In "Masochism, Masculinity, and the Pleasures of Troilus," Holly Crocker and Tison Pugh explore the dichotomy between Troilus's masochistic pain and the readers' desire for pleasure. Troilus's pain in courtly love, as well as the ways in which Chaucer hints that Troilus discovers some latent pleasure in his pain, structures the unfolding narrative and multiplies readers' pleasures.

Criseyde's vexed relationship to men and masculinities serves as the basis of the two following chapters. In "'The Dreams in Which I'm Dying': Sublimation and Unstable Masculinities in *Troilus and Criseyde*," Kate Koppelman investigates Criseyde and her particular relationship to the creation and maintenance of masculine identity throughout Chaucer's poem. As a focus of the males' sublimated desires and the locus of their sense of identity, Criseyde reveals (through her fears, dreams, and reading) the fantasies that highlight the instability of those masculine subject positions that look to her for confirmation and sanction. In "'A Mannes Game': Criseyde's Masculinity in *Troilus and Criseyde*," Angela Jane Weisl examines Criseyde's occupation of the male space of the narrative that is vacated by Troilus through his courtly love behavior. The essay maintains that Criseyde is condemned in the later books because of her acts of self-protection and that the condemnation results not from her rejection of her position as the masculinized lady created by the romance genre, but rather in her at least partially successful attempt to preserve it.

In many ways, spectatorship is a gendered act, and the subsequent two essays of *Men and Masculinities in Chaucer's* Troilus and Criseyde explore the dynamics of vision and masculinity in the text. In "Troilus's Gaze and the

Collapse of Masculinity in Romance," Molly Martin asserts that Chaucer purges the romance of genre conventions that threaten masculine hegemony, with these changes functioning on the axes of vision and gender. Exploring the interconnection of gender and genre in the text, Martin explains how Chaucer attempts to solve the visual incompatibility of masculinity and romance. Richard Zeikowitz explores the link between homoerotically charged visual dynamics and masculinity in *Troilus and Criseyde* by applying the cinematic mechanism of *suture* – the shot/reverse shot whereby a character is "stitched into" the frame, giving the impression that the character is the viewing point in the initial shot – as a hermeneutic of desire. His "Sutured Looks and Homoeroticism: Reading Troilus and Pandarus Cinematically" examines the scene in Book 1 between Pandarus and Troilus and reveals the unstable power relations between the two by problematizing the concept of the gazer as active/masculine and the object of the gaze as passive/feminine.

The final two chapters of *Men and Masculinities in Chaucer's* Troilus and Criseyde explore Chaucerian masculinities in tandem with those of contemporary and descendant texts – William Langland's *Piers Plowman* and Shakespeare's *Troilus and Cressida*. In "Being a Man in *Piers Plowman* and *Troilus and Criseyde*," Michael Calabrese considers these two late fourteenth-century poems as parallel stories of men journeying, questing, and suffering as men in search of truth. Masculinities and male bodies relate the experiences of these two eponymous characters who dominate medieval fiction but whose names are seldom heard in the same sentence. R. Allen Shoaf's essay, " 'The Monstruosity in Love': Sexual Division in Chaucer and Shakespeare" is a parallel analysis of Chaucer's and Shakespeare's versions of the Troilus legend that isolates and demonstrates their respective realizations of the failure of the heroic ethos to code predictable gender in men and women. Shakespeare's understanding of the collapse of prescriptive gender roles, Shoaf maintains, finds its source in his awareness of the complex gender confusion in Chaucer's poem.

In sum, the essays of *Men and Masculinities in Chaucer's* Troilus and Criseyde ask readers to look with fresh eyes at the masculinities of this text and how they create and undermine narrative meaning. Mythologies of masculinity prevalent in the Middle Ages still bear enormous influence in today's society, and not merely in the recreational re-enactments of Hollywood blockbusters or societies of creative anachronism. Mythologies create roles through which real people measure their lives, and the need to examine them can hardly be overestimated. To this end, we turn to Chaucer's *Troilus and Criseyde*.

1

"Beautiful as Troilus": Richard II, Chaucer's Troilus, and Figures of (Un)Masculinity

JOHN M. BOWERS

In his description of Richard II's royal entry into London in 1392, Richard Maidstone, in his *Concordia*, lavishes praise upon the youthful king's handsomeness and sex-appeal by likening him to Troilus:

> Iste velud Troylus vel ut Absolon ipse decorus,
> Captivat sensum respicientis eum.
> Non opus est omnem regis describere formam:
> Regibus in cuntis non habet ille parem.
> Larga decoris ei si plus Natura dedisset,
> Clauderet hunc thalamis invida forte Venus!
>
> (He himself, beautiful as Troilus or as Absalom,
> Captures the attention of the onlooker.
> It takes no effort to describe the king's every feature:
> Among all earthly rulers he has no equal.
> If generous Nature had given him more beauty,
> Jealous Venus might have locked him in her bedroom!)[1]

This literary allusion raises the obvious question of what Maidstone implied when comparing the English king with the Trojan prince.[2]

The name Troilus did not enjoy wide currency in England before Chaucer's *Troilus and Criseyde* began circulating among metropolitan readers during the mid-1380s, although the semantic implications of Troilus as the nickname "Little Troy" would have gained resonance amid contemporary discussions celebrating London as the "New Troy." *St. Erkenwald* made this comparison explicit

[1] Richard Maidstone, *Concordia (The Reconciliation of Richard II with London)*, ed. David Carlson, trans. A. G. Rigg (Kalamazoo, MI: Medieval Institute, 2003), pp. 56–7 (lines 112–17); my translations throughout. See Gordon Kipling, "Richard II's 'Sumptuous Pageants' and the Idea of Civic Triumph," *Pageantry in the Shakespearean Theater*, ed. David Bergeron (Athens: University of Georgia Press, 1985), pp. 83–103.

[2] Not part of the brief reference by Virgil (*Aeneid*, 1.475), the depiction of Troilus as an unusually handsome youth carries over from the Greek tradition in less familiar accounts by Dictys (*De Bello Troiano* 4.9) and Dares (*De Excidio Troiae Historia* 12); see *The Trojan War: The Chronicles of Dictys of Crete and Dares the Phrygian*, trans. R. M. Frazer (Bloomington: Indiana University Press, 1966).

– "Now that London is neuenyd hatte the New Troie"[3] – and Maidstone himself reiterated this claim near the beginning of his *Concordia*: "bona felici sunt, Nova Troia, tibi!" – "blessings are yours, O happy New Troy."[4] John Gower's *Mirour de l'Omme* (*c.* 1377) made one of the earliest references to "the story of Troilus and fair Criseyde," perhaps as a work-in-progress.[5] The completed text was professionally copied by the scribe Adam Pinkhurst probably in the 1380s on evidence of Chaucer's humorous lyric "Adam Scriveyn."[6] The *Testament of Love* by Thomas Usk (d. 1388) cited the work as an authoritative English-language text on the subject of love: "In the *Boke of Troylus* the answere to thy questyon mayste thou lerne."[7] Even Langland's verb *troyledest* for "deceived" was perhaps prompted in the C revision by the name Troilus.[8]

These references indicate that *Troilus and Criseyde* was the primary Chaucerian work known widely among literate Londoners such as the poet's colleagues "moral Gower" and "philosophical Strode," named near the poem's end.[9] Only later does evidence suggest the Trojan love-tragedy became a staple for courtly readers. The Campsall manuscript of *Troilus* bears the arms of Henry V while he was still Prince of Wales between 1399 and 1413,[10] and Cambridge Corpus Christi MS 61 (*c.* 1415) was probably intended for Henry V as monarch.[11] Perhaps entirely fictionalized, this manuscript's famous frontis-

---

3   *The Complete Works of the* Pearl *Poet*, eds. Malcolm Andrew, Ronald Waldron, and Clifford Peterson, trans. Casey Finch (Berkeley: University of California Press, 1993), p. 324, line 25.

4   Richard Maidstone, *Concordia*, line 18. This foundation myth did not lack controversy. Thomas Walsingham reports that in 1388 Nicholas Brembre was accused of intending to rename London "Parva Troja" with himself as its duke (*Historia Anglicana*, ed. Henry Thomas Riley, 2 vols. [London: Rolls Series, 1863–64], 2.174). See D. W. Robertson, *Chaucer's London* (New York: John Wiley, 1968), pp. 2–4; Lee Patterson, *Chaucer and the Subject of History* (Madison: University of Wisconsin Press, 1991), pp. 155–64; and Sylvia Federico, *New Troy: Fantasies of Empire in the Late Middle Ages* (Minneapolis: University of Minnesota Press, 2003), pp. 1–28.

5   John Gower, *Mirour de l'Omme*, trans. William Burton Wilson, rev. Nancy Wilson Van Baak (East Lansing: Colleagues, 1992), p. 76, lines 5245–56.

6   Linne Mooney, "Chaucer's Scribe," *Speculum* 81 (2006): 97–138, gives details of Adam Pinkhurst's career.

7   R. Allen Shoaf, ed., *Thomas Usk: The Testament of Love* (Kalamazoo, MI: Medieval Institute, 1998), pp. 266–67; Shoaf, pp. 14–17, detects even more pervasive borrowing from *Troilus and Criseyde* than originally recorded by Walter W. Skeat, ed., *The Testament of Love* in *Chaucerian and Other Pieces: Being a Supplement to the Complete Works of Geoffrey Chaucer* (London: Oxford University Press, 1897), pp. xviii–xxxi, 1–145, 451–84.

8   Michael Olmert, "Troilus in *Piers Plowman*: A Contemporary View of Chaucer's *Troilus and Criseyde*," *Chaucer Newsletter* 2 (1980): 13–14; see William Langland, *Piers Plowman: A Parallel-Text Edition of the A, B, C and Z Versions*, ed. A. V. C. Schmidt (London: Longman, 1995), p. 679: "Thus with treson and tricherie thow *troyledest* hem bothe" (C.20.319).

9   John Hines, Nathalie Cohen and Simon Roffey, "*Iohannes Gower, Armiger, Poeta*: Records and Memorials of His Life and Death," *A Companion to Gower*, ed. Siân Echard (Cambridge: D. S. Brewer, 2004), pp. 23–41. Ralph Strode moved from Merton College, Oxford, to become a Common Sergeant for the city of London in 1373 but was remembered at his old college as a *nobilis poeta* into the fifteenth century; see J. A. W. Bennett, "Men of Merton," *Chaucer at Oxford and Cambridge* (Oxford: Clarendon Press, 1974), 58–85, at p. 64.

10   Now Pierpont Morgan Library M 817; see Barry Windeatt, ed., *Troilus and Criseyde* (London: Longman, 1984), pp. 68–69.

11   A. I. Doyle, "English Books In and Out of Court from Edward III to Henry VII," *English Court Culture in the Later Middle Ages*, eds. V. J. Scattergood and J. W. Sherborne (New York: St. Martin's Press, 1983), 163–81, at p. 175. Seth Lerer, *Courtly Letters in the Age of Henry VIII* (Cambridge: Cambridge University Press, 1997), charts the continuing influence of *Troilus* in Tudor culture.

piece, showing the poet reciting before an elegantly attired king, fostered the view that Chaucer performed as a court poet and Richard II figured prominently in the original audience of *Troilus and Criseyde*.[12]

Serving as confessor to John of Gaunt, the Carmelite friar Richard Maidstone was positioned to know something about Chaucer's poetry – he himself had written an English paraphrase of the Seven Penitential Psalms[13] – and to make a knowing connection between Troilus and Richard II. But as a Lancastrian adherent, Maidstone periodically exposes his thinly veiled critiques of the royal subject and the morality of the court over which he presided.[14] As a case in point, the adjective *decorus* means "decorated, ornamented, adorned, elegant, fine, beautiful, handsome," and therefore Maidstone's word-choice makes the king seem precious, made-up, and almost feminine in his physical beauty.[15]

The phrase *invida Venus* suggests jealousy of the monarch's beauty, but the allusion to the goddess locking the young man in her bedroom also invokes the myth of Adonis. The allusion generates double irony because Venus redirected her passion from the warlike Mars to the soft Adonis, and then this young man resisted her female sexual aggression only to meet an unheroic death: "I meene Adoun that with the boor was slawe" (*T&C* 3.721). Implicit in this Ovidian allusion, first by Chaucer and then by Maidstone, is the learned joke that Adonis died of a groin wound steadily interpreted by classical authors as emasculation.[16] Although seemingly framed as extravagant compliments on the king's handsomeness, the *Concordia*'s references to Troilus and Absalom as the twin exemplars of male beauty in the classical and biblical traditions more likely encrypted longstanding gossip about Richard II's manliness and his sexual performance – or lack thereof – with Queen Anne.

In his introduction to the collection *Masculinities in Chaucer*, Peter Beidler asks, "Is Troilus effeminate, impotent, or manly?"[17] The question gains urgency in terms of the complex relationship of male potency, sexual performance, and power politics during the late medieval period when a high-status male's role as a phallic penetrator continued to define his masculinity.[18] My own discus-

12 Derek Pearsall, "The *Troilus* Frontispiece and Chaucer's Audience," *Yearbook of English Studies* 7 (1977): 68–74, and Andrew James Johnston, *Clerks and Courtiers: Chaucer, Late Middle English Literature, and the State Formation Process* (Heidelberg: Winter, 2001), esp. pp. 251–61.

13 Richard Maidstone, *Penitential Psalms*, ed. Valerie Edden (Heidelberg: Winter, 1990).

14 Richard Maidstone, *Concordia*, pp. 62–3, lines 247–54, digresses to describe the accident when a cart overturned, and the ladies had their bare thighs exposed, to moralize about the "luxus et malus omnis amor" – "lechery and every evil love" – for which the Ricardian court was notorious among clerical observers; see Carlson's editorial commentary, pp. 28–29.

15 Charlton Lewis and Charles Short, *A Latin Dictionary* (Oxford: Clarendon Press, 1879), p. 523.

16 Maud McInerney, "'Is this a mannes herte?': Unmanning Troilus through Ovidian Allusion," *MC*, 221–35, at p. 232. For the authoritative version of this myth, with its description of the bore sinking its tusk into the young man's groin, see Ovid, *Metamorphoses*, 10.532–59, 708–39, trans. Frank Justus Miller, 2 vols. (Cambridge MA: Harvard University Press for Loeb Classical Library, 1964–66), 2.102–3 and 114–17.

17 Peter Beidler, "Introduction," *MC*, 1–5, at p. 1.

18 Craig Williams, *Roman Homosexuality* (Oxford: Oxford University Press, 1999), p. 7, emphasizes the man's obligation to penetrate in order to prove virility and assert dominance.

sions focus upon a particular aspect of medieval manliness delineated by Daniel Rubey:

> it may make more sense to divide masculinities into an aristocratic patriarchal masculinity involving the production of children and heirs, and a celibate clerical masculinity . . . the distinction revolving around the issue of inheritance and the question of whether values are to be centered in this world or the next.[19]

Born into the royal family of King Priam, Troilus should have been predisposed to the version of aristocratic patriarchal masculinity elsewhere described as normative by Eve Sedgwick: "under its institutional pseudonyms such as Inheritance, Marriage, Dynasty, Domesticity, and Population, heterosexuality has been permitted to masquerade so fully as History itself."[20]

But when Troilus muses on questions of free-will and predestination in passages lifted from Boethius's *Consolation of Philosophy* (*T&C* 4.953–1085), he demonstrates clerical tendencies that blur and confuse this sense of royal male identity. His intellectualism was perhaps meant to recall Richard II's interest in learned books like his *Liber Judicorum* (Bodleian MS Bodley 581) and his practice of surrounding himself with monks and doctors of theology.[21] Even in matters of love, Troilus the obsessive thinker prefers the sort of libidinous fantasy classified by the *Penitential of Theodore* as a perversion of the reproductive act in the same category with masturbation, oral sex, and interfemoral intercourse.[22] Unconcerned with sex as part of the procreative process, Troilus shows even less concern with perpetuating a dynasty and arranging for patrilineal inheritance than does the Reeve's village parson, who intends marrying his granddaughter into "som worthy blood of auncetrye" and enriching his descendants with wealth embezzled from his church's endowment (*CT* 1.3977–86).[23] The Trojan hero's neglect for begetting heirs, shadowed by the specter of male impotence, haunts Chaucer's *Troilus and Criseyde* to its tragic conclusion.

---

19   Daniel Rubey, "The Five Wounds of Melibee's Daughter: Transforming Masculinities," *MC*, 157–71, at p. 166. Chaucer played with this dual distinction when describing the Monk as a "manly man" (*CT* 1.167) and again when the Host praises the virility of the Nun's Priest (7.3450–51). Ruth Mazo Karras, *From Boys to Men: Formations of Masculinity in Late Medieval Europe* (Philadelphia: University of Pennsylvania Press, 2003), investigates these different socially based categories of masculinity while adding the third "workshop model" to the courtly and university categories.

20   Eve Sedgwick, "Gender Criticism," *Redrawing the Boundaries*, eds. Stephen Greenblatt and Giles Gunn (New York: MLA, 1992), 271–302, at p. 293.

21   Richard Jones, *The Royal Policy of Richard II* (Oxford: Blackwell, 1968), pp. 168–69, and Patricia Eberle, "Richard II and the Literary Arts," *Richard II: The Art of Kingship*, eds. Anthony Goodman and James Gillespie (Oxford: Clarendon Press, 1999), pp. 231–53. On Richard II's interests in future contingencies as evidenced by his *Liber Judicorum*, see Hilary Carey, *Courting Disaster: Astrology at the English Court and University in the Later Middle Ages* (New York: St. Martin's Press, 1992), esp. pp. 92–116.

22   Quoted by James Schultz, "Heterosexuality as a Threat to Medieval Studies," *Journal of the History of Sexuality* 15 (2006): 14–29, at p. 19.

23   John Plummer, "'Hooly Chirches Blood': Simony and Patrimony in Chaucer's *Reeve's Tale*," *ChauR* 18 (1983): 49–60.

Chaucer departs from his sources Benoît and Boccaccio when making Troilus a male with no apparent sexual experience prior to Criseyde.[24] While the poet hints at his protagonist's sexual shyness early in the text, Vern Bullough makes clear that impotence represented no laughing matter in late medieval society:

> Male sexual performance was a major key to being male. It was a man's sexual organs that made him different and superior to the woman. But maleness was somewhat fragile, and it was important for a man to keep demonstrating his maleness by action and thought, especially by sexual action. ... Inevitably, there was also concern with his ability to perform and to beget children. While there was a recognition that males as well as females could be sterile, sterility did not hinder the carrying out of the sexual act, and, lacking proof, the blame for sterility could often be assigned to the woman. Failure to perform, however, was a threat not only to a man's maleness but to society. Potency came to be not only the way in which a male defined himself, but how he was defined by society.[25]

Critics have steadily drawn attention to the ineptitude of Troilus's sexual performance when he swoons during his first opportunity with Criseyde in the bedroom.[26] Criseyde gives him a massage – strangely with the help of Pandarus – that brings Troilus out of his faint and amounts to foreplay for arousing him physically:

> Therwith his pous and paumes of his hondes
> They gan to frote, and wete his temples tweyne;
> And to deliveren hym fro bittre bondes
> She ofte hym kiste; and shortly for to seyne,
> Hym to revoken she did al hire peyne. ...
> And therwithal hire arm over hym she leyde,
> And al foryaf, and ofte tyme hym keste. ...
> And with hire goodly wordes hym disporte
> She gan, and ofte his sorwes to comforte.
>
> (*T&C* 3.1114–18, 1128–29, 1133–34)

Only when Troilus revives from his swoon does he appear to achieve an erection, though he seems unsure what to do with it until assisted by the more sexually experienced young widow.[27] Criseyde's response, "'Is this a mannes game?'" (3.1126), serves as an ominous reminder that she and her uncle do not belong to the prince's world of courtly sensibilities. Her baffled impatience

---

24   Stephanie Dietrich, "'Slydyng' Masculinity in the Four Portraits of Troilus," *MC*, 205–20, at pp. 205–6.

25   Vern Bullough, "On Being a Male in the Middle Ages," *MM*, 31–45, at p. 41. Catherine Rider, *Magic and Impotence in the Middle Ages* (Oxford: Oxford University Press, 2006), discusses the more sinister side of male impotence that hardly impinges upon Chaucer's poem.

26   Jill Mann, "Troilus's Swoon," *ChauR* 14 (1980): 319–35, and Maud McInerney, "'Is this a mannes herte?'" pp. 222–25.

27   Maud McInerney, "'Is this a mannes herte?'" p. 224. Lee Patterson, *Chaucer and the Subject of History*, pp. 280–321, discusses the medieval commonplace of a widow's voracious sexual appetite and preference for younger, less experienced men.

looks forward to the poem's end with Pandarus's hard-nosed advice for his friend simply to find another lady (4.401) and Criseyde's preference for taking a new lover instead of dying martyr-like for an old one.[28]

Glenn Burger has exposed medieval conjugality as a much more hybrid, complicated, and negotiable category than accommodated by most prevailing notions of heteronormativity.[29] But it is precisely a lack of fruitful sexual activity from our couple's initial encounter and thereafter, with no births of potential heirs, that compromises Troilus's identity as a man of princely status. Manhood was defined by the triad of impregnating women, protecting dependents, and providing for one's family – three roles in which Troilus proves deficient from start to finish.[30] Biological survival represented a matter of considerable urgency for a bloodline threatened by imminent extinction by the Greeks. Since Trojan refugees were destined to become the founding patriarchs of Rome and other European nations including Britain – an origin myth emblazoned in the opening lines of *Sir Gawain and the Green Knight*[31] – Troilus's shortcomings in terms of his procreative function mark a serious dereliction of his masculine duties, one that established an oblique correlation with the marital failures of Richard II.

Derek Brewer has reckoned that Troilus was fifteen or sixteen and Criseyde about the same age or a little older.[32] These calculations mean that the couple at the start of their love-affair were the same ages as Richard II and Anne of Bohemia when they wed in 1382. Anticipating the role of Pandarus as go-between, Chaucer himself had been active from 1377 onward in negotiations that led to this royal marriage. These diplomatic maneuvers stand somewhere in the background of *Parliament of Fowls*, written in the same rhyme-royal stanzas and presumed to have been composed just prior to *Troilus and Criseyde*.[33] The dream-vision's linkage of the welfare of the kingdom with the natural process of mating and procreation – really the value of sexual performance for *commune profit* – underscores the neglect of these same social and political imperatives in *Troilus and Criseyde*. The Trojan lovers never seriously discuss marriage or the prospect of having children. The couple might have enjoyed a more public liaison, even with offspring outside of wedlock, but they did not.

Since a male's loss of virginity left no physical marks upon his body, fathering children became the clearest indicator of the transition from boyhood to manhood. Richard II's permanent status as a "boy" became an accusation consistently

---

[28] Angela Weisl makes this point in her chapter "'A mannes game': Criseyde's Masculinity in *Troilus and Criseyde*" later in this volume (pp. 127–31).

[29] Glenn Burger, *Chaucer's Queer Nation* (Minneapolis: University of Minnesota Press, 2003), pp. 37–77.

[30] David Gilmore, *Manhood in the Making* (New Haven, CT: Yale University Press, 1990), p. 223.

[31] Richard Waswo, "Our Ancestors, the Trojans: Inventing Cultural Identity in the Middle Ages," *Exemplaria* 7 (1995): 269–90.

[32] Derek Brewer, "Troilus's 'Gentil' Manhood," *MC*, 237–52, at p. 240. Piero Boitani, "Antiquity and Beyond: The Death of Troilus," *The European Tragedy of Troilus*, ed. Piero Boitani (Oxford: Clarendon Press, 1989), 1–19, at p. 5, quotes the First Vatican Mythographer on the prophecy that Troy would fall if Troilus reached twenty, an age that he must not have achieved even after some years of his affair with Criseyde.

[33] Larry Benson, "The Occasion of the *Parliament of Fowls*," *Contradictions: From Beowulf to Chaucer*, eds. Theodore Andersson and Stephen Barney (Aldershot: Scolar Press, 1995), pp. 175–97.

lodged against him, for example, in Archbishop Arundel's sermon delivered at the king's deposition and in John Gower's revision of the *Vox Clamantis*: "The king, an undisciplined boy, neglects the moral behavior by which a man might grow up from a boy."[34] Troilus shared this characterization as an immature male throughout the classical tradition and was described as still a "boy" when killed by Achilles in Virgil's *Aeneid*: "Unfortunate boy and unequal in his encounter with Achilles."[35] Chaucer's late inset portrait of Troilus emphasizes the word *yong* first in the series of adjectives: "Yong, fressh, strong, and hardy as lyoun" (5.830). Although the narrative has followed the hero's life for several years by this point, Troilus does not seem to have matured. The late classical tradition represented by Quintus of Smyrna (fourth century AD) described the prince as "beardless yet," "almost a child," "virgin of a bride," and at the time of his premature death "barren of all issue" with the sense that his tragic fate included not perpetuating his royal bloodline.[36]

As evidence of mature sexual potency among royal males, instances of illegitimate offspring were common enough during the second half of the fourteenth century to enter the documentary record.[37] Before he married Blanche of Lancaster at age nineteen, John of Gaunt had already fathered his first bastard child with one of the queen's Hainault ladies-in-waiting, Marie de Saint-Hilaire, and by the beginnings of the 1370s he started his long-term relationship with Chaucer's sister-in-law Katherine Swynford, who became his third wife in 1396 after the death of Constanza of Castile. Their four children were legitimized by king, parliament, and pope during 1397 and became the powerful Beaufort half-royals. Richard II's father, Edward the Black Prince, had at least one bastard son by his mistress, Edith de Willesford. The fact that Sir Roger de Clarendon was made a chamber knight attests to Richard II's willingness to acknowledge the social standing as well as the blood kinship of his illegitimate half-brother. Sir Roger's royal pedigree was sufficiently well established to pose a threat to Henry IV, who found legal grounds for having the potential pretender to the throne hanged in 1402. In contrast to these older male relatives, Richard II seems to have kept no mistress and fathered no bastards. His most recent biographer makes a point of observing "no record of illegitimate royal progeny for the twenty years of the reign."[38]

---

[34] *The Major Latin Works of John Gower*, trans. Eric Stockton (Seattle: University of Washington Press, 1962), p. 232, translates from *The Complete Works of John Gower: The Latin Works*, ed. G. C. Macaulay (Oxford: Clarendon Press, 1902), p. 246: "Rex, puer indoctus, morales negligit actus / In quibus a puero crescere possit homo" (6.555–56). Christopher Fletcher, "Manhood and Politics in the Reign of Richard II," *Past & Present* 189 (2005): 3–39, at pp. 4–6.

[35] *Aeneid* 1.475, in Virgil, *Eclogues, Georgics, Aeneid, I–VI*, trans. Rushton Fairclough, rev. G. P. Goold (Cambridge MA: Harvard University Press for Loeb Classical Library, 1999), p. 294 (translation mine): "Infelix puer atque impar congressus Achilli."

[36] Quintus Smyrnaeus, *The Fall of Troy* (4.430–31), trans. Arthur Way (New York: Macmillan for Loeb Classical Library, 1913), pp. 198–99.

[37] C. Given-Wilson and Alice Curteis, *Royal Bastards* (London: Routledge, 1984), pp. 135–59. Edward III had three illegitimate children by Alice Perrers during the last fifteen years of his reign, and his bastard son Sir John de Southeray lived long enough to have a checkered career during John of Gaunt's Spanish campaigns.

[38] Nigel Saul, *Richard II* (New Haven, CT: Yale University Press, 1997), p. 94. Given-Wilson and

These retrievable records of mistresses and illegitimate children have several implications. First, courtly love between a high-status male and a subservient female included sexual relations largely free from the moral complications endlessly rehearsed in literary accounts.[39] Second, because chronicles and other official documentation make possible the reconstruction of these relationships, no absolute legal or social prohibition forced Troilus to conceal his liaison with Criseyde. In pagan Troy without the condemnations of Christian morality, his concubinage might have continued as smoothly as it did for pre-conversion Augustine of Hippo with the begetting of his natural son, Adeodatus. Any children born of the relationship between Troilus and his mistress might have assumed some semi-respectable existence potentially leading to greater things. The power and prestige of the Beauforts during the Lancastrian era would provide a signal example.[40]

Public knowledge of these sexual liaisons must have come mostly from the men involved, since sexual conquests bolstered a man's reputation for virility and power. Ruth Mazo Karras nicely describes the homosocial dynamic: "Success in love was an important part of knighthood. This did not mean that the knight's goal was to impress women. Rather, he used women, or his attractiveness to women, to impress other men."[41] According to the script of noble endeavor, Troilus's male identity would have been enhanced by his role-playing as a lover in camaraderie with other men privy to his initial frustrations and later sexual triumphs.[42] The Black Knight's well-rehearsed account of his courtship of Fair White in the *Book of the Duchess* both confirms his chivalric identity and establishes his hierarchical nexus with the dreamer as a male confidant. By contrast, Troilus's tragedy resulted from his willingness to obey Criseyde's plans for secrecy instead of following this standard script of male solidarity, boastfulness, and even the good-natured teasing that he directed at young knights in his entourage: "God wot, she slepeth softe / For love of the, when thow turnest ful ofte!" (1.195–96).

The positive example of a man's openness to female counsel figured in another work written by Chaucer presumably during the 1380s, his prose rendering of Renaud de Louens' *Le Livre de Melibee et Prudence* later adapted as the *Tale of Melibee* in the *Canterbury Tales*. Scholars have long recognized that the text fits into the political context of the first decade of Richard II's reign when the young

---

Curteis, *Royal Bastards*, p. 142, debunk the rumor that Richard II had a bastard son named Richard Maudelyn.

39   Ruth Mazo Karras, *Sexuality in Medieval Europe: Doing unto Others* (New York: Routledge, 2005), pp. 124–28. James Schultz, *Courtly Love, the Love of Courtliness, and the History of Sexuality* (Chicago: University of Chicago Press, 2006), esp. pp. 79–98.

40   G. L. Harriss, *Cardinal Beaufort: A Study of Lancastrian Ascendancy and Decline* (Oxford: Clarendon Press, 1988), traces the career of the most influential of Gaunt's four children by Katherine Swynford.

41   Ruth Mazo Karras, *From Boys to Men*, "Mail Bonding: Knights, Ladies, and the Proving of Manhood," p. 25.

42   David Aers, "Masculine Identity in the Courtly Community: The Self Loving in *Troilus and Criseyde*," *Community, Gender, and Individual Identity: English Writing 1360–1430* (London: Routledge, 1988), pp. 117–52.

king struggled with the older magnates over the direction of foreign policy.[43] Thomas Walsingham's famous contempt for Richard II's courtiers as "knights of Love rather than War, more capable in the bedchamber than on the battlefield" figures as part of this widespread criticism of Richard II's peace policies with France.[44] Slurs upon Richard II's political weakness typically focused upon his youthfulness and physical softness, although these post-deposition attacks are contradicted by his bravery in front of the rebels at Smithfield in 1381 and his jousting skills at the Smithfield tournament in 1390.[45] Furthermore his knightly courage was proven during his Scottish campaign of 1385 and his two invasions of Ireland in 1394–95 and 1399.[46] Christopher Fletcher makes the convincing case that Richard II offered all of the right military responses during the invasion scare of 1386, intending to assemble an army and take the fight to the French on their own territory, but the king was deterred only by the refusal of the Commons to grant revenues and then the collapse of the French campaign itself. Chancellor Michael de la Pole told parliament that the king intended to make war on his enemies "in person" (*en propre persone*) as evidence that – like Chaucer's Troilus – he did not lack battlefield bravery as one key marker of aristocratic manliness.[47]

Central to *Melibee*'s moral argument is the woman's role as peacemaker modeled after the real-life activities scripted for the king's grandmother Queen Philippa and his mother Princess Joan. Paul Strohm has explored the function of the petitionary mediatrix whose humble femininity leaves intact a sovereign's maleness:

> This new form of queenly influence was *petitionary*, in the sense that it cast the queen as one seeking redress rather than one able to institute redress in her own right, and *intercessory*, in that it limited its objectives to the modification of a previously determined male resolve.[48]

Maidstone crafts his narrative so that the *Concordia* culminates with exactly such a scene in Westminster Hall, where Queen Anne begs for mercy on London's behalf by appealing to Richard II's two roles as king and husband. Whether in the *Concordia* or *Melibee* – or later in the Prologue to the *Legend of Good Women* – such scripts risked the perception of the wife's dominant position when

[43] Gardiner Stillwell, "The Political Meaning of Chaucer's *Tale of Melibee*," *Speculum* 19 (1944): 433–44; Lynn Staley Johnson, "Inverse Counsel: Contexts for the *Melibee*," *SP* 87 (1990): 137–55; and Carolyn Collette, "Heeding the Counsel of Prudence: A Context for the Melibee," *ChauR* 29 (1995): 416–33.

[44] Thomas Walsingham, *Historia Anglicana*, 2.156. Daniel Rubey, "Five Wounds," pp. 162–65, relates these slanders to the king's pacifist policies.

[45] *The Westminster Chronicle*, eds. and trans. L. C. Hector and Barbara Harvey (Oxford: Clarendon Press, 1982), pp. 450–51, reports how King Richard won honors during the tournament.

[46] James Gillespie, "Richard II: King of Battles?" *The Age of Richard II*, ed. James Gillespie (New York: St. Martin's Press, 1997), pp. 139–64, adjusts the longstanding view that the king and his knights lacked warrior prowess.

[47] Christopher Fletcher, "Manhood and Politics," pp. 32–39.

[48] Paul Strohm, *Hochon's Arrow: The Social Imagination of Fourteenth-Century Texts* (Princeton, NJ: Princeton University Press, 1992), p. 95.

lecturing her husband, weakening his resolve, and transforming his righteous rage into merciful forgiveness.[49] Already in the 1380s Troilus's willingness to follow Criseyde's plans for a secret affair traveled the thin line between a nobleman's openness to wise counsel and his weakness for allowing himself to be overruled by a woman.[50]

Troilus finally enjoys physical intimacy with his mistress Criseyde but keeps the affair a secret from everyone except his single confidant, Pandarus. By contrast – as discussed at length below – Richard II was quite possibly *not* having sex with his wife, but failed to maintain secrecy about this anomaly from court insiders like Chaucer. A medieval king enjoyed no real privacy, in the modern sense, bur rather collective privacy within the confines of his household.[51] Any problems in the royal bedroom necessarily became the sort of open secret that D. A. Miller describes as "the secret that everyone hides because everyone holds."[52] Chaucer's portrayal of Troilus as a soliloquizing, swooning lover therefore reads like a fulsome *apologia* for his own prince's failed performance blamed upon an intense, refined amatory sensibility.[53]

Historians have consistently praised the marriage of Richard and Anne as a happy companionate union, but Caroline Barron speaks for recent researchers who raise questions about the sexual aspect of their relationship:

> There are no recorded infidelities on either side, but there were no children either. Here again Richard may have deliberately imitated the childless marriage of Edward the Confessor with Edith, the daughter of Earl Godwin. Was Richard, perhaps, striving for chastity within marriage?[54]

Chaste marriage has a long history traced in a fascinating study by Dyan Elliott, who defines it as a legally binding marriage in which sexual relations have been remitted by the consent of both parties for reasons of Christian piety – marriage, that is, without marital relations.[55] Although Edward the Confessor's failure to produce a male heir led to the succession crisis inviting the Norman Conquest, the virginal Saxon king became a figure of special veneration for Richard II, who would have found in him an example of royal saintliness validated by his

---

49   Daniel Rubey, "Five Wounds," p. 158.

50   Henry Ansgar Kelly, "The Pardoner's Voice: Disjunctive Narrative and Modes of Effemination," *Speaking Images*, eds. R. F. Yeager and Charlotte Morse (Asheville, NC: Pegasus, 2001), 411–44, at pp. 415–17.

51   George Duby, ed., *A History of Private Life*, Volume 2: *Revelations of the Medieval World*, trans. Arthur Goldhammer (Cambridge, MA: Harvard University Press, 1988), p. 510: "if private life meant secrecy, it was a secrecy shared by all members of the household, hence fragile and easily violated."

52   D. A. Miller, *The Novel and the Police* (Berkeley: University of California Press, 1988), 192–220, at p. 205.

53   Mary Wack, "Lovesickness in *Troilus*," *Pacific Coast Philology* 19 (1984): 55–61.

54   Barron's introduction, "Richard II: Image and Reality," to Dillian Gordon's *The Wilton Diptych* (London: National Gallery, 1993), 13–19, at p. 5. *Historia Vitae et Regni Ricardi Secundi*, ed. George Stow (Philadelphia: University of Pennsylvania Press, 1977), p. 134, comments on this childless marriage as an aberration.

55   Dyan Elliott, *Spiritual Marriage: Sexual Abstinence in Medieval Wedlock* (Princeton, NJ: Princeton University Press, 1993), p. 3.

sexual purity.[56] Investigating the symbolism of the Wilton Diptych, Katherine Lewis suggests that Richard encouraged this identification as a strategic back-formation during the middle 1390s, following the death of Queen Anne and leading up to his marriage to the child-bride Isabelle of France. As a heroic exercise in chastity, sexual restraint during his first marriage becomes testimony to the monarch's worthiness and even sacredness: "It also becomes a way of turning a potentially divisive personal, intimate failing into a magnificent public triumph."[57]

But Chaucer provides evidence that the sexless marriage of Richard and Anne was already recognized as a problem during the 1380s. As an apologist for the failure of the English royal couple to produce children early in their marriage, Chaucer wrote another work that converts a sexual shortcoming into a spiritual accomplishment. The hagiographic tradition offered its most popular model for chaste marriage in the life of St. Cecilia. The legend exemplifies a couple's resolve to preserve virginity in the circumstances of an arranged marriage,[58] and the best-known Middle English version survives in Chaucer's *Second Nun's Tale*. Yet we know that this translation existed prior to its insertion in the *Canterbury Tales* because the Prologue to the *Legend of Good Women* indicates that the poet had already written his "Lyf of Seynt Cecile" (F.426) at some earlier point in his courtly career. Since this saint's life was composed in the same rime-royal stanzas as *Troilus*, the original version has usually been dated to the mid-1380s – that is, during the years immediately following the marriage of Richard to Anne in 1382.

Hagiographic writing usually took the form of collections such as Chaucer parodies in his *Legend of Good Women*. So why single out this particular *vita*? Like other fourteenth-century versions of St. Cecilia's story written on behalf of virgin couples in regions as widely separated as Provence and Poland, Chaucer's "Lyf of Seynt Cecile" served as literary justification for the sexless marriage practiced by the couple at the center of his own court. Unlike Troilus, however, Cecilia's husband Valerian was eagerly prepared to consummate his marriage, but he was dissuaded from using physical force by his wife's threat that he would be killed by her guardian angel:

> "And if that he may feelen, out of drede,
> That ye me touche, or love in vileynye,
> He right anon wol sle yow with the dede,
> And in youre yowthe thus ye shullen dye."   (*CT*, 8.155–58)

This canonic version of the saint's life from the *Legenda Aurea* places responsibility for the unconsummated marriage primarily upon the wife's determination

---

56 Eric John, "Edward the Confessor and the Celibate Life," *Analecta Bollandiana* 97 (1979): 171–78.
57 Katherine Lewis, "Becoming a Virgin King: Richard II and Edward the Confessor," *Gender and Holiness: Men, Women, and Saints in Late Medieval Europe*, eds. Samantha Riches and Sarah Salih (London: Routledge, 2002), 86–100, at p. 96. Ruth Mazo Karras, *Sexuality in Medieval Europe*, pp. 28–58, explores the Christian ideal of heroically subduing sexual drives for the sake of the soul.
58 Dyan Elliott, *Spiritual Marriage*, pp. 63–73, 270–71, 276, 284.

to maintain her virginity. In real-life arrangements within a courtly household such as England's, concealment became paramount and the truth came out only posthumously – as it did for Edward the Confessor – in order to avoid the inevitable slur upon the husband's manliness. If the rumor of Richard II's sexless marriage did not surface after his death in 1399, Lancastrian propagandists probably did not want to risk an accusation that might have been interpreted as a saintly attribute, as it was with St. Edward, and preferred the tactic of alluding to the king's same-sex activities.

Surely the holy example of Cecilia and Valerian sometimes provided camouflage for marriages unconsummated because the husband was impotent or disinclined to have sexual relations with his wife. Clerical warnings that chaste unions might induce husbands to "unnatural vices" – Dante's second category of sodomites was composed of husbands denied sex by shrewish wives[59] – may have concealed the reality that many of these husbands already had same-sex preferences and married only because of social pressures.[60] Scarcely into puberty when contracted to wed the daughter of the Holy Roman Emperor, Richard II may already have preferred male partners, perhaps after the model of the "intimate association" between his chamber knights Sir William Neville and Sir Thomas Clanvowe.[61] The 1380s is when Richard entered into a well-documented intimacy with his court favorite Robert de Vere. Walsingham gave voice to monastic homophobia when he described the "obscene familiarity" of their friendship,[62] and the Evesham chronicler also implied sexual indecency when describing how Richard II conducted all-night parties with drinking and other unspeakable acts.[63] Because sodomy was the vice so abominable that it should never be mentioned,[64] the monastic writer's "unspeakables" (*non dicendis*)

---

[59]   Charles Singleton, *Inferno Commentary* (Princeton, NJ: Princeton University Press, 1970), pp. 280–81 for Canto 16 (lines 44–5).

[60]   Dyan Elliott, *Spiritual Marriage*, pp. 123, 281.

[61]   K. B. McFarlane, *Lancastrian Kings and Lollard Knights* (Oxford: Clarendon Press, 1972), pp. 165–66: "The really intimate association between Clanvowe and Neville began in 1378" when they entered the king's household. Their example is discussed by Ruth Mazo Karras, *From Boys to Men*, p. 63, and *Sexuality in Medieval Europe*, pp. 144–49, on the basis of Siegrid Düll, Anthony Luttrell, and Maurice Keen, "Faithful unto Death: The Tomb Slab of Sir William Neville and Sir John Clanvowe, Constantinople 1391," *Antiquaries Journal* 71 (1991): 174–90.

[62]   Thomas Walsingham, *Historia Anglicana*, 2:148: "tantum afficiebatur eidem, tantum coluit et amavit eundem, non sine nota prout fertur, familiaritatis obscoenae" – "as much was Richard affected by De Vere, just as much did he love and worship him, widely noted as it was displayed, with obscene familiarity." Carolyn Dinshaw, "A Kiss Is Just a Kiss: Heterosexuality and Its Consolations in *Sir Gawain and the Green Knight*," *Diacritics* 24 (1994): 205–26, at pp. 222–23, discusses the poem's unnatural erotic situations, which she associates with allegations of sexual irregularity in Richard II's behavior with De Vere.

[63]   *Historia Vitae Ricardi*, p. 166: "totam noctem in potacionibus et aliis non dicendis in sompnem duceret" – "all night he would spend in drinking and other unspeakable acts until passing out."

[64]   Allen Frantzen, "The Disclosure of Sodomy in *Cleanness*," *PMLA* 111 (1996): 451–64, and Elizabeth Keiser, *Courtly Desire and Medieval Homophobia: The Legitimation of Sexual Pleasure in* Cleanness *and Its Contexts* (New Haven, CT: Yale University Press, 1997), pp. 41–70, examine the theme of homosexuality in a text close to Richard II's court and probably contemporary with Chaucer's *Troilus and Criseyde*.

implied the most scandalous version of sodomy as homosexual acts between men.[65]

Karma Lochrie and others have demonstrated that sodomy was not opposed categorically to heterosexuality in medieval legal and theological writings,[66] and Boccaccio's commentary on the first group of sodomites in Dante's *Divine Comedy* assumes that sexual perversion became a crime of opportunity for those like teachers confined in a same-sex environment, what today might be termed situational homosexuality.[67] The question remains whether English monastic writers fictionalized their slanders about Richard II and De Vere or whether they published a widely circulated rumor during the Lancastrian regime when the new dynasty welcomed testimony that further discredited the deposed monarch. Written during King Richard's ongoing intimacy in the 1380s, however, Chaucer's *Troilus and Criseyde* testifies to a roughly similar relationship between Pandarus and Troilus. Pandarus represents the active, aggressive seducer while Troilus enacts the role of the passive, vulnerable seduced. Perhaps the least masculine aspect of the Trojan prince's character is his masochistic passivity: he submits to his disease of love-sickness, he submits to Pandarus's advice for gaining his lady's love, he submits to Criseyde's conditions for conducting their affair, and finally he submits to the philosophical conclusion that his fortunes were unalterably determined by necessity and he was powerless to change the outcomes. Troilus escapes the taint of man-on-man sodomy only by pursuing so histrionically his doomed relationship with Criseyde, but a line-count within the text indicates that Troilus spends a great deal more time in bed engaged in pillow-talk with Pandarus.[68]

The classical tradition was explicit about the pretty young Troilus as the target of male erotic aggression, although Virgil sanitized these accounts of same-sex contact with the word *congressus* to describe his "coming together" with Achilles. Robert Graves summarizes Troilus's death-scene in two ancient versions quite different from the vignette offered by *The Aeneid*:

> Some say that Achilles fell in love with him as they fought together, and "I will kill you," he said, "unless you yield to my caresses!" Troilus fled and took sanctuary in the temple of Thymbraean Apollo; but Achilles cared nothing for the god's wrath and since Troilus remained coy, beheaded him at the altar. ... Others say that Achilles ... lured him out by offering a gift of doves, and that Troilus died with crushed ribs and livid face, in such bear-like fashion did Achilles make love.[69]

---

[65] V. A. Kolve, "Ganymede / *Son of Getron*: Medieval Monasticism and the Drama of Same-Sex Desire," *Speculum* 73 (1998): 1014–67, offers a finely nuanced study of a monk's homophobic anxiety.

[66] Karma Lochrie, *Covert Operations: The Medieval Uses of Secrecy* (Philadelphia: University of Pennsylvania Press, 1999), pp. 177–227, and Ruth Mazo Karras, *Sexuality in Medieval Europe*, pp. 129–32.

[67] Quoted by James Schultz, "Heterosexuality as a Threat," p. 21.

[68] On the queerness of the two men's relationship, see Richard Zeikowitz, *Homoeroticism and Chivalry: Discourses of Male Same-Sex Desire in the Fourteenth Century* (New York: Palgrave Macmillan, 2003), pp. 131–50, and especially Tison Pugh, "Queer Pandarus?," *Queering Medieval Genres* (New York: Palgrave Macmillan, 2004), pp. 82–95.

[69] Robert Graves, *Greek Myths*, rev. ed., 2 vols. (London: Penguin, 1960), 2:297.

Servius remarked how Virgil bowdlerized his account of Troilus's death: "led by the love of Troilus, Achilles offered him the doves that made him pause with delight to hold them; then seized by Achilles, Troilus perished in his embraces – but the poet changed this disgraceful scene in his heroic song."[70] The explicitness of Servius's commentary meant that the homoerotic pursuit of Troilus by Achilles survived within the Latin scholarly tradition available to Chaucer and his target-audience of Gower and Strode, as well as to Maidstone and his Latin readership.

As a real-life counterpart to the courtly seducer Pandarus, De Vere overcame his status as one of the realm's poorest titled noblemen and succeeded in earning almost limitless access to royal patronage.[71] As the king's chamberlain, De Vere served as Chaucer's superior in the royal household and personally endorsed the poet's 1385 petition for a permanent deputy in the office of controller.[72] Chaucer was therefore positioned socially to know secrets of the king's chamber and to have a personal stake in their protection, concealment, and even their rationalization as chivalric and Christian virtues.[73] The same decade during which the poet produced *Troilus and Criseyde* and *St. Cecilia* also witnessed the first draft of the *Knight's Tale*. This work's original title, preserved in the Prologue to the *Legend of Good Women* (F.420), advertised the ideal of same-sex bonding at the heart of this courtly narrative: *The Love of Palamon and Arcite*. Whereas Boccaccio's full title *Il Teseida delle nozze d'Emelia* anticipated the marriage of Emelia, Chaucer used his title in the 1380s version to focus instead upon the love of Palamon and Arcite – their competitive love for Emelye, to be sure, but also the love of the two young knights for each other.[74]

Other cultural evidence attests that the sexless relationship between King Richard and Queen Anne persisted into the 1390s.[75] In recent efforts at explicating the esoteric contents of the Wilton Diptych, Pamela Tudor-Craig notes "there are numerous indications that the married life of Richard and Anne was

---

70 Servius, *Servii Grammatici Qvi Fervntvr in Vergilii Carmina Commenarii*, ed. Georgius Thilo and Hermmanus Hagen, 3 vols. (Hildesheim: Olms, 1961), 1.151: "Troili amore Achillem ductum palumbes ei quibus ille delectabatur obiecisse: quas cum vellet tenere, captus ab Achille in eius amplexibus periit. sed hoc quasi indignum heroo carmine mutavit poeta." On the widespread tradition of "Achilles' homosexual love for Troilus," see Piero Boitani, "The Death of Troilus," pp. 16–18, and Timothy Gantz, *Early Greek Myth: A Guide to Literary and Artistic Sources*, 2 vols. (Baltimore, MD: Johns Hopkins University Press, 1993), 2.601–02. Medieval manuscripts of the *Aeneid* routinely came equipped with Servius's commentary, itself plentifully preserved in its own copies; see John Savage, "The Manuscripts of Servius's Commentary on Virgil," *Harvard Studies in Classical Philology* 45 (1934): 157–204.

71 Nigel Saul, *Richard II*, pp. 121–22.

72 J. R. Hulbert, "Chaucer and the Earl of Oxford," *MP* 10 (1912–13): 433–37, and *Chaucer Life-Records*, eds. Martin Crow and Clair Olson (Oxford: Clarendon Press, 1966), pp. 134 and 168–69.

73 As father of one son Thomas and perhaps a second son Lewis, Chaucer shows his homophobic revulsion only when writing his *Canterbury Tales* privately during the 1390s. See my "Queering the Summoner: Same-Sex Union in Chaucer's *Canterbury Tales*," *Speaking Images*, eds. Yeager and Morse, 301–24, esp. pp. 315–18.

74 See my "Three Readings of the *Knight's Tale*: Sir John Clanvowe, Geoffrey Chaucer, and James I of Scotland," *JMEMS* 34 (2004): 279–307, at pp. 279–87.

75 My book *The Politics of Pearl: Court Poetry in the Age of Richard II* (Cambridge: D. S. Brewer, 2001), pp. 151–86, reviews these materials in greater detail.

closely based on that of the Confessor and Edith,"[76] and Ruth Sullivan proposes that these spiritual values of chaste marriage informed other riddling representations in the painting: "Richard deliberately chose to have himself portrayed as a delicately featured, pious youth, suggesting, in effect, the unsullied qualities of a 'virgin king.'"[77] Because the designer of the Wilton Diptych chose Edward the Confessor along with John the Baptist and Edmund of East Anglia – all of them male virgins[78] – to present Richard to the Virgin Mary in the opposite panel, Caroline Barron seems justified in suggesting Richard's efforts at invoking their examples of sexual renunciation in terms of his own marriage (see p. 18 above).

During the year after Queen Anne's death in 1394, Philippe de Mézières dispatched his *Letter to King Richard* (BL Royal 20.B.vi) urging a permanent peace between England and France cemented by Richard II's marriage to Charles VI's six-year-old daughter, Isabelle. Philippe would have been privy to court gossip through Robert the Hermit, the official intermediary between France and England throughout the mid-1390s, and this privileged information apparently prompted him to neglect the obvious concern for a childless king's need to produce an heir to the throne.[79] This dynastic imperative figures as the starting-point for the story of Walter in the *Clerk's Tale*, and Philippe knew this political parable intimately because he had translated Petrarch's version of the story of Patient Griselda during the 1380s. His *Letter to King Richard* in fact alludes to Griselda as the model of a pliable bride.[80] But rather than lamenting the ruin of kingdoms left without a clear line of succession, such as England following the death of the childless Edward the Confessor, Philippe praises rulers such as Alexander the Great and Julius Caesar who died without begetting natural heirs. And rather than placing responsibility upon a sterile or virginal wife, Philippe makes the extraordinary gesture of praising Richard II for maintaining the "state of abstinence in order to win the aureole."[81]

The *Legend of Good Women* signals Chaucer's estrangement from court culture when the God of Love, transparently a representation of King Richard, rejects *Troilus and Criseyde* because the poem commits "heresy" by portraying Criseyde's treachery and thus fostering a sense of anxiety among men:

---

[76] Pamela Tudor-Craig, "The Wilton Diptych in the Context of Contemporary English Panel and Wall Painting," *The Regal Image of Richard II and the Wilton Diptych*, eds. Dillian Gordon, Lisa Monnas and Caroline Elam (London: Miller, 1997), 207–22, at p. 219.

[77] Ruth Sullivan, "The Wilton Diptych: Mysteries, Majesty, and a Complex Exchange of Faith and Power," *Gazette des Beaux-Arts* 129 (1997): 1–18, at p. 11.

[78] Shelagh Mitchell, "Richard II: Kingship and the Cult of Saints," *The Regal Image of Richard II*, eds. Gordon et al., pp. 115–24.

[79] The fifteenth-century Lancastrian *Eulogium Historiarum sive Temporis*, ed. Frank Haydon, 3 vols. (London: Longman, 1858–63), 3.384, points to Richard II's dual failures to make war and make babies: "prole careret et animo bellicoso" – "he lacked offspring and a warlike spirit."

[80] Amy Goodwin, "The Griselda Story in France," *Sources and Analogues of the* Canterbury Tales: Volume I, eds. Robert M. Correale and Mary Hamel (Cambridge: D. S. Brewer, 2002), pp. 130–39. Philippe de Mézières, *Letter to King Richard II: A Plea Made in 1395 for Peace between England and France*, ed. and trans. G. W. Coopland (Liverpool: Liverpool University Press, 1975), p. 42, says that the ultimate satisfaction of a second marriage for Richard would be the possession of a virtuous wife "such as Griselda, the wife of the Marquis of Saluzzo."

[81] *Letter to King Richard II*, pp. 37 and 40.

> "And of Creseyde thou hast seyd as the lyste,
> That maketh men to wommen lasse triste,
> That ben as trewe as ever was any steel." (*LGW* Prologue, F.332–34)

The God of Love's assault upon the dreamer recalls the temperamental rages for which Richard II became notorious, while dramatizing the insecurity and stifled resentment that must have been felt by those like Chaucer attending upon this volatile monarch.[82] The charge of heresy became more explosive by 1395 when Richard II proclaimed his official opposition to Lollardy by adding this inscription to his tomb in Westminster Abbey: "he crushed heretics and laid low their friends."[83] Michael Calabrese's comparison of Criseyde with Langland's Lady Mede reveals a materialist, self-interested creature so wholly alien to courtly idealism that her decision to survive Troy's fall by attaching herself to Diomede would have struck the God of Love as a betrayal of his core beliefs, hence "heresye ayeins my lawe" (*LGW*, F.330).[84] Yet this charge obscures a more obvious source of consternation arising from the poem's description of Troilus's – and by inference Richard II's – sexual clumsiness and even possibly his impotence with a woman.

The problem of feminized men persists throughout Chaucer's last dream-vision poem. "What is most dangerous about heterosexual desire according to the *Legends*," Elaine Hansen observes, "is the feminine position, itself a divided one – vulnerable, submissive, subservient and self-sacrificing on the one hand, crafty and duplicitous on the other – that men in love or lust for a woman seem forced to assume."[85] While these male sex-offenders suffer because driven by erotic forces, the God of Love himself emerges as a strangely neutered figure, untouched by the sexual energy that he explicitly represents, and too willing to soften and bend to the forceful mediations of a woman. Like the uxorious King Arthur in the feminist narrative of the *Wife of Bath's Tale*, the God of Love turns judicial authority over to the queen: "'Al lyeth in yow, dooth wyth hym what yow leste'" (*LGW*, F.449). Even the penance imposed upon the dreamer expresses some "emasculated courtly response," born of deep misogynist anxiety and producing only stories of women whose goodness is proven by their willingness to die and disappear.[86]

Not many critics have noted that the God of Love and his consort Alceste, although dramatized as a couple, are not really husband and wife. Admetus was the husband of Alcestis. The line that introduces them – "The god of Love and

82 David Wallace, *Chaucerian Polity* (Stanford, CA: Stanford University Press, 1997), pp. 337–78, goes further in investigating the correspondence between the God of Love and Queen Alceste and the King and Queen of England.

83 The complete inscription is translated in Terry Jones with Robert Yeager, Terry Dolan, Alan Fletcher and Juliette Dor, *Who Murdered Chaucer?: A Medieval Mystery* (New York: St. Martin's Press, 2004), p. 93.

84 See Michael Calabrese's essay in this volume, "Being a Man in *Piers Plowman* and *Troilus and Criseyde*," pp. 176–79.

85 Elaine Hansen, *Chaucer and the Fictions of Gender* (Berkeley: University of California Press, 1992), p. 3.

86 Carolyn Dinshaw, *Chaucer's Sexual Poetics* (Madison: University of Wisconsin Press, 1989), p. 67.

in his hand a quene" (*LGW*, F.213) – identifies Alceste as *a* queen but not *his* queen. The God of Love himself reminds the dreamer of Alceste's example as a wife loyal to her husband beyond death: "She that for hire housbonde chees to dye / And eke to goon to helle, rather than he" (*LGW*, F.513–14).[87] Some mysterious elision therefore lurks at the juncture of their domestic debate over the fate of the dreamer. While the G Prologue represents the poet as a figure of flagging erotic energies – "As olde foles when here spiryt fayleth" (262) – Chaucer implicitly ridicules the God of Love himself as a sham of all that his name suggests.[88] What the companionate couple Love and Alceste lacks is precisely what destroys tragic lovers in the later *Legends* themselves: full sexual congress. What excludes the couple from true wedlock is what constituted legal grounds for a marriage's annulment: failure to consummate.[89]

Maidstone's praise of Richard II's handsomeness operated by comparison with two paragons of male beauty: "Iste velud Troylus vel ut Absolon ipse decorus" – "beautiful as Troilus or as Absalom." Working on his *Canterbury Tales* during the 1390s at some remove from the royal court and very likely with the intention of posthumous publication, Chaucer, always the most courageous of cowards, proceeded far more boldly when satirizing a variety of Ricardian irregularities.[90] Here I have in mind particularly the comical fusion of the clerkly and courtly embodied in Absolon in the *Miller's Tale*. Whereas Troilus's sexual career was disabled by clerical inhibitions and paralyzed by philosophical musings, Absolon's romantic ambitions are rendered ludicrous by a courtly script grossly at odds with his identity as an Oxford clerk.[91] As a suitor made ridiculous by his reliance upon bookish accounts of courtship, Absolon shows himself so unfamiliar with real-life women that when he kisses Alison's "naked ers," he thinks he has kissed someone with a beard (*CT*, 1.3730–37) – with the added comic implication that he has some practical experience kissing partners with beards.[92]

With his well-groomed blond hair, Chaucer's Absolon resembles Richard II as shown with his own blond hair parted in the middle in the royal portraits of the Wilton Diptych, the Westminster portrait, and the tomb effigy in West-

---

87 Louise Fradenburg investigates the implications of "rescue" in *Legend of Good Women* in "The Love of Thy Neighbor," *Constructing Medieval Sexuality*, eds. Karma Lochrie, Peggy McCracken, and James Schultz (Minneapolis: University of Minnesota Press, 1997), pp. 135–57.

88 In 1395 when Richard II was promoting his image as the virgin king in the Wilton Diptych, Froisssart reported presenting him with a volume of poetry: "The King asked me what it was about and I told him: 'About love!' He was delighted by this answer" (*Chronicles*, trans. Geoffrey Brereton [London: Penguin, 1978], p. 408).

89 Christopher Brooke, *The Medieval Idea of Marriage* (Oxford: Clarendon Press, 1989), pp. 132–34. Ruth Mazo Karras, *Sexuality in Medieval Europe*, pp. 70–75, discusses the prevailing view of the canonists that consent validated a marriage, not consummation, otherwise Mary and Joseph would not have been legally wedded.

90 Derek Brewer, "Chaucer's Anti-Ricardian Poetry," *The Living Middle Ages*, eds. Uwe Böker, Manfred Markus, and Rainer Schöwerling (Stuttgart: Belser, 1989), pp. 115–28.

91 Ruth Mazo Karras, "Sharing Wine, Women, and Song: Masculine Identity Formation in the Medieval European Universities," *BMMA*, 187–202, creates a sociohistorical context for Absolon's farcical sexual ambitions; see also her *From Boys to Men*, pp. 67–108.

92 Elaine Hansen, *Chaucer and the Fictions of Gender*, pp. 223–36, and Martin Blum, "Negotiating Masculinities: Erotic Triangles in the *Miller's Tale*," *MC*, 37–52, at pp. 46–49.

minster Abbey.[93] The biblical Absalom represented the longstanding paragon of male beauty – "from the sole of his foot to the crown of his head there was no blemish in him" (2 Samuel 14.25) – and his beautiful long hair was the feature shared by his Chaucerian namesake:[94]

> Crul was his heer, and as the gold it shoon,
> And strouted as a fanne large and brode;
> Ful streight and evene lay his joly shode. (*CT*, 1.3314–16)

The biblical Absalom appears elsewhere in Chaucer's writings during the 1390s. In both versions of the *Legend* Prologue, the poet inserted a ballade that begins with a similar reference to the golden hair of Absalom, although the reference is strangely designed to praise Queen Alceste's beauty:

> Hyd, Absolon, thy gilte tresses clere;
> Ester, ley thou thy meknesse al adown;
> Hyd, Jonathas, al thy frendly manere. (*LGW*, F.249–51)

The odd blending of Absalom's masculine beauty and Esther's meekness, along with the problematic reference to Jonathan as the exemplar of same-sex attachment in the Old Testament,[95] serves as a connection back to the gender-slippage and sexual irregularity lurking at the heart of the Ricardian household.

The Bedford Psalter-Hours pictures Richard II as a beardless youth with a note comparing him to Absalom.[96] The king was also lampooned by the Lancastrian historian Adam Usk as "the most beautiful of all mortal men, like a second Absalom," in the opening lines of his *Chronicle*.[97] These two comparisons depend upon what must have become a cultural commonplace. Fully mindful of the biblical Absalom's prideful fall, Usk's caustic characterization expresses a jibe only partially repressed when Maidstone praised King Richard as "beautiful as Absalom" during the royal entry into London in 1392 and more fully exploited by Chaucer's use of Absolon to caricature Ricardian effeteness and sexual bungling in the *Miller's Tale*. On a more sinister note, Absolon's fierce obsession with avenging his wounded pride by attacking the offenders with his "hoote kultour" invites comparison to King Richard's long-simmering resentment that led finally to his lethal retaliation against the Appellants who had humiliated him during the political crisis of 1387–88.[98]

Maidstone's comparison of Richard II to Troilus must also have drawn upon some common satiric understanding. Throughout the 1380s, Chaucer had played

93   Jonathan Alexander, "The Portrait of Richard II in Westminster Abbey," *The Regal Image of Richard II*, ed. Gordon et al., pp. 197–206.
94   Paul Beichner, "Absolon's Hair," *Medieval Studies* 12 (1950): 222–33.
95   John Boswell, *Christianity, Social Tolerance, and Homosexuality* (Chicago, IL: University of Chicago Press, 1980), pp. 238–39.
96   Sylvia Wright, "The Author Portraits in the Bedford Psalter-Hours: Gower, Chaucer and Hoccleve," *British Library Journal* 18 (1992): 190–201 at pp. 195–96 for BL Add. 42131, fol. 210a.
97   *The Chronicle of Adam Usk, 1377–1421*, ed. and trans. C. Given-Wilson (Oxford: Clarendon Press, 1997), pp. 1–2: "inter omnes mortales ac si secundus Apsalon pulcherimus."
98   Nigel Saul, *Richard II*, pp. 366–404.

a cagy literary game by normalizing and redefining in highly praiseworthy terms the irregularities of Richard II's domestic life – what Karma Lochrie has recently described as "heterosyncrasies."[99] *Troilus and Criseyde* invested the youthful prince with handsomeness and battlefield bravery but also with the high-mindedness and fearful regard for his lady's honor that forced him to struggle awkwardly with the script of amatory endeavors. His intensely emotional reverence for Criseyde accounted for his restraint as well as his sexual shortcomings in the bedroom, at worst a victim of the love-sickness or "stage fright" known to infect only the noblest heart. In the earlier version of the *Knight's Tale* known as *The Love of Palamon and Arcite*, the theatricality of male rivalry masked the affectionate bonds of knightly brotherhood as the true driving force for these two noblemen, who paid absurdly little attention to the Amazon princess they were fighting over. And in the 1380s version of the *Second Nun's Tale* known as *The Life of St. Cecilia*, the rejection of sex within wedlock was enshrined as an admirable spiritual ideal, while the wife's insistence upon keeping her virginity spared the husband's reputation for manly performance. Denied sex by his wife, Valerian turned to another man for comradeship, and his conversion led almost immediately to martyrdom shared not with his wife but with his "brother deere" Tiburce (*CT*, 8.302–71).

Only in the 1390s did Chaucer feel freer to expose the comic pretenses of failed masculinity in his characterization of Absolon in the *Miller's Tale*. Also writing in the mid-1390s as a Lancastrian dependent, Richard Maidstone invoked the same two figures of Troilus and Absalom in his *Concordia* to praise the beauty of Richard II and – traveling the same thin line as Chaucer – to hint at the king's shortcomings, specifically his failure to produce a male heir, which would eventually contribute to his tragic downfall in 1399. Maidstone's metaphorical language that described Richard II exercising a husband's conjugal rights over London like his wife in the bedroom "gives a new meaning to the phrase *royal entry*," as Paul Strohm has wittily remarked.[100] But for all of its veiled humor, the imagery also contributes nervously to the national anxiety arising from the king's failure to fulfill these same manly duties of penetration and procreation with his actual wife, Queen Anne.

[99] Karma Lochrie, *Heterosyncrasies: Female Sexuality When Normal Wasn't* (Minneapolis: University of Minnesota Press, 2005).
[100] Paul Strohm, *Hochon's Arrow*, p. 108.

2

The State of Exception and Sovereign Masculinity in *Troilus and Criseyde*

ROBERT S. STURGES

Troilus and Criseyde, though one of Chaucer's most overtly political texts, nevertheless leaves an unanswered political question at the heart of its plot: where can sovereignty be located in this romance?

Its characters variously attribute a metaphorical sovereignty to personified abstract forces such as love, fortune, and providence: "thilke sovereyne purveyaunce / That forwoot al withouten ignoraunce" (4.1070–71). The two lovers also claim to treat Criseyde's desires as sovereign within the context of their love relationship: "'O my Criseyde, O lady sovereigne'" (4.316), says Troilus, and Criseyde too reserves decisions about sovereignty to herself: "'A kynges sone although ye be, ywys, / Ye shal namore han sovereignete / Of me in love, than right in that cas is'" (3.170–72).

These metaphorical invocations exhaust the occurrences of the terms "sovereign" and "sovereignty" in *Troilus and Criseyde*. Literal political sovereignty in wartime Troy is thus more difficult to pin down precisely. Does it rest with King Priam, the titular sovereign, but one who remains a shadowy background figure? Does it rest with his eldest son Hector, to whom matters of state are normally referred in the course of the romance? Does it rest with the Trojan council or "parliament" that collectively overrules Hector and chooses to exchange Criseyde for Antenor in Book 4? Or is sovereignty in *Troilus and Criseyde* less an absolute power residing in any one individual or political body than a more diffuse system of relations? In this essay I examine the latter possibility, and suggest some ways in which these power relations are gendered, as well as some of the ways in which Chaucer critiques the gendering of power.

I begin by asking what is meant by the concept of sovereignty, which Chaucer invokes regularly, although, except in the instances cited above, without naming it as such. To start answering this question, I turn to the works of the political philosopher Giorgio Agamben, whose theories of sovereignty have played an increasingly important role in medieval literary studies in recent years.[1] For

---

[1] For example Sylvia Huot, *Madness in Medieval French Literature* (Oxford: Oxford University Press, 2003), pp. 65–96; Robert Mills, "Sovereign Power and Bare Life in Poetry by François Villon," *Exemplaria* 17.2 (2005): 445–80; Robert Sturges, "'Wols-hede and outhorne': The Ban, Bare Life, and Power in the Passion Plays," *Mindful Spirit in Late Medieval Literature*, ed. Bonnie Wheeler (New

Agamben, drawing on ancient and medieval as well as modern political theory, sovereignty is neither in essence a matter of governance nor the product of a social contract, but rather the biopolitical power of life and death, specifically the power to decide whose life is protected by the state and whose is not:

> The *puissance absolue et perpétuelle*, which defines state power, is not founded ... on a political will but rather on naked life, which is kept safe and protected only to the degree to which it submits itself to the sovereign's (or the law's) right of life and death. ... The state of exception, which is what the sovereign each and every time decides, takes place precisely when naked life – which normally appears rejoined to the multifarious forms of social life – is explicitly put into question and revoked as the ultimate foundation of political power.[2]

"Naked life" – or, as it is usually translated, "bare life" – is not some natural state of simple biological life in itself, but rather a political relation: it is life that has been reduced to bare biological existence by means of the sovereign decision.[3]

This decision, which founds sovereign power, is the decision to suspend law, and thus the rights possessed by citizens or subjects under the law, in a "state of exception." Individuals under a "ban" exist as bare life because they can be killed with impunity, as Agamben suggests with regard to early medieval law:

> the bandit could be killed (*bannire idem est quod dicere quilibet possit eum offendere*, "'To ban' someone is to say that anyone may harm him") ... or was even considered to be already dead (*exbannitus ad mortem de sua civitate debet haberi pro mortuo*, "Whoever is banned from his city on pain of death must be considered as dead").[4]

The ban is the abandonment of specific citizens/subjects by the sovereign state, the declaration that they exist in a state of exception to the rights and protections normally accorded them. An exception to all normal legal frameworks, such an individual's existence is purely biological, devoid of social relations except for the ban itself, and thus inhuman, comparable to the life of animals – aside from that sole remaining political relation, the sovereign decision that withdraws the

---

York: Palgrave, 2006), pp. 93–108; and Ruth Evans, "*Sir Orfeo* and Bare Life," *Medieval Cultural Studies*, eds. Ruth Evans, Helen Fulton, and David Matthews (Cardiff: University of Wales Press, 2006), pp. 198–212.

2   Giorgio Agamben, "Form-of-Life," *Means without End: Notes on Politics*, trans. Vincenzo Binetti and Cesare Casarino (Minneapolis: University of Minnesota Press, 2000), 3–12, at p. 5–6.

3   Both "bare life" and "naked life" are translations of Agamben's Italian phrase *la nuda vita*; "bare life" has gained wider acceptance because it is used in the English translation of Agamben's most influential book: *Homo Sacer: Sovereign Power and Bare Life*, trans. Daniel Heller-Roazen (Stanford, CA: Stanford University Press, 1998).

4   Giorgio Agamben, *Homo Sacer*, pp. 104–5, citing, first, Jacobus de Arena, *Lectura super Cod.*, 1. *Reos capitalium*, C. de accusationibus, n. 1, and, second, Baldus, *Consilia* (Venice: 1575), V, 54, n. 1 *Modo quaeritur*, both quoted in Desiderio Cavalca, *Il bando nella prassi e nella dottrina giuridica medievale* (Milan: Giuffrè, 1978), pp. 42, 50.

protection of life. Sovereignty is therefore power specifically over the body, a biopolitical power, as Foucault also suggests.[5]

For Agamben, indeed, bare life and the state of exception emphasize the ambiguity of political relations: the state of exception in particular places the sovereign both within and outside the juridical order, since it is in some sense legal for the sovereign to suspend the workings of the law. Subjects thus resemble sovereigns in their existence at the frontiers of law and of politics: bare life, too, has been cast outside the normal political order, but it is a political decision that has done so. This decision thus creates "a zone of absolute indeterminacy between anomie and law, in which the sphere of creatures and the juridical order are caught up in a single catastrophe."[6]

Scholars who link Agamben's political theories to medieval literature tend to emphasize the ways in which medieval texts represent the production of bare life itself, but the preceding and necessary condition, the state of exception, is at least as important as its product, bare life, in Agamben's thought.[7] The state of exception may also be applied to entire communities, particularly in declarations of a state of siege and similar conditions, in which normal laws and rights are suspended; thus, "[t]he state of exception is ... a space devoid of law, a zone of anomie in which all legal determinations – and above all the very distinction between public and private – are deactivated."[8] Again, this power to decide on a state of exception is foundational of sovereignty itself: "Therein consists the essence of State sovereignty, which must therefore be properly juridically defined not as the monopoly to sanction or to rule, but as the monopoly to decide."[9]

Although Agamben's primary concern is with the implications of understanding sovereignty for the post-Auschwitz world, his ideas may also help us understand the operation of power in *Troilus and Criseyde*. Rather than asking where "sovereignty" is located in Chaucer's text – as we have seen, the term itself is typically understood in only a metaphorical sense – we may ask where the power of life and death lies, how the romance imagines states of exception, who in this text risks reduction to bare life, and how this reduction is imagined as coming about. This is not, of course, to suggest that Chaucer is in some sense "Agambenian": *Troilus and Criseyde* does not offer any representation of an originary sovereign decision on the state of exception as Agamben describes it, nor do any of its characters fully qualify as a sovereign in Agam-

5   See Giorgio Agamben, *Homo Sacer*, pp. 187–88, referring to Michel Foucault, *History of Sexuality*, Volume I: *An Introduction*, trans. Robert Hurley (New York: Random House, 1978). See also Giorgio Agamben, "What Is a People?," *Means without End*, pp. 29–35.
6   Giorgio Agamben, *State of Exception*, trans. Kevin Attell (Chicago, IL: University of Chicago Press, 2005), p. 57.
7   For critiques of Agamben's connection of the state of exception to bare life, see two essays in *Politics, Metaphysics, Death: Essays on Giorgio Agamben's* Homo Sacer, ed. Andrew Norris (Durham, NC: Duke University Press, 2005): Peter Fitzpatrick, "Bare Sovereignty: *Homo Sacer* and the Insistence of Law," pp. 49–73, and Andrew Norris, "The Exemplary Exception: Philosophical and Political Decisions in Giorgio Agamben's *Homo Sacer*," pp. 262–83.
8   Giorgio Agamben, *State of Exception*, p. 50.
9   Giorgio Agamben, *Homo Sacer*, p. 16.

ben's sense. Instead, Chaucer represents wartime Troy as a "zone of anomie," in which the public/private distinction has been deactivated, and therefore as a source of cultural anxiety precisely because there is no clear sovereign power to which Trojan subjects might take recourse. Sovereignty is contested in Chaucer's Troy, and his critique of the state of exception echoes Dante's in Book 2 of his *Monarchia*, which suggests that the goals of law can be achieved only by means of the law. Agamben takes this to mean that "[t]he idea that a suspension of law may be necessary for the common good is foreign to the medieval world."[10] Nevertheless, the potential ramifications of such an idea were of the utmost concern to late medieval political thinkers,[11] and Agamben's analysis of them provides a set of concepts and a vocabulary that may prove helpful in understanding Chaucerian sovereignty.

Troilus and Criseyde themselves like to speak and behave as if their relationship were controlled by the ethos of *fin'amors* or "courtly love," a system that conventionally assigns power over the male lover to his lady. Not only do they both use the terminology of sovereignty in understanding Criseyde's role in their relationship (as in the quotations above), they also behave throughout the romance as if this sovereignty did indeed grant her a biopolitical power over their bodies. Thus Criseyde famously declares herself to be her "owene womman" (2.750), while perhaps the most pleasurable aspect of her conversation with Pandarus in Book 2, as he talks her into accepting Troilus's love service, is the belief that she has the power "[t]o mowen swich a knyght don lyve or dye" (2.1594). Such sentiments are echoed by Troilus in the scene of their meeting in Book 3, when he first directly confesses his love:

> "Thus muche as now, O wommanliche wif,
> I may out brynge, and if this yow displese,
> That shal I wreke upon myn owen lif
> Right soone, I trowe, and do youre herte an ese,
> If with my deth youre wreththe may apese.
> But syn that ye han herd me somwhat seye,
> Now recche I nevere how soone that I deye." (3.106–12)

This is undoubtedly literary-conventional language, but this particular literary convention would be incomprehensible if the metaphor of sovereignty did not refer to a real-life political power over bodies, a relation in which the death of the subject can serve to appease the wrath of the sovereign. Troilus's metaphor imagines that Criseyde, by withholding her love, has the power to impose a ban and thus to recreate his existence as bare life. Immediately after this declaration, Criseyde reminds Troilus that, in spite of his real-life status as a "kynges sone," he lacks "sovereignete / ... in love" (3.171–73), a reminder made concrete in his

---

[10] Giorgio Agamben, *State of Exception*, p. 26. See Dante, *Monarchia*, ed. and trans. Prue Shaw (Cambridge: Cambridge University Press, 1995), 2.5.23: "finem iuris intendentem oportet cum iure intendere" (p. 70) – "one who seeks the purpose of right must seek it with right" (p. 69).

[11] Most late medieval political thinkers were concerned to limit sovereign power over individual bodies. In addition to Dante, see, for one influential example, Marsilius of Padua, *Defensor Pacis*, trans. Alan Gewirth (1956; repr. Toronto: University of Toronto Press, 1980), pp. 31–33, 41–43.

gesture of kneeling obeisance, from which "she bad hym nought rise" (3.967). The passage from Book 4 cited in the first paragraph above also links Criseyde's figurative sovereignty to Troilus's imagined death (4.316–22). For Chaucer as for Agamben, in the sadomasochistic love relation, "the very physiological life of bodies appears, through sexuality, as the pure political element."[12]

This apparent, metaphorical feminine sovereignty of *fin'amors* – a sovereignty here ideally exercised by a redoubled, excessive femininity, as in the phrase "wommanliche wif" – despite its sadomasochistic effects on Troilus, often seems no more than a worn-out courtly illusion in the world of Greek/Trojan *realpolitik* that *Troilus and Criseyde* depicts. The deception practiced on Criseyde by Pandarus and Troilus is a more effective response than *fin'amors* to the realities of that world: they trick Criseyde into a love relationship, and their deceit emphasizes how powerless she is in Troy after her father's treason, which sets the plot in motion. In the infamous scene following the consummation of her and Troilus's love, Pandarus himself acknowledges that her sovereignty is a joke:

> With that she gan hire face for to wrye
> With the shete, and wax for shame al reed;
> And Pandarus gan under for to prie,
> And seyde, "Nece, if that I shal be ded,
> Have here a swerd and smyteth of myn hed!"
> With that his arm al sodeynly he thriste
> Under hire nekke, and at the laste hire kyste. (3.1569–75)

Whatever may be going on here erotically, politically the illusion of Criseyde's sovereignty is now revealed as a comedy, the product of masculine deceit: the power of life and death that Pandarus mockingly offers her reads more like a sexual assault. That she is complicit in the joke ("'Fox that ye ben!'" [3.1565]) is significant, because Criseyde pursues her own agenda in the politics of love, which turns out, especially from her perspective, to be intimately related to the *realpolitik* of the Trojan War. Criseyde's real lack of power can also be understood in terms of a biopolitical sovereignty, and her response to her own powerlessness emphasizes the ways in which claims of sovereign power are truly gendered in Chaucer's Troy: the political action of *Troilus and Criseyde* in every instance reveals the courtly metaphor's feminization of sovereign power for the illusion it is. It is an illusion that Criseyde herself seems to understand better than she is often willing to admit.

As I suggested earlier, real sovereign power is difficult to locate in wartime Troy, a difficulty that may suggest that Troy, at the time of the romance's action, exists in a state of exception, in that "zone of anomie" described by Agamben, in which the distinction between public and private is "deactivated." The source of sovereign power is so difficult to locate in *Troilus and Criseyde* because

---

12   Giorgio Agamben, *Homo Sacer*, p. 134.

the reader nowhere witnesses this deactivation, the sovereign decision itself. However, we can observe its effects throughout the romance.

In the first encounter between Criseyde and her uncle, Pandarus observes that "'love of frendes regneth al this town'" (2.379): politics, indeed sovereignty itself, has been redefined as a relation of personal protection rather than of law. We may observe here the effects of Agamben's deactivization of the distinction between public and private. Its further effects are evident in Pandarus's assembly of royal friends against Poliphete, who, he alleges, will bring legal charges against Criseyde (2.1467–69). Although this allegation suggests that some system of civil law may still be functioning in Troy, Criseyde is not surprised that the way Pandarus deals with it is entirely personal, bustling around to make powerful individuals, including Hector and his brother Deiphebus, Poliphete's "foo" (2.1482). Although Pandarus's allegations against Poliphete appear to be trumped up simply to frighten Criseyde into her first meeting with Troilus – certainly the text provides no evidence that these allegations are true – nevertheless, Pandarus's personal politics have potentially serious consequences for Poliphete: "'Anhonged be swich oon, were he my brother! / And so he shal, for it ne may nought varien!'" (2.1620–21), declare Pandarus's friends. Because the public/private distinction has been dissolved, what appears to be a trumped-up accusation exposes Poliphete to bare life; this attempt at a sovereign decision has been made not through law but through personal relations.

That the public/private distinction has been deactivated in wartime Troy is especially clear in Criseyde's case. Because of her father's originary crime, she is, from the first, presented as living in a state of exception, one which, according to the Trojan viewpoint, places her in precisely the position described by Agamben, that of the one who may be killed with impunity:

> Gret rumour gan, whan it was first aspied
> Thorough al the town, and generaly was spoken,
> That Calkas traitour fled was and allied
> With hem of Grece, and casten to be wroken
> On hym that falsly hadde his feith so broken,
> And seyden he and al his kyn at-ones
> Ben worthi for to brennen, fel and bones. (1.85–91)

Chaucer's typical distaste for mob violence is displayed here: his editors date *Troilus and Criseyde* to the period immediately following the experience, traumatic for Chaucer and his aristocratic patrons, of the Peasants' Revolt of 1381.[13]

---

13   On Chaucerian responses to the Peasants' Revolt, see Alfred David, *The Strumpet Muse: Art and Morals in Chaucer's Poetry* (Bloomington: Indiana University Press, 1976), p. 92; Lee Patterson, *Chaucer and the Subject of History* (Madison: University of Wisconsin Press, 1991), p. 279; Paul Strohm, *Social Chaucer* (Cambridge, MA: Harvard University Press, 1989), pp. 152–54; Susan Crane, "The Writing Lesson of 1381," *Chaucer's England: Literature in Historical Context*, ed. Barbara Hanawalt (Minneapolis: University of Minnesota Press, 1992), pp. 201–22; Steven Justice, *Writing and Rebellion: England in 1381* (Berkeley: University of California Press, 1994), pp. 225–31; and Robert Sturges, *Chaucer's Pardoner and Gender Theory* (New York: St. Martin's Press, 2000), pp. 1–14.

In the romance as in reality, the anonymous people rise up, though at this point only linguistically, in violent reaction against members of the aristocracy, and claim sovereign power for themselves; the fantasized burning of Calchas and his family – which is to say of Criseyde, who is introduced immediately in the following stanza – suggests that they have been imaginatively placed outside the juridical order. The voice of the people does not imagine Criseyde's death as murder, but as something of which she is "worthi" because of her father's crime. But nor does it imagine her death as sanctioned by law; that is to say, this anonymous mass voice fantasizes the imposition of a ban.

This first attempt at sovereign decision-making is oddly anonymous. The original grammatical subject of the seven-line sentence is neither an individual nor even the people as a collectivity, but rather "rumour" itself (or, in a variant reading, "noise"[14]) rises up of its own accord and is, passively, spoken; this grammatical subject is then, by stylistic sleight-of-hand, succeeded by an unexpressed plural subject that "casten to be wroken" on Calchas and his family, and that "seyden" they deserve death by burning.[15] The text's first attempt at a sovereign decision thus floats free of any specific agent, ready to be taken up by this anonymous crowd. In *Troilus and Criseyde*, Troy itself always already exists in a state of exception. The virtual absence of the titular king Priam from the poem's action also contributes to this sense of instability.

Criseyde's response to the threat that she will be placed under a ban also suggests the extent to which the distinction between public and private has been erased in Troy's state of siege: she pleads her case not with King Priam, but with Hector. This is the first of several matters of state that are referred to Hector's personal intervention in the course of the romance. Falling on her knees before him in the gesture of obeisance that Troilus later performs before her, Criseyde makes, not a legal case, but a personal plea for mercy: "With pitous vois, and tendrely wepynge, / His mercy bad, hirselven excusynge" (1.111–12). There seems to be no law in effect to which Criseyde can appeal; her only recourse is the personal protection of a powerful individual.

Hector, in fact, seems a good candidate in this text for the location of sovereign power as Agamben defines it. Criseyde accepts that he will take power over her body, specifically the power of life and death; in return, Hector will afford her protection and that safekeeping of her bare life – the protection from a state of exception – that defines sovereignty.[16] Hector sees that Criseyde is not only "sorwfully bigon" but also "so fair a creature," and

---

[14]   The *Riverside Chaucer*'s textual note on this line gives "The noise up rose" as a possible authorial revision of "Gret rumour gan"; Barry Windeatt adopts the variant in his edition, *Troilus and Criseyde* (London: Penguin, 2003).

[15]   Windeatt notes that Chaucer's version of these events differs from Boccaccio's in its awareness of contemporary English laws concerning treason, but also demonstrates that the imagined extension of his punishment to his family contradicts legal practice: see Windeatt's edition of *Troilus and Criseyde*, p. 355, note on ll. 87–91. In any case, the people's judgment on Criseyde is not presented as a legal decision.

[16]   Commentators on Agamben's political theories typically emphasize the withdrawal of such protections, but the necessary obverse of the decision on a state of exception is the decision to protect bare

> Of his goodnesse he gladede hire anon,
> And seyde, "Lat youre fadres treson gon
> Forth with meschaunce, and ye youreself in joie
> Dwelleth with us, whil yow good list, in Troie.
>
> "And al th'onour that men may don yow have,
> As ferforth as youre fader dwelled here,
> Ye shul have, and youre body shal men save,
> As fer as I may ought enquere or here." (1.116–23)

Criseyde's safety in Troy comes not from any legal recourse, but from Hector's personal "goodnesse" and his word that he himself will afford her protection. Specifically, he declares that her body will be safe from other men. In dissociating her from Calchas's treason, indeed in simply letting her father's crime go, Hector here assumes the power of life and death, and, motivated at least in part by the beauty of the subjected body kneeling before him, stakes his claim to sovereignty over her, keeping Criseyde's body safe from the status of bare life to which the anonymous voice of the Trojan people sought to expose her. She will, indeed, retain the same status she has always enjoyed in Troy, all due to Hector's personal protection.

Hector is generally the one who acts the sovereign part throughout the romance, with regard to Troy as a whole as well as to Criseyde. When she and Troilus are brought together at the end of Book 2, Hector has, by letter, asked his brother's counsel on a sovereign decision; Troilus tricks Helen and Deiphebus into leaving by asking them to take the letter and advise him in turn:

> And fond, as hap was, at his beddes hed
> The copie of a tretys and a lettre
> That Ector hadde hym sent to axen red
> If swych a man was worthi to ben ded,
> Woot I nought who; but in a grisly wise
> He preyede hem anon on it avyse. (2.1696–701)

Again, whether this anonymous man – like Criseyde in Book 1 – lives or dies is presented as a matter for Hector's personal decision. One might wonder whether this man, whom the narrator refuses to name, might not be the hapless Poliphete; in that case, the others whom Pandarus has interested in the case have referred the sovereign decision on Poliphete to Hector. Here he asks Troilus only for his "red" or advice; Hector alone will make the decision, and he alone claims the sovereign power of life and death. The reader never learns the fate of this man, nor even what he is supposed to have done to deserve death, any more than we learn his name, and this very lack of legal information increases the impression that Hector's word alone is now the law. Like Poliphete's, this anonymous figure's bare life hangs disturbingly in the balance, its vulnerability

---

life from such a state, as Agamben makes clear in the passage from "Form-of-Life" quoted above, p. 29.

to the extra-legal, or supralegal, sovereign decision remaining poignantly in the background for the remainder of the poem.

Hector's claim of sovereignty, in contradistinction to the metaphorical feminine sovereignty in love, cannot be detached from an ideal of masculinity. Hector, indeed, is the poem's ideal of manhood, and his masculine power is regularly associated with the protection of Troy – especially by Criseyde. When Pandarus first approaches her concerning Troilus's love in Book 2, the siege is among their first topics of conversation; Criseyde, terrified of potential Trojan violence in Book 1, is equally – to the point of death – afraid of the Greeks in Book 2: "'I am of Grekes so fered that I deye'" (2.124). Hector, it turns out, is her (and the city's) protector from the latter as he is from the former: Criseyde asks Pandarus "how Ector ferde, / That was the townes wal and Grekes yerde" (2.153–54). Significant here is not only her concern about Hector, but also how she, in indirect discourse, imagines him: both as a protective wall and as a "yerde" – a rod used to beat or scourge a rival, but also figuratively the phallus, a metaphorical usage familiar in the period of *Troilus and Criseyde*.[17] Criseyde imagines Hector asserting a specifically masculine, phallic dominance over their Greek enemies – even, given that the "yerde" is imagined as an offensive weapon, as raping them. And Criseyde can fantasize loving such a man: shocked that her uncle is urging her to love Troilus, she complains that she would instead have expected him to reprove her if she "'[h]adde loved outher hym or Achilles, / Ector, or any mannes creature'" (2.416–17). "Hym" presumably refers to Troilus, but the fantasized lovers that she actually names – those she has apparently already imagined as lovers – are the greatest Greek and Trojan heroes, Achilles and Hector. In her doubly dangerous situation with regard both to Troy and to the Greeks, Criseyde imagines that only heroic masculinity can safeguard her bare life. Indeed, in Troy's cultural imaginary as a whole, as we shall see, only masculinity can lay claim to real sovereignty.

What makes Troilus attractive to Criseyde is the heroic masculinity reflected onto him from his brother Hector. Throughout the romance, Troilus is imagined as participating in a comparable heroic masculinity – though always secondarily to Hector's. In Book 3, Troilus among the Greeks is "[s]ave Ector most ydred of any wight" (3.1775); in Book 5, again on the battlefield, Troilus is "withouten any peere, / Save Ector" (5.1804). The comparison with Hector is also the first aspect of Troilus's love service mentioned in Book 1, immediately after he declares himself Criseyde's "man while he may dure" because she alone now provides "his lif, and from the deth his cure" (1.468–69):

> The sharpe shoures felle of armes preve
> That Ector or his othere brethren diden
> Ne made hym only therfore ones meve;
> And yet was he, where so men wente or riden,
> Founde oon the beste. (1.470–74)

---

[17]   The *OED*, s.v. "yard," gives 1379 as the earliest instance of this usage.

Hector sets the standard of manliness here, one to which Troilus more or less lives up – if not as the best man, at least as one of the best – but in Troilus's case he acts the traditional masculine role not for reasons of manly competition, but rather because of his newly declared allegiance to Criseyde's sovereignty in love. His own manhood as a courtly lover, indeed, becomes more complex than Hector's: by the end of Book 1 he is still a lion on the field of battle (1.1074), but now also "the frendlieste wight, / The gentilest, and ek the mooste fre, / The thriftiest" (1.1079–81).

Such nuances of masculinity, however, are not what first attract Criseyde; in wartime Troy, Troilus's more complex masculinity can easily be called into question: if heroic masculinity threatens violence, sensitive masculinity is threatened with weakness.[18] When in Book 2 Criseyde inquires of Pandarus about Hector in his manly role as "yerde" and defender of Troy, her uncle praises Troilus as "'[t]he wise, worthi Ector the secounde'" (2.158), emphasizing both his martial prowess and his moral virtue. In both, Troilus remains secondary to Hector; Troilus is a good knight, according to Pandarus, precisely because of his similarity to Hector: "'Of Troilus the same thyng trowe I'" (2.184). From this point, Pandarus moves into an account of Troilus's power on the battlefield, and only then reveals Troilus's love for Criseyde. Troilus's warrior image, armed on his bleeding horse, finally convinces Criseyde to think of him as a potential lover:

> But swich a knyghtly sighte trewely
> As was on hym, was nought, withouten faille,
> To loke on Mars, that god is of bataille.
>
> So lik a man of armes and a knyght
> He was to seen, fulfilled of heigh prowesse,
> For bothe he hadde a body and a myght
> To don that thing, as wel as hardynesse. (2.628–34)

Criseyde eventually remembers his other virtues too, but the first visual impression Troilus makes on her is the image of heroic masculinity – a "weldy" masculinity (2.636) that can, ambiguously, do "that thing," whether martial or sexual – that has previously been associated with his brother Hector.[19]

---

18 Scholarship on masculinity in *Troilus and Criseyde* has tended to focus on this complex (or compromised) masculinity of Troilus himself. Several such scholars may be cited at this point: David Aers, *Community, Gender and Individual Identity: English Writing 1360–1430* (New York: Routledge, 1989), pp. 117–52; Elaine Hansen, *Chaucer and the Fictions of Gender* (Berkeley: University of California Press, 1992), pp. 143–55, 166–67, and 180–82; Jill Mann, *Feminizing Chaucer* (Cambridge: D.S. Brewer, 2002), pp. 129–32; R. D. Eaton, "Gender, Class and Conscience in Chaucer," *English Studies* 84.3 (2003): 205–18; and three essays in *MC*: Stephanie Dietrich, "'Slydyng' Masculinity in the Four Portraits of Troilus," pp. 205–20; Maud McInerney, "'Is this a mannes herte?': Unmanning Troilus through Ovidian Allusion," pp. 221–35; and Derek Brewer, "Troilus's 'Gentil' Manhood," pp. 237–52.

19 On the implied sexual sense of these lines, see E. Talbot Donaldson's classic essay "Criseide and Her Narrator," in his *Speaking of Chaucer* (New York: Norton, 1970), pp. 65–83, at p. 66 n. 1; Windeatt cites the same source in his note on these lines, p. 385n.

If Hector's claim to sovereignty is inseparable from that heroic masculine ideal, the reader is now reminded once again that Troilus's masculine prowess is a secondary reflection of Hector's: "And ay the peple cryde, 'Here cometh oure joye, / And, next his brother, holder up of Troye'" (2.643–44). Like Hector, Troilus is Troy's protector; if Troilus's masculinity reflects his brother's, perhaps he can share in Hector's claim of sovereignty as well. Hector's protection of Troy has already been associated with his protection of Criseyde's body. It is thus significant, first, that the anonymous people of Troy who threatened Criseyde with the prospect of a ban are the ones acclaiming Troilus, and second, that Criseyde utters her famous line "'Who yaf me drynke?'" (2.651) precisely when these same people – the ones whose claim to sovereignty over her body has been superseded by Hector's – have compared Troilus to his brother and her protector. Criseyde's recognition of sovereign masculinity has been displaced from Hector to Troilus, not exactly because of love, but because "his distresse / Was al for hire" (2.663–64). Feminine sovereignty in love gives access to masculine political sovereignty, even apparent power over it, since feminine sovereignty at this point has not yet been exposed as an illusion fostered by masculine deceit.

Hector's masculine heroism against the Greeks is displayed once again as he and his men ride out to battle at the beginning of Book 4, to the beat of Chaucer's own unusually heroic alliteration:

> Ector and many a worthi wight out wente,
> With spere in honde and bigge bowes bente;
> And in the berd, withouten lenger lette,
> Hire fomen in the feld hem faste mette. (4.39–42)

The language of spears, big bows, and beards emphasizes the image of Hector that has developed throughout the romance: not merely of sovereign masculinity, but of an aggressive hypermasculinity that his brother Troilus possesses only as a reflection of Hector. But this time, Hector's masculine power and his claims to sovereignty both prove illusory, just as Criseyde's metaphorical sovereignty in love proved earlier. Hector, for the first time in *Troilus and Criseyde*, fails this crucial test of masculine power: "The folk of Troie hemselven so mysledden / That with the worse at nyght homward they fledden" (4.48–49). "[H]emselven … mysledden" suggests a collective failure of leadership, and the plural person demonstrates the degree to which Hector has failed to remain in charge. He must ignominiously flee homeward, now only as one of the anonymous crowd, and his failed hypermasculinity is ultimately responsible for the Greek capture of Antenor and the other Trojan heroes (4.50–54), which drives the remainder of the romance's plot.

Hector's failure of masculinity is followed, inevitably, by a failure of sovereignty: having failed to control the Greeks in battle, Hector also fails to control his own Trojan people in their response to the battle's outcome. Indeed, once more it is the people of Troy who claim decision-making power over Criseyde's body. This time the Trojan parliament with Priam presiding, rather than the anonymous rumor or noise of Book 1, claims the right of decision, as the narrator insists at several points (4.142–43, 211, 217); nevertheless, when the question of exchanging Criseyde for Antenor is debated, with Hector's as the sole voice opposing the exchange, Chaucer's language recalls the anonymous attempt to pass judgment on her in Book 1:

> The noyse of peple up stirte thanne at ones,
> As breme as blase of straw iset on-fire;
> For infortune it wolde, for the nones,
> They sholden hire confusioun desire. (4.183–86)

The parliament is here linguistically transformed back into the anonymous people of Book 1, and once again the "noyse" itself is the grammatical subject, starting itself up like a fire just as the noise or rumor rose up of its own accord earlier. The effect of the people's decision-making in this case too recalls the madness of mob violence, irrationally desiring the return of Antenor, who will eventually betray them; if Chaucer and his patrons found the Peasants' Revolt traumatic, they perhaps found the parliaments of the mid-1380s no less so.[20]

This time, the people are successful, despite Hector's attempt to reassert his claim to sovereign status as protector of Criseyde's bare life:

> "Syres, she nys no prisonere," he seyde;
> "I not on yow who that this charge leyde,
> But, on my part, ye may eftsone hem telle,
> We usen here no wommen for to selle." (4.179–82)

Hector now tries to define Criseyde's status legally – she is not a prisoner, but a Trojan subject – but in the Trojan "zone of anomie," at the frontier of the juridical order, no such legal status can be acknowledged. Hector recognizes that this parliamentary decision is a matter of control over Criseyde's body – of her bare life – in the last line of his brief speech: its overtones of slavery and prostitution in the "selling" of women suggest a future of concubinage for Criseyde. Having sacrificed his masculine potency, Hector thus loses his claim to sovereignty as well; in the Trojan "zone of anomie," sovereignty is still up for grabs. The parliament, with its recollection of mob violence, now successfully seizes it, and the sign of its power is its ability to dispose of Criseyde's body, just as the sign of the failure of Hector's claim to sovereignty is the loss of his power to protect that body.

---

[20] On Chaucer's prudent responses to "the first stirrings of parliamentary discontent in 1385 and their aftermath in the Wonderful Parliament of 1386" – the period of the composition of *Troilus and Criseyde* – see Paul Strohm, "Politics and Poetics: Usk and Chaucer in the 1380s," *Literary Practice and Social Change in Britain, 1380–1530*, ed. Lee Patterson (Berkeley: University of California Press, 1990), pp. 83–112; this quotation is on p. 91. See also S. Sanderlin, "Chaucer and Ricardian Politics," *ChauR* 22.3 (1988): 171–84, especially pp. 172–73; Lee Patterson, *Chaucer and the Subject of History*, pp. 157–59. Scholars date the completion of *Troilus and Criseyde* to 1387 at the latest: see the introduction to Barry Windeatt's edition, p. xx; Sylvia Federico, *New Troy: Fantasies of Empire in the Late Middle Ages* (Minneapolis: University of Minnesota Press, 2003), takes this to mean that "the moment of the poem's completion is also the moment at which Chaucer himself began to fall" (p. 97). Federico also discusses some general relations between this romance and contemporary politics (pp. 71–72 and 90–93), and suggests that "[t]he concluding movements of *Troilus and Criseyde* become, in retrospect, part of the record of the disintegration of Ricardianism" (p. 93).

What the people desire in this new claim to sovereignty is, ironically, what Criseyde herself desired – the protection and safeguarding of bare life by the exercise of masculine power:

> "Ector," quod they, "what goost may yow enspyre
> This womman thus to shilde and don us leese
> Daun Antenor – a wrong way now ye chese –
>
> "That is so wys and ek so bold baroun?
> And we han nede to folk, as men may se.
> He is ek oon the grettest of this town.
> O Ector, lat tho fantasies be!" (4.187–93)

Hector's own claim to sovereignty, defined by his protection of Criseyde's body, is here redefined not once, but twice, as merely a "fantasie" inspired by a "goost": he can no longer shield "this womman" – Criseyde defined in terms of bodily sex rather than self – in favor of a great and "bold baroun" – Antenor defined in terms of his heroic masculinity – when men are so desperately needed to defend the city. The parliament's sovereign decision gives value to heroic masculinity, and renders other gendered positions – femininity, Troilus's more complex manhood, and even Hector's recently compromised masculinity – valueless. The very sovereign masculinity in which Criseyde placed her hope of protection, in a crushing irony, now sacrifices her to an image of itself. Antenor, Troy's new masculine ideal, will also, in a further irony, become the betrayer of Troy, as the narrator keeps reminding us: "For he was after traitour to the town / Of Troye" (4.204–5). The sovereignty of masculinity, like the other forms of sovereignty explored in Troy's "zone of anomie," is always a fantasy of protection, and is always exposed as an illusion: it never protects in the long run, but only exposes the subject to bare life, over and over again.

The bare life of outlawry is the only other fate Troilus can now imagine for Criseyde and himself, as he, at the suggestion of Pandarus, urges elopement as a possible response to the parliamentary decision. " 'And lat us stele awey bitwixe us tweye'" (4.1503), he suggests; Criseyde rejects his plan precisely because it fails to safeguard her bare life: "'If this were wist, my lif lay in balaunce'" (4.1560).[21] Criseyde's attempt to find her own new masculine ideal in Diomede, with his "sterne vois and myghty lymes square, / Hardy, testif, strong, and chivalrous / Of dedes" (5.801–3), is thus merely a repetition of the same fantasy of a protective sovereign masculinity, one that she particularly needs as she imagines the renewed possibility of reduction to bare life should she try to escape back to her previous protectors: " 'lo, this drede I moost of alle – / If in the hondes of some wrecche I falle, / I nam but lost'" (5.704–6).

---

21 On this episode and Criseyde's vulnerability, see Carolyn Dinshaw, "Rivalry, Rape and Manhood: Gower and Chaucer," *Violence against Women in Medieval Texts*, ed. Anna Roberts (Gainesville: University Press of Florida, 1998), pp. 137–60. Angela Gibson, "The Captivity Narrative and English National Identity in *Troilus and Criseyde*," a paper delivered at the December, 2005 convention of the Modern Language Association in Washington, DC, argues that Criseyde's decision might be read as consent to, and ratification of, the parliamentary decision.

Diomede understands Criseyde's status among the Greeks as bare life and takes full advantage of it, imagining her heart and body not as human attributes but rather in terms of fish to be caught: "To fisshen hire he leyde out hook and lyne" (5.777).[22] And Diomede too claims sovereign power over her body, the last of the series who have staked that claim: "'whoso myghte wynnen swich a flour / From hym for whom she morneth nyght and day, / He myghte seyn he were a conquerour'" (5.792–94). That Diomede is potentially a literal political sovereign as well, "'[o]f Calydoyne and Arge a kyng'" (5.934), furthers his case with Criseyde, who, in a replay of her desire for the protective masculinity of Hector and Troilus, finally responds to Diomede's advances because of "[h]is grete estat, and perel of the town" (5.1025).

Robert Henryson, an early and sensitive reader of Chaucer, understands that the illusion of sovereign masculinity exposed in *Troilus and Criseyde* can end only in the very exposure to bare life that Criseyde hoped to avoid:

> Quhen Diomeid had all his appetyte,
> And mair, fulfillit of this fair ladie,
> Upon ane-uther he set his haill delyte,
> And send to hir ane lybell of repudie,
> And hir excludit fra his companie.
> Than desolait scho walkit up and doun,
> And sum men sayis into the court commoun.[23]

For Diomede, in Henryson's view, Criseyde is never more than a body, and his masculine sovereignty over it can protect and safeguard, but can equally well expose, its bare life: the "court commoun" of this passage suggests that Hector's prediction of concubinage or prostitution as Criseyde's fate was accurate, as she here becomes a "common woman."[24] The trajectory of Criseyde's career that Henryson projects follows the logic of sovereign masculinity, as understood by Chaucer, to its inevitable conclusion: defined by a "zone of anomie," its protective aspect is always a fantasy, one that leads invariably to the exposure of bare life for those who trust in it.

Another ending to the story is suggested in Chaucer's controversial Christian conclusion to *Troilus and Criseyde*, which in my reading is a political as well as a religious one:

> Thow oon, and two, and thre, eterne on lyve,
> That regnest ay in thre, and two, and oon,
> Uncircumscript, and al maist circumscrive,
> Us from visible and invisible foon
> Defende, and to thy mercy, everichoon,

---

[22] Agamben's own consideration of human–animal relations can be found in his *The Open: Man and Animal*, trans. Kevin Attell (Stanford, CA: Stanford University Press, 2004).

[23] Robert Henryson, *The Testament of Cresseid*, in *Poems*, ed. Charles Eliott, 2nd edn. (Oxford: Clarendon Press, 1974), pp. 90–107, at p. 92, ll. 70–77.

[24] On the implications of this term, see Ruth Mazo Karras, *Common Women: Prostitution and Sexuality in Medieval England* (Oxford: Oxford University Press, 1996).

> So make us, Jesus, for thi mercy, digne,
> For love of mayde and moder thyn benigne. (5.1863–69)

The reader is here placed, alongside the narrator, in the position previously occupied by Criseyde: like her, we are all now the ones who need a defense from our foes. By the same token, Jesus here takes the place of Criseyde's various failed masculine protectors, a reigning sovereign who can be imagined as safeguarding our bare lives as Hector, Diomede, and Troy itself failed to defend hers. And while Jesus' sovereignty may be gendered masculine, it becomes accessible and comprehensible only through feminine love. The illusions of sovereignty and gender on the earthly level are finally reintroduced as heavenly realities, and the production of bare life by gendered sovereignty is once again concealed. Whether Chaucer reimplicates himself in the logic of gendered sovereignty or offers a devastatingly ironic critique of it is one of the questions remaining at the romance's conclusion.

3

Revisiting Troilus's Faint[1]

GRETCHEN MIESZKOWSKI

> Because there is neither an "essence" that gender expresses or exter-
> nalizes nor an objective ideal to which gender aspires, and because
> gender is not a fact, the various acts of gender create the idea of
> gender, and without those acts, there would be no gender at all.
> Gender is, thus, a construction that regularly conceals its genesis; the
> tacit collective agreement to perform, produce, and sustain discrete
> and polar genders as cultural fictions is obscured by the credibility
> of those productions – and the punishments that attend not agreeing
> to believe in them.
>
> Judith Butler, *Gender Trouble*[2]

With a crash that shattered the last manifestations of the notion that some inner core renders human beings male or female, an ancient concept of the self fell to the axe of Judith Butler, one of the most important theorists rewriting identity and sexuality today. Gender is the bedrock of personal identity in Butler's conception, but, jettisoning conventional notions altogether, she argues that it is the acts of gender and only the acts of gender that constitute its reality. Gender emerges from the repetition of such acts. It is constructed in and through that repetition, with each iteration altering slightly the act it enacts. No additional "essence" lies behind this performance. Gender is thus the product of the "reiterative power of discourse to produce the phenomena that it regulates and constrains."[3] People, speaking subjects, "I's" emerge only as always already gendered, as already existing within gender relations, where those relations are themselves the products of the utterances that constitute the substance of "gender" and "relation" in the first place. Gender identity is performatively brought into being "by the very 'expressions' that are said to be its results."[4]

---

[1] An earlier version of this paper was presented at the 41st International Congress on Medieval Studies, Medieval Institute, Kalamazoo, MI, May 6, 2006. Its core idea about fainting lovers in the Middle Ages appears in my *Medieval Go-Betweens and Chaucer's Pandarus* (New York: Palgrave, 2006), p. 169.

[2] Judith Butler, *Gender Trouble: Feminism and the Subversion of Identity* (1990; New York: Routledge, 1999), p. 178.

[3] Judith Butler, *Bodies That Matter: On the Discursive Limits of "Sex"* (New York: Routledge, 1993), p. 2.

[4] Judith Butler, *Gender Trouble*, p. 33.

Since gendering is "the differentiating relations by which speaking subjects come into being," it is so primary that "sex" is reduced to a fiction or a fantasy, prelinguistic and therefore inaccessible.[5] Sex is no more than "a performatively enacted signification" without independent being. There is no "interior 'truth' of dispositions and identity" behind sex.[6] Sex is merely "one of the norms by which the 'one' becomes viable at all, that which qualifies a body for life within the domain of cultural intelligibility."[7] With sex reduced to a fiction, gender can no longer be understood through the feminist idea, popular since the 1980s, of a cultural construct imposed on "the body" or the body's sex. For Butler, no aspect of gender can be thought of as "natural," a "given," part of the core of what it is to be a man or woman, because there is no such core; there are only gendered acts within "the matrix of gender relations."[8]

If gender is brought into being performatively, rather than as the expression of a gendered human core, then specific behaviors will not by necessity be male or female, and actions can acquire or lose their status as one or the other (or both) over time. As we read, we participate in these discourses that are generative of gender. When many literary works of a genre contrast the actions of males and females, those acts create gender norms. They determine what it is to be male or female in literature of that genre, an inheritance passed down from one literary work to another. What we call reading is in part the process of being interpellated by these discourses. How manly is Troilus? What are the consequences of his manliness, or lack of manliness, for his role in the poem? When Criseyde turns to Diomede, is her choice understandable because she is choosing a more manly man than Troilus? In reading we are part of the performative dynamic that poses and gives answers to questions of this sort.

Six centuries of reliving literary as well as societal genders intervene between the present and *Troilus and Criseyde*. This essay examines the impact of that six-century gap on what twentieth- and twenty-first-century readers understand as indications of Troilus's masculinity. Two aspects of Troilus have figured more prominently than any others in the debate over his manliness: his passivity as a lover and his faint during his first night with Criseyde. Twenty-first-century Chaucerians will be surprised to learn that there is no basis in medieval literature for reading either Troilus's passivity or his faint as evidence of effeminacy. Neither passive loving nor fainting was identified with women more than with men in the literature of Chaucer's period.

Undebatably, Troilus is a passive lover. Instead of courting Criseyde, he retreats to his bedroom to sing love songs and to prepare to die of love (1.358–60,

---

5   Judith Butler, *Bodies*, p. 7. In response to the objection that biological sex is not a fiction, Butler resists any simple opposition between sex as biology/nature and gender as culture: "there is no reference to a pure body which is not at the same time a further formation of that body. In this sense, the linguistic capacity to refer to sexed bodies is not denied, but the very meaning of 'referentiality' is altered. In philosophical terms, the constative claim is always to some degree performative" (*Bodies*, pp. 10–11).
6   Judith Butler, *Gender Trouble*, p. 44.
7   Judith Butler, *Bodies*, p. 2.
8   Judith Butler, *Bodies*, p. 7.

458–62, 526–27, 758). Since the mid-1990s, more and more commentators have characterized Troilus as effeminate, emasculated, even impotent, and based their judgment on his "feminine" passivity. Diane Steinberg describes falling in love as "a debilitating and a feminizing experience" for Troilus.[9] Stephanie Dietrich begins an article on "'Slydyng' Masculinity in the Four Portraits of Troilus" with: "Recent criticism on Troilus's 'lovesickness' and the resulting passivity suggests that if Troilus is not exactly emasculated, he is at least 'feminized' by his erotic experience."[10] Mary Behrman describes Criseyde as having recognized "that Troilus, playing the courtly-lover role, has been emasculated by his desire,"[11] and Jane Chance writes that "Troilus is effeminized by courtly love."[12] Steinberg talks about Troilus's associating love "with a feminine lack of both strength and sense";[13] Marilyn Moore, arguing that Troilus is excessively self-involved, criticizes him for "not making a move on" Criseyde.[14] Elaine Hansen describes men as plagued by gender instability and role reversal in Chaucer's fiction. Courtly love's impact, she says, is "softening and unmanning." "Agency and power in heterosexual relations" are confused in courtly ideology, and its emphasis on role reversal both conceals and exacerbates them: "The courtly, aristocratic male lover in the very act of falling in love is, by convention and by rhetoric, rendered to some degree passive and submissive; he is … feminized and interiorized by love, or by the language of love."[15]

The assumptions that empower these judgments are that passivity is the woman's part in courtship, a manly lover is active and aggressive, and manly men show their feelings through strong, assertive acts. However, none of these assumptions match the loving depicted in typical medieval romances. Romance men and women suffer equal passivity as lovers. When portraying even their manliest heroes, medieval romances lavish attention on how paralyzed they are and how excessively they suffer. Alexander, heir to the throne of Constantinople in Chrétien de Troyes's *Cligés* (*c.* 1176), for instance, is a superlative warrior, honored by King Arthur with magnificent gifts for his outstanding military exploits, but when he falls in love at the sight of Soredamors, Queen Guinevere's beautiful, blond lady-in-waiting, he does not tell anyone that he loves her – neither her nor anyone else.[16] Ironically, she is equally in love with him, but since neither one reveals his or her feelings toward the other, all they can do is suffer. During a sea voyage, they turn pale, sweat, sigh, and tremble so obvi-

9   Diane Steinberg, "'We do usen here no wommen for to selle': Embodiment of Social Practices in *Troilus and Criseyde*," *ChauR* 29.3 (1995): 259–73, at p. 264.

10 Stephanie Dietrich, "'Slydyng' Masculinity in the Four Portraits of Troilus," *MC*, 205–20, at p. 205.

11 Mary Behrman, "Heroic Criseyde," *ChauR* 38. 4 (2004): 314–336, at p. 324.

12 Jane Chance, *The Mythographic Chaucer* (Minneapolis: University of Minnesota Press, 1995), p. 110.

13 Diane Steinberg, "'We do usen here,'" p. 264.

14 Marilyn Moore, "Who's Solipsistic Now? The Character of Chaucer's Troilus," *ChauR* 33.1 (1998): 43–59, at p. 43.

15 Elaine Hansen, *Chaucer and the Fictions of Gender* (Berkeley: University of California Press, 1992), pp. 17, 150, 148–49.

16 Chrétien de Troyes, *Cligés, Les Romans de Chrétien de Troyes*, ed. Alexandre Micha, 2 vols. (Paris: Champion, 1957), 2.435–2315. For the dating of the text, see p. viii.

ously at the sight of each other that Guinevere decides they must be seasick. Alexander analyzes and laments his feelings as a lover: the much desired wound and love's arrow that enters the eye; his eyes like a glass window the sun passes through without leaving a trace; his loving heart like a candle burning inside a lantern. He describes the arrow that pierces his heart in a traditional head-to-toe portrait of his beloved: Soredamors's golden hair, her forehead brighter than an emerald, her coloring lilies and roses, and her breasts as white as snow. Nevertheless, half a year passes and Alexander still cannot bring himself to exchange a glance with Soredamors. Finally Guinevere recognizes the symptoms of love in the couple's mutual paling and trembling, she at once confronts them about loving each other, and she arranges their immediate marriage. A less aggressive lover than Alexander is unimaginable. Troilus, spurred on by Pandarus, writes letters to Criseyde and finally speaks to her. Alexander far outdoes Troilus in unassertiveness.

If Alexander is a more passive lover than Troilus, William of Palerne surpasses him in incapacitating lovesickness.[17] William nearly dies. He loves Melior, an emperor's daughter, who is equally in love with him although neither realizes that the other one loves. William suffers devastatingly, paralyzed by love. He languishes, lies awake all night, goes nearly mad from grief, and looks ravaged. He finally stations himself beneath a dense apple tree in a high-walled garden where he can gaze at Melior's chamber window. The apple tree is covered with new leaves and blossoms and for seven days William hides beneath it unseen, eating and drinking nothing, sustaining himself altogether by the sight of Melior's window: "but held him finliche ifed his fille to loke / on the mayde Meliors chaumber, for wham he s[o] morned."[18] In the evening he returns to his room and grieves. He does not sleep at all, and none of his servants can discover either the cause of his misery or where he spends the day. Only the intervention of Melior's cousin saves his life. She brings the equally love-stricken Melior, also near death, to the garden, and helps the couple declare their mutual love. Beside William's incapacitating lovesickness, Troilus's seems moderate.

Although *William of Palerne* was written in Middle English in the mid-fourteenth century, it is a reworking of a late twelfth-century French romance, and its conventions of love behavior derive from the same period as those of *Cligés*.[19] *Sir Eglamour of Artois*, however, another Middle English romance, dates from the middle of the fourteenth century, and it is not a translation.[20] Nevertheless, its spectacular warrior-hero is as unaggressively lovesick as Alexander, William, and Troilus. Sir Eglamour loves Cristabelle, his earl's daughter, and he fights off the unwelcome suitors who come for her hand, but instead of telling her he loves her, he takes to his bed to die. His squire appeals to Cristabelle as follows:

---

[17] *William of Palerne: An Alliterative Romance*, ed. G. H. V. Bunt (Groningen: Bouma's Boekhuis, 1985), lines 509–1059.

[18] *William of Palerne*, lines 768–69.

[19] Bunt dates *William of Palerne* between 1335 and 1361, at pp. 14–15.

[20] *Sir Eglamour of Artois*, ed. Frances Richardson (London: Oxford University Press, 1965). Richardson discusses dating at p. xxx.

> "He ys seke and deed full nere:
>   He prayes yow of a syght.
>   He ys kest into such care
>   Butt ye hym help he wyll mysfare –
>   He lyues not tyll nyghth!"[21]

Cristabelle and the dying Sir Eglamour discover that they love each other, and her love saves his life. Even condensed to a single stanza, the passive non-courting of Sir Eglamour is clearly in the tradition of William of Palerne's and Alexander's performances.

These lovers' unassertive enduring of love's pain, with no attempt to reach out to the women who could save them from their self-destruction – very often women who in fact love them equally – could be multiplied many times over. As its presence in as derivative and unsophisticated a romance as *Sir Eglamour* underscores, this typical courtly behavior is ascribed to heroes of all sorts. But the most important point about its gendering is that none of these works questions the manliness of its protagonist. These men are not feminized by their suffering; they are merely suffering. Their spectacularly unaggressive courting is taking an extravagant – and by twenty-first-century notions ridiculous and effeminate – form, but there is nothing effeminate about it as this literature presents it. This is the way manly heroes love in medieval romance. Moreover, passive loving is not gendered either female or male in these stories. Soredamors and Melior, for instance, love as passively and as devastatingly as Alexander and William.

Between the fourteenth and the late twentieth century, passive loving became gendered so exclusively female that its earlier stature as a powerful and appropriate form of male loving in romance sank out of sight. Male fainting follows a similar but more extravagant trajectory. Late twentieth- and twentieth-first-century critics offer Troilus's faint as the strongest evidence of his masculine inadequacy. More than any other episode in *Troilus and Criseyde,* the faint generates critiques of his manliness and speculations about his sexual problems. In one of the classics of Chaucerian commentary, David Aers describes Troilus as suffering from "fear lest his masculine identity, so heavily dependent on performance in the sexual domain, might not, as it were, stand up."[22] Barry Windeatt categorizes the swoon as "a deflation of male stereotypes of sexual conquest and mastery" and "the extreme instance of that setting aside of conventional masculine initiative and assertiveness that has characterized Troilus as a lover: male fear and shame trigger sexual consequences rather than a male 'advance.'"[23] Edward Condren describes Troilus as swooning "like a Victorian maiden under a vapour attack," and argues that the swooning stanza describes

21 *Sir Eglamour*, Cotton MS, lines 116–20.
22 David Aers, *Community, Gender, and Individual Identity: English Writing, 1360–1430* (London: Routledge, 1988), p. 129.
23 Barry Windeatt, *Oxford Guides to Chaucer:* Troilus and Criseyde (Oxford: Oxford University Press, 1992), pp. 225–26.

Troilus experiencing a premature ejaculation.[24] Maud McInerney, on the other hand, understands the reason for Troilus's faint as "Troilus, at this critical moment, is unable to get an erection: the 'in-knetting' of his vigour strongly suggests detumescence," and she argues that when Troilus faints, his problem is "the threat of impotence and the loss of manhood." She sees his faint as funny "precisely because it suggests not restraint, which is voluntary, but impotence, which is involuntary, and a favorite source of Chaucerian humour."[25] Hansen connects impotence and courtly conceptions of loving:

> Troilus's conventional, unmanly behavior reaches new heights in Book III, where the infamous bedroom scene, as Chaucer shapes it, confirms the real difficulty: if the lover is as conventionally submissive, frightened, infantilized, and unmanned by love as he is supposed to be, he will not be able to perform like a man in an actual heterosexual encounter.[26]

Contemporary readers see Troilus as sexually inadequate in so many varied ways in this episode in part because they think of fainting as a behavior peculiar to women. In the Middle Ages, however, there was no such conception. Fainting was not gendered either male or female. Both men and women faint in medieval literature, heroes in particular faint, and there is nothing remotely unmanly about the act of fainting. "Traunce," "swelte," and most often "swouen" in various forms precede "faint" as the words for losing consciousness in Middle English, and even a cursory reading of the pronouns in the *Middle English Dictionary*'s citations for them shows how much more often the swooners are male than female. Some faint because they are wounded in battle, but others faint for strong feelings of all sorts: joy, misery, humiliation, remorse, and particularly love. Christ swoons on the cross in a verse of great power in *Piers Plowman*: "'*Consummatum est*,' quod Crist, and comsede for to swoune."[27] Hawkin, the Active Man, swoons over his guilty soul. Weeping about how hard it is to live and sin, displeasing God, Hawkin "Swouned and sobbed and siked ful ofte."[28] Even Sloth swoons in *Piers Plowman*. At the close of Sloth's lengthy confession, Repentance calls him to account, "and right with that he swowned" so severely that Vigilate has to throw cold water on him.[29] Apollonius, in Gower's *Confessio Amantis*, swoons so deeply when he learns his wife has died in childbirth that everyone believes him dead, and when he revives, kissing her corpse a thousand times, he swoons again, begging for death.[30] One of the most famous medieval male swoons is Dante's faint from pity at the end of Canto

---

24   Edward Condren, "Transcendent Metaphor or Banal Reality: Three Chaucerian Dilemmas," *PLL* 21.3 (1985): 233–57, at pp. 248 and 252–54.
25   Maud Burnett McInerney, "'Is this a mannes herte?'": Unmanning Troilus through Ovidian Allusion," *MC*, 221–235, at pp. 222–25.
26   Elaine Hansen, *Chaucer and the Fictions*, p. 149.
27   William Langland, *The Vision of Piers Plowman*, ed. A. V. C. Schmidt, 2nd edn. (London: Everyman, 1995), B.18.57.
28   William Langland, *Piers Plowman*, B.14.326.
29   William Langland, *Piers Plowman*, B.5.443–45.
30   John Gower, *Confessio Amantis*, ed. Russell Peck (Toronto: University of Toronto Press, 1980), 8.1059–61, 1076–78.

Five of the *Inferno* after he hears the story of the beginning of the love affair of Francesca and Paolo, murdered by her husband: "di pietade / io venni men cosi com' io morisse; / e caddi come corpo morto cade" ("for pity I swooned as if in death and dropped like a dead body").[31] Boccaccio's Troilo swoons when he hears that Criseida is to be exchanged for Antenor in the *Filostrato*, and his swoon illustrates both proper treatment for someone who has fainted and what medieval people thought occurred during a faint. As Priam, Hector, and Troilo's other brothers rub Troilo's wrists, bathe his face, and weep over his seemingly dead body, Troilo's soul wanders; after a long time, his soul returns to his body and he revives.[32]

In medieval allegories, swoons frequently yield visions or conclude visions; they are important moments of spiritual clarity and access to truth. In *Piers Plowman*, for instance, Will hears about the tree of charity and vows that he would travel two thousand miles for a sight of it. Instead he sees it in a "love-dreem," a swoon.[33] *Pearl* ends in a similar swoon, religiously grounded but emotionally inspired, this time by a lost heavenly vision and by love. The dreamer-narrator sees his little queen in the Lamb's procession and, overcome by love-longing, rushes to the bank to cross the water that separates them, only to awaken on the mound where he had first fallen asleep. Exiled from her and from that heavenly region, he faints, grief-stricken: "A longeyng hevy me strok in swone."[34]

While many different strong emotions incite faints in men in medieval literature, the most usual precipitator is love. Secular love allegories combine wounds with swoons to express at once falling in love and visionary insight into the heart of things. In Chaucer's translation of the *Roman de la rose*, when the God of Love sees the Lover admiring the blossom, the God shoots an arrow deep into the Lover's heart. The Lover shivers, falls flat on the ground, "And longe tyme a-swoone I lay" (1736). When he regains consciousness, he pulls out the feathered arrow shaft, but its hooked head, Beauty, has gone so far into his heart that he cannot extricate it. This process, including the swoon and the inextricable arrowhead, is repeated both when Love shoots the third arrow, Courtesy (1804–5), and a third time when Company hits the Lover (1867). John Gower's *Confessio Amantis* reverses this allegorical sequence. The Lover, Gower, is too old for love, as Venus spells out for him in painful detail. He swoons at that news and is granted a vision of famous lovers from the past. Finally old men who have loved beg Venus to take pity on the swooning Lover.[35] Cupid extracts the fiery arrow, Venus heals his wounded heart, mind, and kidneys with magic ointment, and as the lover awakens from his swoon, his reason returns.

---

31 Dante Alighieri, *The Divine Comedy of Dante Alighieri: Inferno*, trans. John D. Sinclair (1939; repr. New York: Oxford University Press, 1961), Canto Five, 140–42.
32 Giovanni Boccaccio, *Il filostrato*, ed. Vincenzo Pernicone, trans. Robert apRoberts and Anna Seldis (New York: Garland, 1986), Part 4, stanzas 18–21.
33 William Langland, *Piers Plowman*, B.16.18–20.
34 *Pearl*, line 1180. *Pearl and Sir Gawain and the Green Knight*, ed. A. C. Cawley (London: Everyman, 1962).
35 John Gower, *Confessio Amantis*, 8.2449 and 8.2749.

Men faint from love troubles in Chaucer's poetry as well. Arcite faints repeatedly when he is exiled from Athens to Thebes in the *Knight's Tale*: "Ful ofte a day he swelte and seyde 'Allas!'" (*CT*, 1.1356). After Arcite's return to Athens disguised as Philostrate, at the close of his lament over being unable to court Emily – the lament that the escaped Palamon overhears from his hiding place in the bushes – Arcite "fil doun in a traunce / A longe tyme" (1.1572–73). Aurelius, in the *Franklin's Tale*, faints similarly after he prays to Apollo to submerge the rocks so that he can win Dorigen's love: "And with that word in swowne he fil adoun, / And longe tyme he lay forth in a traunce" (*CT*, 5.1080–81). In "The Complaint of Mars," Mars nearly faints when he is separated from Venus: "So feble he wex for hete and for his wo / That nygh he swelte, he myghte unnethe endure" (127–28). And in his own "Compleynt," characterizing his pain, Mars laments: "'O herte swete, O lady sovereyne! / For your disese wel oughte I swowne and swelte'" (215–16). The redundant, alliterating "swowne and swelte" appears again, this time satirically, when Damian, the knight's squire in the *Merchant's Tale*, falls in love at first sight of May, the knight's new wife: "Almoost he swelte and swowned ther he stood" (*CT*, 4.1776). This combination may also be echoing beneath the joke when Absolon, who claims to be fainting from love in the *Miller's Tale*, tells Alison: "'No wonder is thogh that I swelte and swete'" (*CT*, 1.3703).

Men often faint for love in Old French romances and their Middle English progeny, the works that lie directly behind much of Chaucer's poetry. These fainting men are typically near death. Paridès, for instance, a young nobleman in *Éracle*, a late twelfth-century romance, is so ill from hopeless yearning that his family is digging his grave when he faints at hearing the woman he loves named.[36] Partonopeu, another of these fainting twelfth-century lovers, has accidentally destroyed his lady's magical powers in *Partonopeu de Blois*. His lady's sister finds him deep in a forest, overcome by guilt and grief over his worthlessness, and when he realizes who she is, he faints so profoundly that she believes he is dying.[37] In the twelfth-century romance *Florimont*, when Delfin begs Florimont, his comrade-in-arms, to forget the princess he loves, Florimont faints and does not revive until Delfin promises to carry a love message to the princess, no matter what harm comes to them from it.[38]

Being capable of extraordinarily intense, idealizing love is an attribute of greatness in these romances, and fainting is a sign of that capacity. By romance convention, it is the greatest warriors and the greatest lovers who faint. The greatest of them all, both warrior and lover, is Lancelot, in the early thirteenth-century Prose *Lancelot*. Lancelot is so decisively the greatest of lovers that his loving is honored magically. When he and Guinevere consummate their love for the first time, a mysterious split shield given to Guinevere by the Lady of

---

[36] Gautier d'Arras, *Éracle*, ed. Guy Raynaud de Lage (Paris: Champion, 1976), line 4181.

[37] *Partonopeu de Blois: A French Romance of the Twelfth Century*, ed. Joseph Gildea (Villanova, PA: Villanova University Press, 1967), vol. 1, 6041–54.

[38] Aimon de Varennes, *Florimont*, ed. Alfons Hilka (Göttingen, 1932), lines 8139–252.

the Lake reunites so that the knight and lady painted on it are embracing.[39] In the middle of his first interview with Guinevere, this greatest of all lovers faints and must be supported by his comrade-in-arms, Galehot. When Guinevere has Galehot bring Lancelot to her at dusk in a meadow where she is walking with her ladies-in-waiting, she discovers that he is the nameless knight in black armor who has been performing the major military exploits of their time. Love inspires Lancelot's battle feats, but love is also destroying him. In the meadow, he is so pale he looks ill, he cannot lift his eyes, he trembles so that he can hardly speak, and he weeps continuously so that his silk garment is soaked to his knees. To tease Lancelot, Guinevere suggests that he is attracted to one of her ladies-in-waiting, and he is so shocked that he starts to faint. Guinevere must call Galehot to come catch Lancelot, and the rest of her conversation is with Galehot, who answers for Lancelot while Lancelot hangs his head between them. Lancelot himself, then, is one of the fainting heroes of the western Middle Ages, and he faints at the most important moment in his emotional life.[40]

A remarkable episode in another thirteenth-century Old French work drama-tizes how explicitly fainting had become a conventional signal that a man or woman was very seriously in love. In *Floriant et Florete*, Floriant loves and is loved by Florete, whose father, the emperor of Constantinople, is waging war against Floriant. Gauvain, Floriant's comrade-in-arms, loves and is loved by Blanchandine, Florete's lady-in-waiting and daughter of the King of Hungary. Although Floriant and Florete both fell in love when they exchanged a few words, neither suspects the other's feelings. In the middle of a battle, Floriant sees Florete for the second time and is so overcome by emotion that he faints and has to be carried off the field. When Gauvain discovers that the unconscious Floriant is not wounded, Gauvain understands, with no additional information, that Floriant must be in love. Occurrences on the women's side match these exactly. When Florete sees Floriant fall in battle, she too faints, and Blanchan-dine recognizes that Florete is in love and comforts her.[41]

A number of aspects of these romance episodes match elements of the fainting scene in *Troilus and Criseyde*. In *Claris et Laris*, another thirteenth-century romance, when Claris falls into a deadly faint because the woman he loves has refused him, her brother pressures her to kiss Claris until she revives him, just as Pandarus appeals to Criseyde to help him revive Troilus.[42] In both *Claris et Laris* and another romance, *Generydes*, men faint in as physically intimate situations as in *Troilus and Criseyde*. Claris is in bed when he faints, and Troilus, via Pandarus's ministrations, ends up in bed once he has fainted. Pandarus strips Troilus "al to his bare sherte" (3.1099); Claris "se gisoit toz nuz" (lay completely naked).[43] Claris faints in his own bed, but in a second male

---

[39] *Lancelot do Lac: The Non-Cyclic Old French Prose Romance*, ed. Elspeth Kennedy, 2 vols. (Oxford, 1980), 1.556.

[40] *Lancelot do Lac*, 1.340–64.

[41] *Floriant et Florete*, ed. Harry F. Williams (Ann Arbor: University of Michigan Press, 1947), lines 3949–88.

[42] *Li romans de Claris et Laris*, ed. Johann Alton (Tübingen, 1884), lines 7885–8184.

[43] *Claris et Laris*, line 8060.

fainting scene in a romance bedroom, the woman is in bed, as is Criseyde. This episode occurs in the mid-fifteenth-century Middle English *Generydes*, which is believed to have been adapted from a lost Old French original that circulated in England in Chaucer's lifetime.[44] Clarionas, the lady, is sick because she believes her fiancé, Generydes, has fallen in love with another woman. When he comes to her bedroom to convince her of his fidelity, she denounces him. He faints, and, urged into action by her confidante Mirabell, just as Criseyde is by Pandarus, Clarionas kisses the man who loves her and he revives.[45]

There is nothing unmanly, then, about fainting in this literature. A faint most often indicates very strong feelings, frequently feelings of love or feelings associated with love: pity for lovers, grief at the loss of love, fear of not being loved, or, most often of all, incapacitating yearning for love. If Boccaccio's cultural heritage had suggested that fainting was effeminate, he surely would not have risked comparing his grief-stricken, swooning Troilo to a flower: a lily turned up by the plough, withering in the sun.[46] If a medieval audience were likely to consider fainting a sign of emasculation, Chaucer's Arcite, Aurelius, and Mars, and the romances' Lancelot, Florimont, Partonopeu, Generydes, Claris, and other battle-hardened, tournament-winning, giant- and dragon-slaying heroes would not have been depicted fainting. Similarly, the great moments of spiritual vision and transition in love allegories and religious allegories alike would not have been imaged by swoons.

And yet fainting is firmly gendered female for twentieth- and twenty-first-century readers. Although a faint is a physiologically uncontrollable response and neither females nor males can faint at will, in a spectacular instance of an act's acquiring gender, very probably primarily through literature, women became the swooners in the middle of the eighteenth century. The sentimental heroine regularly collapses in fainting fits and must be resuscitated with smelling salts. Fainting, valued as a sign of woman's "delicacy," attested to "physical fragility, vulnerability, and infirmity" and "a heightened perceptibility and emotionality in women," as Christiane Zschirnt explains, describing this stock feature of the eighteenth-century courtship novel.[47] The most spectacular eighteenth-century fainter is Samuel Richardson's Pamela, who swoons on at least six occasions, sometimes remaining unconscious for two hours, sometimes for three, and repeatedly nearly dying, hovered over by Mrs. Jervis with her bottle of salts. Pamela's faints are brought on by the sexual advances of Mr. B., the rake who employs her, with "I found his hand in my bosom" the sure-fire instigator of a lengthy faint.[48]

---

[44] *Generydes* ed. W. A. Wright (London: EETS, 1873, 1878). Dating, derivation from French original: Carol Meale, "The Morgan Library Copy of *Generides*," *Romance in Medieval England*, eds. Maldwyn Mills, Jennifer Fellows, and Carol Meale (Cambridge: D. S. Brewer, 1991), lines 89–104, at pp. 90–91.

[45] *Generydes*, lines 4623–734.

[46] Boccaccio, *Il filostrato*, Part 4, stanza 18.

[47] Christiane Zschirnt, "Fainting and Latency in the Eighteenth Century's Romantic Novel of Courtship," *Germanic Review* 74.1 (1999): 48–66, at p. 48.

[48] Samuel Richardson, *Pamela*, 2 vols. (London: Everyman, 1957), 1, Letters 25, 50.

Men rarely faint in late eighteenth- and nineteenth-century novels. When they do, it is usually because they are bleeding hard or are very ill. Nineteenth-century novelists clearly assume their audiences consider male fainting unmanly. Mr. Sedley, in *Vanity Fair*, for instance, ridicules his very fat son with: "'Undo his stays! ... Fling some water in his face, Miss Sharp, or carry him upstairs: the dear creature's fainting.'"[49] When Heathcliff, in *Wuthering Heights*, denounces Catherine's husband Linton to her – "'I wish you joy of the milk-blooded coward, Cathy! ... the slavering, shivering thing you preferred to me!'" – his final sneer is "'Is he weeping, or is he going to faint for fear?'"[50]

Women, on the other hand, faint often. Some, like Pamela, faint at the advances of men who desire them. Charlotte Temple, for instance, in an eponymous early American novel, shrieks and faints when a seducer carries her off for sex; her mother faints when she learns her seduced daughter is not married; and Charlotte's death follows a protracted fainting fit brought on by learning that her seducer has married another woman.[51] Most women in these novels faint at hearing dreadful news, or from fear or extreme exertion, or at their own distressing feelings, or even from great joy. Fainting is the sign of both woman's weakness and her capacity for emotional response. Rosamond, in George Eliot's *Middlemarch*, remains faint for hours when she realizes that Will Ladislaw is not in love with her.[52] In Mary Shelley's *Frankenstein*, on three occasions women faint from terror from their encounters with the monster.[53] In Dickens's *Bleak House*, Lady Dedlock faints, overcome by grief when she recognizes the handwriting of the former lover she believed to be dead,[54] Esther Summerson faints twice, and Mrs. Snagsby faints in a comic imitation of upper-class sensibility.[55] In *David Copperfield*, Mrs. Micawber's fainting is similarly mocked as a class affectation: "'I have known her to be thrown into fainting fits by the king's taxes at three o'clock, and to eat lamb-chops, breaded, and drink warm ale (paid for with two tea-spoons that had gone to the pawnbroker's) at four.'"[56] Also in *David Copperfield*, Dora – weak, emotional, and ineffective – faints from fright while visiting a prison and faints out of guilt each time David's name is mentioned after the death of her father who has forbidden her to love David.[57]

Several women, both free and slave, faint in *Uncle Tom's Cabin*. After Eliza leaps from ice-block to ice-block across the half-frozen Ohio River with her son

49 William Makepeace Thackeray, *Vanity Fair* (New York: Random House, 1950), ch. 4, p. 26.
50 Emily Brontë, *Wuthering Heights*, ed. David Daiches (New York: Penguin, 1980), ch. 11, p. 154.
51 Susanna Rowson, *Charlotte Temple* and *Lucy Temple*, ed. Ann Douglas (New York: Penguin, 1991), ch. 12, p. 48; ch. 14, p. 55; ch. 27, p. 106.
52 George Eliot, *Middlemarch*, ed. W. J. Harvey (New York: Penguin, 1988), ch. 78, p. 837.
53 Mary Shelley, *Frankenstein*, ed. Johanna M. Smith (Boston: St. Martin's Press, 1992), ch. 7, p. 69; ch. 11, p. 95; ch. 15, p. 117.
54 Charles Dickens, *Bleak House*, ed. Morton Dauwen Zabel (Boston: Houghton Mifflin, 1956), ch. 2, p. 11.
55 Charles Dickens, *Bleak House*, ch. 36, p. 385; ch. 57, p. 593; ch. 22, p. 242.
56 Charles Dickens, *David Copperfield* (New York: Penguin, 1980), ch. 11, p. 167.
57 Charles Dickens, *David Copperfield*, ch. 48, pp. 688–89; ch. 38, p. 560.

in her arms, she faints when an Ohio family takes her in, and later she nearly faints from joy when she hears that her husband has escaped from his owner.[58] A quadroon, long mistress to her owner, faints at learning that he has sold her and their two children to another man to pay off his gambling debts, and little Miss Eva nearly faints at hearing the story of a slave who was beaten to death.[59]

Although women who faint are usually admired for their delicacy by the conventions of these novels, their heightened sensitivity has its costs. Occasional episodes compare weak women who faint to stronger, more competent women who do not faint. In *Vanity Fair*, for instance, when Becky Sharp and Amelia Sedley listen to the young officers talk about war, glory, and how much they hope to be part of a victory, "Miss Sharp kindled with this exciting talk, but Miss Sedley trembled and grew quite faint as she heard it."[60] When Cassy and Emmeline run away from Simon Legree in *Uncle Tom's Cabin*, Emmeline says she is about to faint. " 'If you do, I'll kill you!' said Cassy, drawing a small, glittering stiletto." Emmeline revives and they escape into the swamp.[61] When St. Clare, Miss Eva's father, is dying of a stab wound, his southern wife, Marie, "whose nervous system had been enervated by a constant course of self-indulgence," swoons to incapacitation, while Miss Ophelia, St. Clare's Vermont cousin, eases his dying.[62]

These instances of fainting women from famous mid-eighteenth- and nineteenth-century English and American novels could be multiplied many times over. As Carroll Smith-Rosenberg writes, "The Victorians asserted gender complementarity and male dominance as 'eternal verities' rooted in human biology."[63] Included in those "eternal verities" were the weak, fragile, vulnerable, fainting female, subject to vapors, and the strong male who does not faint. These swooning eighteenth- and nineteenth-century heroines created a powerful legacy: twentieth- and twenty-first-century readers expect people who faint to be women.

Both fainting and passive loving, then, acquired feminine gender between the fourteenth and the twentieth centuries. Behaviors that had been appropriate for men as well as women in medieval romance turned into evidence of male effeminacy. With that change, part of the immensely complex tonal and conceptual construction that is *Troilus and Criseyde* was lost.

In the romances, fainting and passive loving ordinarily depict idealized love straightforwardly. No alien voice intervenes to evaluate these behaviors from a contrary perspective. No one, for instance, interjects to appraise realistically

58   Harriet Beecher Stowe, *Uncle Tom's Cabin* (New York: Harper and Row, 1965), ch. 9, p. 84; ch. 13, p. 140.
59   Harriet Beecher Stowe, *Uncle Tom's Cabin*, ch. 34, p. 365; ch. 19, pp. 220–21.
60   William Thackeray, *Vanity Fair*, ch. 5, p. 48.
61   Harriet Beecher Stowe, *Uncle Tom's Cabin*, ch. 39, p. 407.
62   Harriet Beecher Stowe, *Uncle Tom's Cabin*, ch. 29, pp. 319–20.
63   Carroll Smith-Rosenberg, *Disorderly Conduct: Visions of Gender in Victorian America* (New York: Knopf, 1985), p. 178.

whether inaction will help a lover succeed with a lady. Viewed rationally, passive loving makes no sense. If Alexander, William, Melior, and Sir Eglamour had spoken about their feelings, Alexander would have spared himself and Soredamors half a year of agony, and the other three would not have almost died. But romances ordinarily do not honor common sense. Reasonableness in loving is not one of their values.

Troilus and Criseyde, on the other hand, articulates in all its unreasonableness the practical consequences of Troilus's elevated, solitary loving. Pandarus's assessment is down-to-earth and accurate: "'Thow mayst allone here wepe and crye and knele – / But love a womman that she woot it nought, / And she wol quyte it that thow shalt nat fele'" (1.806–8). Idealized loving is inspired and spiritual; commonsensical courting is result-driven. *Troilus and Criseyde* is only from time to time a romance.

And yet while realistic, result-driven courting raises issues that will not be silenced in *Troilus and Criseyde*, it does not nullify the worth of idealized passive loving. Their virtues are from different aspects of being human, but both are real and have their strengths, as the contrast between Diomede and Troilus illustrates. Diomede's courting is entirely result-driven, and he is the one who possesses Criseyde when *Troilus and Criseyde* concludes. His first words in the poem as he leads Criseyde's horse to the Greek camp are his startlingly callous rationale for his initial declaration of love: at least it will make the trip seem shorter (5.94–98). Passive loving like Troilus's may be absurd, judged by its probable effectiveness, but at least it is the loving of a man who loves. Its opposite is Diomede's unidealized seduction, unmediated by caring. And then there is "hende" Nicholas's approach to Alison in the *Miller's Tale*: "And prively he caughte hire by the queynte ... And heeld hire harde by the haunchebones" (*CT*, 1.3276, 3279). Romance's idealized passivity differentiates lovers' feelings from responses like Diomede's and Nicholas's. Passive loving is important in the discourse about ways of loving and valuing in *Troilus and Criseyde*. If passive loving is dismissed as effeminate, one of the poles of value of the poem is diminished. Moreover, it is worth noting that when Pandarus ridicules Troilus's passive loving, he accuses him of unreasonableness, but not effeminacy.

Passive loving is of value, but so is fainting. In the consummation scene, as Chaucer maneuvers between sexual comedy and high romance, Troilus's faint is one of his pivots, and the tradition of the fainting lovers of romance is an important context. Within that context, Troilus's faint is neither comic nor inappropriate. It establishes him as capable of intense idealizing feelings like the other lovers of romance. In the midst of this scene based on lies, guilty as Troilus is, his faint would have reminded medieval readers of his sensitivity and devotion. Like Paridès, Partonopeu, Florimont, Lancelot, Floriant, Claris, Generydes, Arcite, and Aurelius, Troilus faints because he is a lover.

When Troilus's faint is treated as farce, it is easy to forget that in the fourteenth century, unlike the nineteenth, a fainting man was not a joke. According to medieval ideas, fainting represented a medical emergency that could end in death. As Elizabeth Liggins has documented, that "crampe of deth" (3.1071) around Troilus's heart is no exaggeration, and Pandarus and Criseyde respond to it medically correctly.[64] Troilus is kneeling when he faints and would have collapsed in a heap. When Pandarus throws Troilus into Criseyde's bed and takes off his clothes, he gives Troilus air by laying him out flat and loosening constricting material.[65] When Criseyde, to counteract the apparent reason for Troilus's faint, whispers in his ear that she has forgiven him, and Pandarus and Criseyde wet Troilus's temples and rub his pulse, they are following the best medieval medical practices for helping a patient regain consciousness.

Twentieth- and twenty-first-century ideas about the effeminacy of fainting have had such a strong impact on attitudes toward Troilus's faint that it is repeatedly interpreted as brought on by his inability to perform sexually. McInerney, Hansen, and Aers argue that he fears or experiences impotence.[66] Condren contends that he has had a premature ejaculation.[67] Such readings, however, overlook the issues Troilus faces at the moment of his faint. When Troilus faints during his tête-à-tête with Criseyde, not only is he not in bed with Criseyde, he has no hope of becoming her lover despite being in her bedroom. He is so overwhelmed by misery that he is cursing ever having been born and expects to die on the spot. Criseyde's despairing Boethian speech on false felicity and the impossibility of earthly happiness, followed by her forty-one verses about jealousy and her declaration of innocence and loyalty, culminates in her tears and submerges Troilus beneath the weight of his responsibility for the lies that have caused her grief. Although he says he is not to blame for what has occurred, he clearly knows how guilty he is (3.1084–85). Troilus faints because he has made the woman he loves cry. As Jill Mann describes the process that yields Troilus's faint,

> Unable to discover an issue in speech or action, Troilus' mind is turned in on itself, trapped in deadlock, and this condition of his mind is so acute that it transfers itself to his body. ... The swoon is an expression of Troilus' acceptance of – and indeed absolute identification with – the contradictory and destructive implications of the situation, to which, unlike Pandarus, he is fully alive.[68]

Troilus faints from love and guilt, not fear of sexual inadequacy.

Before Pandarus's intervention, the bedroom scene between Troilus and Criseyde is full of solemn material like Criseyde's declaration that she loves Troilus for his "grete trouthe," his goodness, his daily service, and because his heart is all hers (3.992–95). But as every reader of *Troilus and Criseyde* experiences indelibly, when Pandarus throws the unconscious Troilus into Criseyde's bed, comedy crashes through romance. " 'O thef, is this a mannes herte?' " (3.1098), Pandarus explodes, and when Troilus revives, Criseyde matches

64 Elizabeth Liggins, "The Lovers' Swoons in *Troilus and Criseyde*," *Parergon* 3.3 (1985): 93–106, at pp. 96, 99–100.
65 Elizabeth Liggins, "The Lovers' Swoons," p. 100.
66 Maud McInerney, " 'Is this a mannes herte?' " pp. 222–25; Elaine Hansen, *Chaucer and the Fictions*, p. 149; David Aers, *Community, Gender*, p. 129.
67 Edward Condren, "Transcendent Metaphor," p. 248.
68 Jill Mann, "Troilus' Swoon," *ChauR* 14 (1980): 319–35, at p. 327.

Pandarus's outburst with "'Is this a mannes game? / What, Troilus, wol ye do thus for shame?'" (3.1126–27). What they are condemning as unmanly is not Troilus's fainting; it is that Troilus is not making love to Criseyde. Pandarus, who had no use for passive loving, sees nothing at all positive about fainting, and Criseyde follows his lead. Tossing Troilus, unconscious, into Criseyde's bed parallels Pandarus's tough-minded dismissal of passive loving, and as with that dismissal, there is truth in his action. The point of his lies and machinations has always been to get Troilus into Criseyde's bed. Pandarus substitutes his own style of effectiveness for what he sees as Troilus's ridiculous and counterproductive overvaluing of Criseyde's unhappiness.

Finally, just as the realistic, result-driven courting that is Pandarus's idea of how a lover should act does not cancel out the worth of Troilus's idealized passive loving, turning Troilus's faint into farce as Pandarus does leaves intact its medical seriousness, its ethical importance, and its positioning of Troilus within romance tradition. When contemporary critics write about Troilus as an inadequate, effeminate lover, they are overlooking the three years he and Criseyde spend as a couple and her desperate grief when she learns she is to be exchanged (4.1128–246). They are also overlooking the ecstasy of Troilus and Criseyde's first night of love. The most difficult piece of discourse magic in all of *Troilus and Criseyde* is the movement from "'Is this a mannes game?'" (3.1126) to entwined woodbine and the nude Criseyde. Chaucer's counter-balancing of the idealized loving enacted by fainting in romance with Pandarus's comic tossing of Troilus into Criseyde's bed paves the way to the alternating idealism and comedy that make that first night of ecstatic love so powerful.

"Male and female created He them" (Genesis 1). The Middle Ages and the early nineteenth centuries were secure in this concept; the twenty-first century no longer is. If, as Judith Butler argues, the genesis of gender is "the tacit collective agreement to perform, produce, and sustain discrete and polar genders as cultural fictions," it is crucial for readers of medieval literature to distinguish as best we can between medieval collective agreements and our own. And if the "acts of gender" that "create the idea of gender" express neither an "essence" nor "an objective ideal," then nothing necessitates that these gender conceptions take one form as opposed to another; these collective agreements are virtually free-floating.[69] Passivity in courting was as honorable a behavior for a man as for a woman in medieval romance. Fainting, restricted so exclusively to females by the nineteenth century, was equally appropriate for men five centuries earlier. What other cultural fictions performing "discrete and polar genders" are we imposing retroactively on the literature of Chaucer's period? And if neither passivity as a lover nor fainting is evidence of effeminacy, then what evidence remains for the argument that Troilus is unmanly?

---

[69] Judith Butler, *Gender Trouble*, p. 178.

4

What Makes a Man? Troilus, Hector, and the Masculinities of Courtly Love

MARCIA SMITH MARZEC

A survey of the chivalric literature contemporary with Chaucer suggests it is largely true that by Chaucer's time, "chroniclers and poets had long been recording elaborate – and contradictory – notions of what it meant to be a member of the knightly estate, notions such as that a true knight must be a lover as well as a soldier," as Craig Berry argues.[1] Thus, for example, Geoffroi de Charny's *Book of Chivalry* cites "Deeds Undertaken for Love of a Lady" as one method of winning "great honor" through "deeds of arms";[2] yet Charny also argues that "All Honors Come from God's Grace" (187), and he urges the knight to live in such a way as to please God. In contrast, the earlier, thirteenth-century anonymous *Ordene de Chevalerie*, in recounting the advice of the fictional Hue de Tabarie to Saladin on the nature of knighthood, makes clear its position on knightly chastity, quoting the crusader:

> you should preserve in holiness your pure flesh, your loins, and your whole body, and keep your name pure, as in a state of virginity. You should not prac- tice lechery, for a knight should cherish his body and keep it pure so that he does not incur shame therefrom, for God much hates such filth. (172)[3]

While there is a clear ambivalence in Chaucer's time toward both chivalry and masculinity, an ambivalence which admitted constituents of the masculine ideal as various as heroic prowess, piety, chastity, and romantic love, and while Chau- cer's own ambivalence may be observed in his corpus, in *Troilus and Criseyde*, the poet hearkens back to an older, more clearly defined, sexually stringent notion of chivalry and masculinity, arguing the inverse relationship between martial and sexual prowess. In *Troilus and Criseyde*, Chaucer demonstrates that

---

[1] Craig Berry, "The King's Business: Negotiating Chivalry in *Troilus and Criseyde*," *ChauR* 26 (1992): 236–65, at p. 248.

[2] Richard Kaeuper and Elspeth Kennedy, eds., *The Book of Chivalry of Geoffroi de Charny* (Philadel- phia: University of Pennsylvania Press, 1996). All subsequent references to Charny's work are to this edition and cited parenthetically by page. Parenthetical citations are also used for other primary texts addressing medieval epics, romance, and chivalry, including those of Joseph of Exeter, Dares, Dictys, Ramon Lull, Boccaccio, Benoît, the *Gest Hystoriale,* and *Le Roman de Troi.*

[3] Keith Busby, ed., *Raoul de Hodenc:* Le Roman des Eles*; The Anonymous* Ordene de Chevalerie (Amsterdam: Benjamins, 1983).

makes sens
in regard
to Pg AC

far from proving manhood, sexual involvement outside marriage weakens and feminizes a knight.

Chaucer articulates this theme through the implied contrast between Troilus and his hero-brother Hector. While Hector appears only twice in the work, he is ever-present by way of allusions, none of which appears in Chaucer's immediate source, Boccaccio's *Filostrato*, and none of which advances the action. The poet introduces these passing references to recall to his audience those aspects of the hero that were familiar from the literary Troy tradition. These allusions contrast Hector's character and actions with those of the courtly lover Troilus to reveal the devastating effects of courtly love on an otherwise noble and heroic knight.

Although Chaucer's audience was not familiar with Homer's Hector, the story of the Trojan hero was well known to medieval audiences through the accounts of the first-century Greek Dares Phrygius, known in the Middle Ages in a Latin translation dating to at least four hundred years later; the fifth-century Latin work said to be the translation of a first-century Greek writer, Dictys Cretensis; from Benoît de Sainte-Maure's twelfth-century poetic *Roman de Troie*, based loosely on Dares and introducing the story of Troilus and his lover Briseyde to the Trojan literature; from a Latin prose redaction of Dares by Joseph of Exeter in the late twelfth century; from Guido delle Colonne's thirteenth-century *Historia Destructionis Troiae*, an adaptation of Benoît's narrative in Latin prose; and from Boccaccio's *Filostrato*, Chaucer's immediate source, which focuses on the love story between Troilo and Cressida. Also contemporary with Chaucer is the *"Gest Hystoriale"* of the Destruction of Troye, an alliterative poetic rendering of Guido into Middle English. Moreover, since Jean de Longuyon's early fourteenth-century *Voeux du Paon*, the common theme of the Nine Worthies had established Hector as the first of a list of heroes embodying the ideal of chivalry and aristocratic manhood.

Without exception, the early sources identify Hector as the perfect knight. Not only is he the greatest hero among the Trojans, but, according to Joseph of Exeter, he surpasses the Greek hero Achilles: "Achilles would not have dared to try conclusions with so great a warrior as Hector," Joseph relates, "but when he refused, both Juno and Minerva pricked him to action" (63).[4] Writing from the viewpoint of the Trojans, Dares makes it clear that Phrygian success is dependent solely on Hector: although "[t]he Trojans bravely defended their country … wherever Hector withdrew, the Trojans fled" (149).[5] Joseph calls him "the only hope of the Trojans … once like Mars, Hector, to whom Jove, retiring, would gladly have entrusted his thunderbolts, if only Nature had made him immortal" (63). The *Gest Hystoriale*, too, depicts Hector as the great hope of the Trojans:

[4]   *The Iliad of Dares Phrygius*, trans. Gilas Roberts (Cape Town: Balkema, 1970).
[5]   *De excidio Troiae historia*, in *The Trojan War: The Chronicles of Dictys of Crete and Dares the Phrygian*, trans. R. M. Frazer, Jr. (Bloomington: Indiana University Press, 1966).

> Then [the Grekes] knowen by course of his clene shap,
> That it was Ector the honerable, eddist of knightes.
> Thai fled fro the fase of his felle dynttes ...
> Whill he bode in the batell, the buerne with his honde,
> Mony grekes with grem he gird to the dethe.
>
> (ll. 5949–51, 5954–55)[6]

In the *Gest*, Priam recognizes Hector's superiority when he commissions him as leader of his forces, describing him as "Antrus in armys, ablist of person, – / Boldest in batell, and best of thi hondes" (2186–87), and the narrator compares the hero explicitly with his brothers: "Of all his sones for sothe, that semely were holdyn, / Non was so noble, ne of nait strenght, / As Ector" (ll. 3876–78). The author's Achilles himself must admit that Hector is the major threat to Greek victory:

> this chaunse choisly beheld
> That so mony of thaire men were marrid by hym,
> He hopit but if happely that hardy were slayne,
> That neuer greke shuld haue grace the ground for to wyn;
> Ne neuer Troye for to take, terme of hor lyue. (ll. 8619–23)

Even Dictys, whose bias is clearly with the Greeks, characterizes Hector as a worthy opponent of his Danaan heroes, "whose deeds in war and peace alike were known throughout the world" (87).[7] Dictys's Hector stands his ground when the other Trojans retreat (63); in fact, in one battle "the Trojans in the center would have been completely destroyed if Hector had not arrived and checked their flight" (73).

Not only is Hector the best warrior, he is also a paragon of goodness and wisdom, consistent with the dictates of early chivalric texts. In his thirteenth-century *Book of the Order of Chivalry*, Ramon Lull insists that the central principles of knighthood are "the excellence of the [knight's] manliness and good behavior" (12), and he argues that he is duty-bound "to be good and pleasing to God" (14), to maintain the "nobility of heart" and "excellence of conscience" which sets him apart from the majority of men (26).[8] Similarly, Geoffroi de Charny describes the "man of worth" as one possessing "simplicity of heart," who "would scarcely know how to do wrong," and who "set[s] out to perform" all good actions, who "cannot be criticized for any vile sins nor for any shameful reproach," and who lives "loyally and honestly" (147–49).

In Hector's case, even Dictys admits that Hector's fame is "due to his righteous character no less than his martial spirit" (87). He emphasizes Hector's

---

6   *The "Gest Hystoriale" of the Destruction of Troy* (London: EETS, 1869; rpt. New York: Greenwood, 1969).
7   Dictys Cretensis, *Ephemeridos belli Troiani*, in Frazer, *The Trojan War*, pp. 19–130.
8   Ramon Lull, *The Book of the Order of Chivalry*, trans. Robert Adams from the 1926 EETS publication of William Caxton's *The Book of the Ordre of Chyvalry* (Huntsville, TX: Sam Houston State University Press, 1991).

sense of justice and fairness, a virtue without which, according to the medieval writer Lull, knighthood could not survive (81). Dictys relates how

> Hector was saddened and wept, remembering [Paris's] crime. Nevertheless, he thought that Helen should by no means be given up, for she was a suppliant at his home; good faith intervened and they must keep her. If, however, the envoys would enumerate the various articles that had been carried off with Helen, all of these things, he thought, should be returned. And, to take Helen's place, Cassandra or Polyxena, whichever seemed best to the envoys, should be given in marriage to Menelaus, along with a handsome dowry. (52)

The *Gest Hystoriale* illustrates the integrity of "Ector the Honerable" (6065), relating how when Theseus warns Hector to leave the battle and thus saves his life, Hector repays the debt by insisting that Theseus be spared when the Trojans are about to slay him (6794–803).

The Troy tradition with which Chaucer's audience was familiar depicts the ideal knight as also wise. "Chivalry and bravery are not compatible with each other unless they are joined by intelligence and judgment" (33), says Lull, who calls reason and judgment "the proper habits of chivalry" (95). Geoffroi de Charny describes such men as

> those who, from their youth, strive diligently to learn what is best to do, to distinguish good from evil, and to know what is reasonable to do; and because they recognize what course of action would be against reason, they endeavor to behave loyally, confidently, and according to what is right. ... [T]hese people know well how to advise others honestly and wisely. (151)

The Hector of the Troy tradition exhibits such wisdom, as in the *Gest* when Hector cautions Priam against embarking on the war with Greece: "'What proffet any prowes with a prowde entre, / To begyn any goode, on a ground febill, / And fortune it faile, and haue a fowle ende?'" (ll. 2248–50). Hector's wisdom is vindicated later in his singular dissent against the truce proposed by the Greeks: "'Thai wold stuf hom full stithly, strenkyth hom agayn, / With mete in the meneqwile, & many othir thinges,'" Hector argues wisely, although not persuasively, "'And we oure store schall distroi, & stynt of oure sped'" (ll. 7855–57). Hindsight, of course, proves Hector correct.[9] The subsequent disaster takes place only because the king and his lords assent to the disastrous truce, and in submission to their authority, Hector refuses to oppose them, regardless of his better judgment.

This, then, is the Hector whom Chaucer recalls to his audience with his well-placed allusions to the Trojan tradition. One need only think of Chaucer's Troilus to know that he does not equal his brother. Whereas both are warrior-heroes, Hector is, notably, not a *courtly* hero, a distinction at the very heart of

---

9   Chaucer's literate audiences were, no doubt, familiar with this account as well as with the tradition of advice regarding the perils of deceptive treaty or truce; see, e.g., the treatment of the subject by Christine de Pizan, *The Book of the Deeds of Arms and Chivalry*, trans. Sumner Willard, ed. Charity Willard (University Park: Pennsylvania State University Press, 1999), Part I, Ch. 20.

Chaucer's intent. Although the medieval Troy literature typically emphasizes both Hector's might and his character, the sources do not suggest any great physical attractiveness, unlike their treatment of Troilus, famous as both knight and lover. For example, whereas Benoît's Hector derives his fame from more enduring virtues, his Troilus is drawn in terms of appearance, charm, strength, and amorousness. Calling him "marvelously handsome," he notes Troilus's nature as lover and proclaims him the fairest of the youths of Troy.[10] The *Gest Hystoriale* describes Troilus as "Amirous vnto Maidens, & mony hym louyt, / And delited hym in dole with damsels ofte" (ll. 3926–27). While traditional descriptions of Hector focus on his massiveness, strength, and character (e.g., *Gest Hystoriale*, ll. 3886–90), the histories also make clear that he is not the perfect physical specimen that Troilus is, indeed even acknowledging Hector's imperfections. For example, although Joseph of Exeter describes Hector's lisp as "agreeable," he comments that Hector's crossed eyes "dipped his sight in two directions, and this constant squint marred his steadfast face with a downcast look" (41). The *Gest Hystoriale* describes Hector not only as no golden-mouthed ladies' man but relates that he "a little . . . stotid" (l. 3881).

Just as Hector is not the Lothario that Troilus is presented to be, Troilus in the literature does not have the wisdom that characterizes Hector. William Brown observes that Dares "seems to have a slight reservation about Troilus when he suggests that, if he has Hector's power in arms . . . , he has not attained Hector's wisdom,"[11] and that Benoît, too, "qualifies Troilus' determination [to do battle] with the suggestion of rashness."[12] It is significant that one of the passages illustrative of Hector's sagacity in the *Gest Hystoriale* concerns his advice to Troilus to eschew rashness in battle:

> "I pray the full prestli, with all my pure saule,
> That thou kepe thi corse, for case that may fall,
> And fare not with foli oure fos for to glade,
> Ne wirk not vnwyly in thi wilde dedis,
> That thi manhod be marte thurgh thi mysrewle." (ll. 6124–28)

For Chaucer, Hector's love is identified with his country and his comrades, and connubial love for him is clearly within the confines of marriage. Although he is the greatest of the Trojan heroes, the only woman connected with him is his wife, Andromache, whose depth of devotion is famously illustrated in the episode of her prophetic dream of his death, in her subsequent mourning of his death, and in her supplication to Achilles for his body. Notably, the sources from the Middle Ages depict Andromache as the quintessential courtly lady: according to Benoît, she is beautiful and genteel, whiter than the fleur-de-lis, with a long neck and a fine nose, her body perfectly proportioned (288–89); the

---

10 *Le Roman de Troie Benoît de Sainte-Maure*, Vol. I, ed. Léopold Constans (Paris: Librairie de Firmin Didot et Cie, for the Société des Anciens Textes Français), pp. 281–84.

11 William Brown, "A Separate Peace: Chaucer and the Troilus of Tradition," *JEGP* 83 (1984): 492–505, at p. 494.

12 William Brown, "A Separate Peace," p. 495.

Gest further describes her as white as milk, with roses in her cheeks and lovely red lips (3982–89).

Although Andromache can match any courtly heroine in terms of beauty, the poet makes clear that the love between her and Hector is not a "courtly" love: first, it is within marriage, and second, it does not subordinate the lover to the woman. According to Jo Ann McNamara, "[t]he fighting class . . . were expected to exercise their manly attributes of rationality and potency to control their wives, as they were expected to control the toiling classes."[13] That Hector fulfills this expectation is witnessed in his response to Andromache's dream, recorded in several texts in the tradition. The *Gest*, for example, records Hector's anger when Andromache successfully pleads with Priam to hold Hector back from battle:

> Therat Ector was angry, & angardly wrothe,
> Repreuet the prinses with a pale face:
> With his worshipful wife wrathit hym then …
> To his seruondes he saide in a sad haste,
> To bring hym his bright geire, bownet to feld,
> And arrayed for the rode with a ronke wille. (ll. 8472–74, 8476–78)

With Hector's two sons in her arms, Andromache falls at Hector's feet, begging him to refrain from battle, and she is joined by Hector's mother, Hecuba, by his sisters, Cassandra and Polyxena, and even by Helen. Yet, we are told, "He hade no ruthe of hor remyng, ne the rank teris, / Ne the prayer of tho prise persit not his hert" (ll. 8511–12). Similarly, Dares's Hector "dismissed the vision as due to her wifely concern," and on learning about her appeal to Priam, "bitterly blamed Andromache and told her to bring his armour" (152). Joseph of Exeter recounts that "Hector was not moved by the warnings of a woman, and spurned the presentiments of the timid sex" (62). Unlike Chaucer's Troilus, who must abide by his lady's wishes, the Hector of tradition, who refuses to be governed by the "timid sex," is free to follow his own judgments, such as when he defends Criseyde in the parliament.

The first appearance of Hector in Chaucer's *Troilus and Criseyde* occurs in the passage in which Criseyde begs the hero's protection after her father's treason (1.110ff). This passage, taken directly from Boccaccio, relies on the reputation of Hector as a protector of women, as seen in the story of his refusal to surrender Helen (1.12).[14] The passage recalls Lull's injunction that "[t]he duty of a knight is to support and defend women, widows and orphans" (34), "to help and succor them that approach in tears and require aid and mercy" (36). Whether or not chivalric manuals condone courtly love, they insist on the duty

---

[13] Jo Ann McNamara, "The *Herrenfrage*: The Restructuring of the Gender System, 1050–1150," *MM*, 3–29, at p. 9.

[14] Giovanni Boccaccio, *The Filostrato of Giovanni Boccaccio*, eds. and trans. Nathaniel Griffin and Arthur Myrick (New York: Octagon, 1978), p. 138.

of knights to protect women,[15] and Chaucer makes much of the contrast between Hector and Troilus in this regard.

The majority of the numerous allusions to Hector that Chaucer invents occur in Book 2, with eleven references to the hero, most of which take place in the long scene between Pandarus and Criseyde. In this scene, Hector's praise is readily on the lady's lips, whereas she needs be convinced of Troilus's worth. She asks of Hector first, referring to him as "the townes wal and Grekes yerde" (2.154). Pandarus is eager to shift her attention to Troilus, referring to him as "Ector the secounde" (2.158). He describes Troilus as another Hector, delineating attributes that belong to Troilus's brother and which, the text subsequently shows, are not, finally, applicable to Chaucer's main character.

Interestingly, when Criseyde affirms Pandarus's description of attributes appropriate to a prince (2.164–68), the moral virtue which merits her admiration is the very quality which she later insists motivates her to love Troilus:

> "For trusteth wel that youre estat roial,
> Ne veyn delit, nor only worthinesse
> Of yow in werre or torney marcial,
> Ne pompe, array, nobleye, or ek richesse
> Ne made me to rewe on youre destresse,
> But moral vertu, grounded upon trouthe." (4.1667–72)

The audience is, of course, well aware that Criseyde was, in fact, swayed by "his excellent prowesse, / And his estat, and also his renown, / His wit, his shap, and ek his gentilesse" (2.660–62), besides the ego-affirming knowledge that "his distresse / Was al for hire" (2.663–64). Clearly, what draws her to Troilus is not what would draw her to a man like Hector. Indeed, Pandarus seems aware of the difference: even though Criseyde's praise beginning with the statement "'God save hem bothe two!'" (2.163) includes both men, Pandarus's reminder, "'the kyng hath sones tweye'" (2.170), indicates that Pandarus takes Criseyde's praise as referring only to Hector.

In this speech, Pandarus acknowledges that Hector is beyond compare ("'Of Ector nedeth it namore for to telle: / In al this world ther nys a bettre knyght'" [2.176–77]), yet only two lines later, Pandarus contradicts himself in telling Criseyde, "'The same pris of Troilus I seye'" (2.181). Criseyde suggests the difference when she responds that this is indeed "sooth" of Hector, but one can merely "trowe" this of Troilus (2.183–84). When Pandarus characterizes Troilus as "the frendlieste man / Of gret estat," and a person of good "felawshipe" (2.204–6), noticeably absent is any mention of "moral virtue."

Regardless of Pandarus's comparisons of the two men, for Criseyde, Troilus is still second best. This can be inferred from the hypothetical statement she makes to Pandarus: "'That if that I, thorugh my dysaventrue, / Hadde loved outher

---

15 For example, the *Ordene de Chivarerie* states, "[O]n no account should [a knight] deprive a lady or damsel of his protection, but if they need him, he should help them as best he can if he wants to have esteem and praise, for one should honour ladies and carry out great deeds on their behalf" (p. 173).

hym or Achilles, / Ector, or any mannes creature'" (2.415–17). The mention of Achilles and Hector is gratuitous, since they are not the object of Pandarus's suit, nor has either hero shown interest in Criseyde. It is significant that the subject of her discourse moves from Troilus to the other two heroes. Her inclusion of them in her hypothetical proposition may, I suggest, be more wishful thinking than argument, the two great heroes the stuff of her girlish daydreams. At any rate, she seems not to have daydreamed of Troilus.

Even later when Criseyde finds herself falling under the spell of Troilus's desire for her, she is mindful of his inferiority to his brother. " 'For out and out he is the worthieste,'" she says, " 'Save only Ector, which that is the beste'" (2.739–40). There are many indications that Criseyde's attraction to Troilus is a selfish one, that she is only in love with being loved, and thus any decent knight will suffice, as long as he validates her. " 'I thenke ek how,'" she notes rather smugly, " 'he able is for to have / Of al this noble town the thriftieste / To ben his love … And yet his lif al lith now in my cure'" (2.736–38, 741). Even her ultimate trading of Troilus for Diomede argues that she has not chosen Troilus for himself. We sense, however, that such men as Hector and Achilles would for her be outstanding for their merit and could never be interchangeable with other men. Hector, however, is not a possibility for her, for he is married and devoted to Andromache.

The episode at Deiphebus's palace in Book 2 also reveals the contrast between Troilus and Hector. In the scene Hector is mentioned four times concerning the protection of Criseyde, but his absence is most significant. The scene is laden with courtly subterfuge as Pandarus carries out his elaborate and dishonest scheme to bring together the two lovers. Further, Helen is a visitor at the house of Deiphebus, and, noticeably, without Paris. Chaucer's audience, familiar with Virgil, would recall Book 6 of the *Aeneid* in which Deiphebus's ghost relates how the prince had been in bed with Helen when he met his gruesome death at the hands of the Greeks as he was betrayed by her.[16] He is, as Rosanne Gasse describes him, "Deiphebus, who died … not on the battlefield but weaponless in bed."[17] Gasse argues that Chaucer draws on Virgil's depiction of a shameful, unheroic death, which identifies Deiphebus as a "model of [un]heroic

---

[16] John Fleming cites both Virgil and Dictys as sources for Chaucer's implication concerning Helen and Deiphebus: "Chaucer would have known [the historical fact], because he would have read it in the fourth chapter of the Trojan history of Dictys Cretensis, one of his cited sources, that after the death of Paris, Helen married Deiphoebus. … Furthermore, he would have known where 'Dictys' got his information from, and that was, surely, from Deiphoebus's most famous appearance in Western literature, in the catabasis of the sixth book of Virgil's *Aeneid*" ("Deiphoebus Betrayed: Virgilian Decorum, Chaucerian Feminism," *ChauR* 21 [1986]: 182–99, at p. 192). Similarly, McKay Sundwall cites evidence from Virgil to argue that the amorous linking of Helen and Deiphebus was known to Chaucer's audience: "When she was married to Menelaus, Helen's eye and her affections wandered to Paris. Now married to Paris, what could be more natural and credible than that her eye is not only roving, but, as in the case of Alisoun the Wife of Bath and Jankyn, that it has found its newest object in Deiphoebus?" Sundwall concludes that Pandarus relies on Helen's and Deiphoebus's extended absence in the garden because "Deiphoebus and Helen are themselves eager for any chance of privacy" ("Deiphoebus and Helen: A Tantalizing Hint," *MP* 73 [1975]: 151–56, at p. 155).

[17] Rosanne Gasse, "Deiphebus, Hector, and Troilus in Chaucer's *Troilus and Criseyde*," *ChauR* 32 (1998): 423–39, at p. 429.

conduct" and Helen as not just a destroyer but an emasculator of men. His death, Gasse concludes, is "a warning example of the fate of the emasculated, 'feminized' man," a "warning for men to beware the weakening passion of love," to "remain self-controlled and strong."[18] The scene at Deiphebus's palace is rife with suggestions of deceit, lust, illicit love, and finally betrayal and shame. Since Chaucer invented the scene and could easily have included Hector in the gathering, Hector's omission suggests that he is in no manner tainted by such corruption.

Book 3, centering on the lovers' consummation, mentions Hector only once, but it is a highly ironic allusion. After Troilus becomes Criseyde's lover, he is seen to be emboldened in battle, thus illustrating the ennobling quality of courtly love: "He was, and ay, the first in armes dyght, / And certeynly, but if that bokes erre, / Save Ector most ydred of any wight" (3.1773–75). The mention of Hector, however, argues that courtly love is not necessary to personal nobility and prowess: clearly, Hector is still the better man, and we know that he does not need courtly love to motivate him. Conversely, we see that courtly love weakens Troilus.

Derek Brewer argues against the recent tide of anti-Troilus criticism, suggesting that Chaucer's depiction of Troilus does indeed accord with what the poet calls "manhood." His fighting prowess, his *gentilesse*, generosity, constancy, patience, goodness, and strength – all these virtues mark "the chivalric ideal of manliness."[19] While this is indeed true of Troilus's natural virtue, his potential for such manliness is impaired when he falls in love. As Diane Steinberg argues, "Before falling in love, Troilus had ... associate[d] love with a feminine lack of both strength and sense" (as when he ridicules lovers), and she refers to his "emasculation" by virtue of love.[20]

Many scholars point out the paradox that while courtly love's *passio* may increase Troilus's testosterone in battle, it has rendered him impotent in a number of ways.[21] Chaucer shows us, as Thomas Kirby asserts, that "the whole concept of courtly love was entirely foreign to the idea of free will," that "as the slave of love, [Troilus] is absolutely powerless and is able to do nothing of his own choice."[22] Similarly, Winthrop Wetherbee describes the Troilus of Book 4 as "powerless to take action in his own behalf and so as vulnerable to the whims of fortune as he has been 'subject' to love and blissful Venus throughout the poem."[23] D. W. Robertson describes such lovesickness as "an extreme form of

---

18   Rosanne Gasse, "Deiphebus, Hector, and Troilus," pp. 429 and 430.

19   Derek Brewer, "Troilus's 'Gentil' Manhood," *MC*, 237–52, at pp. 238, 244.

20   Diane Steinberg, " 'We do usen here no wommen for to selle': Embodiment of Social Practices in *Troilus and Criseyde*," *ChauR* 29 (1995): 259–73, at p. 264.

21   Maud McInerney argues that Troilus's problem is indeed the "threat of impotence" (" 'Is this a mannes herte?': Unmanning Troilus through Ovidian Allusion," *MC*, 221–35, at p. 224). I use the word only metaphorically.

22   Thomas Kirby, *Chaucer's Troilus: A Study in Courtly Love* (Baton Rouge: Louisiana State University Press, 1940), p. 262.

23   Winthrop Wetherbee, *Chaucer and the Poets: An Essay on* Troilus and Criseyde (Ithaca, NY: Cornell University Press, 1984), p. 212.

acedia,"[24] with its concomitant paralysis of the will, and more recently, Gregory Sadlek argues that for Chaucer and his contemporaries, the qualities we see in Troilus – his passivity, his exaggerated fits of melancholy, his characterization as timid – "defined a recognizable constellation of moral characteristics, the characteristics of a person caught in *acedia*";[25] it is a spiritual and physical sloth which leads to inaction, or, as Wetherbee describes it, "a failure of purpose, an irresolution, which [Troilus] interprets as a constraint on him by fortune."[26] Because this *acedia* renders Troilus irrational and helpless, lovesickness is also a feminizing disease. Vern Bullough points out that according to Isidore's discussion of *femina*, "love beyond measure was called 'womanly love'" and that "a man in love acted as a woman and thereby lost status as a man."[27] Similarly, locating the sensations of love in the brain rather than the heart, the eleventh-century translations by Constantine the African of Ovid's *Art of Love* argue that men who fall in love are suffering from a "woman's disease."[28] According to Maud McInerney, "Love might increase the woman's 'natural' tendencies (toward irrationality, passivity, weakness), but in the man it caused an inversion of nature," unmanning him, so to speak.[29] For this reason, "freedom from women," or at least from their mastery, was "the true test of a fighting man."[30] As David Aers reminds us, the fulfillment of the man's quest to possess the lady ironically opens the male to a "sense of dependency on the woman."[31]

Chaucer's use of love's malady differs from the literary tradition inasmuch as the illness, merely a literary convention in most romances, is "posited as a literal fact" in *Troilus and Criseyde*.[32] Charlotte Otten argues that the symptoms of courtly love as seen in Troilus correspond to the medieval understanding of the incapacitation caused by the actual disease *amor heroes*, a disease defying "[e]radication because body and mind collaborate to create physical and spiritual disequilibrium."[33] As Otten points out, Troilus does not even wish an escape from the disease that enthralls him: "his mind and volition [act as] co-conspirators in the thrilling agony inflicted on and induced by himself." "A person in the throes of lovesickness," Otten explains, "is not capable of redirection or of recognition. The disease disrupts both body and soul: upsets the humoral balance; breeds frenzy, discord, distrust; and can cause physical and spiritual

24 D. W. Robertson, "The Doctrine of Charity in Medieval Gardens," *Speculum* 26 (1951): 24–49, at p. 44.
25 Gregory Sadlek, "Love, Labor, and Sloth in Chaucer's *Troilus and Criseyde*," *ChauR* 26 (1992): 350–68, at p. 351.
26 Winthrop Wetherbee, *Chaucer and the Poets*, p. 212.
27 Vern Bullough, "On Being a Man in the Middle Ages," *MM*, 31–45, at p. 38.
28 Vern Bullough, "On Being a Man," p. 38.
29 Maud McInerney, "'Is this a mannes herte?'" p. 223.
30 Jo Ann McNamara, "The *Herrenfrage*," p. 17.
31 David Aers, *Community, Gender, and Individual Identity: English Writing 1360–1430* (London: Routledge, 1988), p. 145.
32 Giles Gamble, "Troilus Philocaptus: A Case Study in *Amor Hereos*," *Studia Neophilologica* 60 (1988): 175–78, at p. 176.
33 Charlotte Otten, "The Love-Sickness of Troilus," *Chaucer and the Craft of Fiction*, ed. Leigh Arrathoon (Rochester, MI: Solaris, 1986), 22–33, at pp. 22–23.

death."³⁴ Pointing out that "many of the same ideas of love [as found in the courtly romances] appear in the medieval medical treatises where the phenomenon of much the same kind of love is treated as an illness,"³⁵ Carol Heffernan explains the connection between Chaucer's idea of courtly love (*amor heroes* of the medical treatises) and mania, as attested by medieval physicians. Heffernan's description of the progress of the pathology from corruption of the faculty of estimation, to obsessive desire for sexual gratification that overthrows the reason, finally to mental fixation would seem to be borne out in the character of Troilus,³⁶ who, after seeing Criseyde in the temple, "thought ay on hire so, withouten lette" (1.361), making "a mirrour of his mynde / In which he saugh al wholly hire figure" (1.365–66).

On the one hand, Troilus is said by the narrator to be ennobled and emboldened by love. We are told that "was he, where so men wente or riden, / Founde oon the beste, and longest tyme abiden / Ther peril was ... / To liken hire the bet for his renoun" (1.473–75, 481). Such references are counterbalanced, however, by the evidence of Troilus's powerlessness. Book 1 makes clear that, regardless of "his excellent prowesse," Troilus is in bondage to love, which holds him "as his thral lowe in destresse" (1.438–39). For the most part of Books 1 and 2, Troilus is supine, suffering the effects of love's malady, bereft of sleep and appetite, and "wel neigh wood" (1.499). He feels so helpless and hopeless that he is suicidal: "'God wold,'" he says, "'I were aryved in the port / Of deth, to which my sorwe wol me lede!'" (1.526–27). In Books 2 and 3, not only does he lie in chamber at Deiphebus's palace "sik in ernest, douteles / So that wel neigh [he] sterve[s] for the peyne" (2. 1529–30), but when he finally meets his lady, he can barely speak. It may be arguable whether Chaucer intends this episode simply as conventional romance hyperbole in illustration of the lover's submission to his lady, but Troilus's swoon at the critical point in the later love scene is decidedly unconventional.³⁷

---

³⁴ Charlotte Otten, "The Love-Sickness of Troilus," pp. 23, 28.

³⁵ Carol Heffernnan, "Chaucer's *Troilus and Criseyde*: The Disease of Love and Courtly Love," *Neophilologus* 74 (1980): 294–309, at p. 294.

³⁶ Carol Heffernnan, "Chaucer's *Troilus and Criseyde*," pp. 296–97.

³⁷ Jill Mann, "Troilus' Swoon," *ChauR* 14 (1980): 319–35, describes this swoon as "demonstrat[ing], in the clearest possible way, [Troilus's] subjection to Criseyde and his love for her, and his dissociation from the idea that she is not still her 'owene womman'" (p. 328), but she argues that "Troilus' swoon is not ... a piece of behavior designed to show his ineffectuality, either as an individual or as a 'courtly lover'" (p. 331). The swoon, Mann says, is "crucial in ensuring that when the consummation does take place it does not represent the maneuvering of one partner into an admission of 'thraldom' but the natural surrender of each partner to the other" (p. 326). The comedy of the very next stanza (3.1093–99) would, it seems to me, argue against this conclusion. While Troilus's swoon quells Criseyde's fear of male "maistrye," the antics of Pandarus render the scene burlesque for the reader and sexually embarrassing for the hero. A number of scholars argue that the swoon is the result of Troilus's fears concerning impotence. For example, Maud McInerney states that "Troilus, at this critical moment, is unable to get an erection" ("'Is this a mannes herte?'" p. 222). While this fact would certainly be consistent with the notion of courtly love as emasculating and feminizing, I agree with Derek Brewer, that "there is simply no evidence nor any reason to suppose that Troilus may fear sexual impotence" ("Troilus's 'Gentil' Manhood," p. 239). Regardless of the reason for Troilus's behavior here, the swoon itself renders Troilus as passive, vulnerable, and less manly.

Troilus's reticence and his inability to act due to the workings of *amor heroes* may be rather fetching in the hero's tongue-tied adoration or comic in his bumbling appeal in Criseyde's bedchamber, but in Book 4, we see the serious consequence of Troilus's thralldom to love: he cannot save the very woman he is committed to. It is clear from the text that it is not a flaw in Troilus's character that prevents him from acting, but rather the imposition upon him of the strictures of courtly love: his first concern is Criseyde's honor, and only next "what weye / He myghte best th'eschaunge of hir withstonde" (4.158–60). Although he rehearses his arguments against Criseyde's notion of temporarily acquiescing to the trade, he finally gives in to his lady's will – against his better judgment, but nevertheless as a good courtly lover should. It is this moment, Rosanne Gasse argues, upon which the destruction of Troy turns: "The tragic moment for Troilus is ... when he fails to act as a prince, to be a second Hector."[38] Chaucer's audience, familiar with the Troy tradition, would be aware of Hector's refusal to be so dictated to by Andromache as consistent with his princely though vain attempt to prevent the trade.

Finally, Troilus's helplessness is epitomized in the hero's lengthy solilioquy on predestination, a close rendering of Boethius's *Consolatione*, in which Troilus ironically concludes that he indeed has no free will. D. W. Robertson explains that

> Fortune represents the variation between worldly prosperity and worldly adversity. Reason is able to discern that however superficially disappointing this variation may be, it is due neither to chance nor to destiny, but is a manifestation of the divine will, a function of the chain of love which holds creation together. To love the uncertain and transitory rewards of the world is to subject oneself to their fluctuations. To love God is to acquire freedom and peace of mind.[39]

Fortune, Troilus feels, has conspired against him, and he has no freedom of will to make things happen. It is no wonder, then, that in Book 5 he decides, again against his better judgment, to forego fighting Diomede, who comes to escort Criseyde to the Greeks, for fear that something will "happen" to her. His helpless agony during his subsequent ten-day wait only further illustrates his inability to summon the strength to direct his own life.[40]

Because Hector is not a courtly lover, he is free to take his honorable stand in Book 4 and object to Criseyde's trade for Antenor:

> "Syres, she nys no prisonere," he seyde;
> "I not on yow who that this charge leyde,
> But, on my part, ye may eftsone hem telle,
> We usen here no wommen for to selle." (4.179–82)

---

[38] Rosanne Gasse, "Deiphebus, Hector, and Troilus," p. 436.

[39] D. W. Robertson, "Chaucerian Tragedy," *ELH* 19 (1951): 1–37, at p. 5.

[40] Kevin Keirnan argues that "[i]naction is the key to Troilus' misfortunes, and it is his primary deficiency as a lover and as a human being" ("Hector the Second: The Lost Face of Troilustratus," *Annuale Mediaevale* 16 [1975]: 52–63, at p. 61.). The deficiency, I would argue, is not an inherent flaw in Troilus but rather a failure caused by the demands and the strain of courtly love.

Whereas Hector upholds his principles, the courtly lover Troilus only suffers in silence the news of the proposed exchange, regardless of his putative growth in virtue and courage: it is the illicitness of his and Criseyde's love that keeps him from saving her and averting the subsequent events. Troilus must betray his love for Criseyde so as not to betray her honor. The vote is taken, and Hector is the only nay.[41] We are not told whether Troilus painfully abstained or reluctantly voted with the majority so as to avoid suspicion. At any rate, he does not speak against the trade.

The final book of the poem only alludes to Hector, but both allusions are significant additions by Chaucer. The first is a summary account of Hector's death (5.1548–54), related in the context of Fortune's turning against Troy, and recalling the historians' insistence that Trojan success depends on Hector. The passage makes clear that Hector's demise is the beginning of the end for Troy, and that lesser Trojans – including Troilus – will fail to save the city.

The last mention of Hector is probably the most striking for its context. It occurs in the stanza narrating – actually, paraphrasing – the death of Troilus. After Troilus's agonizing wait for Criseyde, Chaucer slights Troilus in rendering his death scene a one-liner: "Despitously hym slough the fierse Achille" (5.1806). Not only is Troilus's death robbed of any possible drama and grandeur, but the gratuitous comparison with his brother – Troilus "was withouten any peere, / Save Ector" (5.1803–4) – undercuts Troilus's image: even in his final epic moment, he is upstaged.

As a number of scholars argue, in *Troilus and Criseyde*, Chaucer uses romance conventions, but to the effect of subverting the romance itself, particularly the element of courtly love.[42] Romance conventions work only when the characters are similarly conventional so that the demand for verisimilitude in action and psychological motivation in character need not arise. We are willing to suspend our disbelief in romance, but we cannot when the characters are flesh-and-blood realistic and, thus, show the conventions to be empty. As Barry Windeatt argues, "Chaucer is exploring … the limitations and inconsistencies in any attempt to associate life with literary forms of idealized behaviour."[43] This realism and its discordance with the romance conventions undo the courtly love depicted in *Troilus and Criseyde*. And "uncourtly" characters such as the happily married Hector only emphasize that discord, revealing not just the emptiness of courtly love but its perniciousness.

I would not argue that courtly love is what keeps Troilus from being another Hector, for it is clear in both *Troilus and Criseyde* and the medieval Troy tradition that Hector is superior to all other Trojan knights: even before Chaucer's Troilus is smitten with love, he has not achieved Hector's renown, and Criseyde

41   See Rosanne Gasse, "Deiphebus, Hector, and Troilus," p. 432, who points out that Deiphebus certainly was present at the parliament, and the fact that Hector's was the sole objection indicates that Deiphebus, who was not restrained by courtly secrecy, failed to speak up for Criseyde.

42   See, e.g., James Wimsatt, "The Medieval and Modern in Chaucer's *Troilus and Criseyde*," *PMLA* 92 (1977): 203–16.

43   Barry Windeatt, "'Love That Oughte Ben Secree' in Chaucer's *Troilus*," *ChauR* 14 (1979): 116–31, at p. 130.

is significantly unaware of his prowess. I would argue, however, that courtly love keeps Troilus from what he could himself be. A love that Chaucer's narrator describes as "feynede" (5.1848), courtly love is false and harmful because it is at heart self-directed and self-defeating.

As Robertson and others have argued for more than half a century, Chaucer's *Troilus and Criseyde* explores the irony of an *amor* that purports, with its religion of love, to be patterned on *caritas*, a "love of kynde" which mirrors God's love: it is freely given and cannot be earned; it is sufficient for happiness; it saves from death; it causes a growth in virtue. But unlike true human sacramental love, which does indeed mirror *caritas* and is a vehicle of grace, courtly love perverts both *caritas* and *amor*.[44] Although the courtly lady may be said to be the lover's *leche*, saving him from sure death from pining, Troilus in love is, in fact, suicidal; further, although Troilus, like Hector, dies in the war, Troilus suffers more, due to his obsession with Criseyde. We also see how Troilus's virtue has not increased but rather diminished: his lust causes the overthrow of his reason,[45] as is seen in his accepting Criseyde's decision to acquiesce to the trade and in his faulty conclusions when he rehearses the line of reasoning from the *Consolation of Philosophy* in Book 5 concerning free will. It causes him to refrain from virtuous acts, such as his refusal to join Hector in defending Criseyde from the trade; it causes him to share the vices of Pandarus, such as his suggesting rewarding Pandarus with one of his own sisters (3.407–13). The fact that the marriage debt precludes a love "freely given," the courtly love that Troilus seeks is an adulterous love, unlike Hector's marital love. Although it may appear ideal to the naïve Troilus, Chaucer affords us Pandarus's perspective to remind us of what this love really is. Finally – and most significantly – the love that Troilus believes to be sufficient for his happiness causes his unhappiness. When Troilus pleads with Fortune, "'Why ne haddestow my fader, kyng of Troye, / Byraft the lif, or don my bretheren dye, / Or slayn myself'" (4. 276–78), Chaucer ironically reveals the cause of Troilus's misery to be his attachment to Criseyde.[46]

Throughout the poem, Troilus has been like Plato's prisoner who, in the ignorance of the cave, seeks out shadows rather than reality. As Alfred David declares,

---

[44] David Aers indicates the misdirection of Troilus's love in the ambiguity of line 1.934: "for now myself I love" (*Community, Gender, and Individual Identity*, p. 124).

[45] D. W. Robertson observes that "[t]he stages of tragic development – subjection to Fortune, enjoyment of Fortune's favor, and denial of Providence – correspond to the three stages in the tropological fall of Adam, the temptation of the senses, the corruption of the lower reason in pleasurable thought, and the final corruption of the higher reason" ("Chaucerian Tragedy," p. 13).

[46] John Steadman demonstrates how the "greater part of Dame Philosophy's catalogue of false goods recur in Chaucer's reflections on Troilus's *fyn*; by placing them in this context," he argues, "the poet emphasizes the fact that his hero had mistaken his true end" (*Disembodied Laughter:* Troilus *and the Apotheosis Tradition* [Berkeley: University of California Press, 1972], p. 124); Alfred David cites Troilus's description of Criseyde as his "suffisaunce" (3.1309), suggesting that the term is meant as an ironic allusion to Book 3 of Boethius's *De consolatione*, where the term *sufficientia* is used in addressing the question of what constitutes true happiness (*The Strumpet Muse: Art and Morals in Chaucer's Poetry* [Bloomington: Indiana University Press, 1976], p. 31).

[t[he feeling we are left with is not that the vanities of this world are not worth possessing but that they are the shadowy, ephemeral intimations of a greater love and a permanent harmony, the desire for which is implanted within the human spirit and is the object of its constant striving.[47]

Similarly, Winthrop Wetherbee observes that Troilus's lack of knowledge of wherein lies true happiness causes his "worship[ping] a deceiving, ephemeral incarnation of that divine presence he had sensed so strongly at the heart of his experience of love."[48] Robertson notes this counterpointing of the ideal and the actual in the fact that Troilus's hymn of praise to love "is a paraphrase of Dante on the Blessed Virgin Mary, in the original an aspect of the new Song of Jerusalem, but in Troilus' version a song to Cupid, who is ironically called 'Charite.'"[49] Ida Gordon cites the irony by which Chaucer uses the hymns to love "to subject Troilus' own love to a comparison it cannot bear, by the use of language that is applicable only to a higher kind of love – the universal love that binds all things [including matrimonial ties, Boethius tells us] in a holy bond of harmony."[50] Troilus's ode, Alan Gaylord maintains, "reflects a confusion between two kinds of love Chaucer would not be guilty of, but it entirely reflects Troilus' estimation of his arrival at heaven" in the arms of Criseyde.[51]

Chaucer's *Troilus and Criseyde* argues that only divine love is perfect and lasting, and that earthly love is a reflection of divine love only inasmuch as it imitates it. Chaucer capitalizes on the distinction between the husband Hector and the lover Troilus to show that whereas the love between husband and wife reflects the other-centered commitment at the heart of true love, courtly love is revealed as self-directed and self-destructive. Although courtly convention posits the growth in virtue of the lover, Chaucer's poem insists that sexual love is true, virtuous love only within marriage. Hector's virtue and prowess, his absence from the love-intrigue scenes, and his freedom from the strictures of courtly love advance Chaucer's argument that courtly love is insufficient for true happiness and incompatible with true manliness.

47 Alfred David, "The Hero of *Troilus*," *Speculum* 37 (1962): 566–81, at p. 567.
48 Winthrop Wetherbee, *Chaucer and the Poets*, p. 238.
49 D. W. Robertson, "Chaucerian Tragedy," p. 27.
50 Ida Gordon, "The Process of Characterization in Chaucer's *Troilus and Criseyde*," *Studies in Medieval Literature and Languages in Memory of Frederick Whitehead*, ed. W. Rothwell et al. (Manchester: Manchester University Press, 1973), pp. 117–31, at p. 123.
51 Alan Gaylord, "Chaucer's Tender Trap: Troilus and the 'Yonge, Fresshe Folkes,'" *English Miscellany* 15 (1964): 25–42, at p. 40.

5

Masculinity and Its Hydraulic Semiotics in
Troilus and Criseyde

JAMES J. PAXSON

In one of its grandest gestures of homage to the classical tradition of Ovidian love literature, Chaucer's *Troilus and Criseyde* fixes the early depiction of its protagonist on the act of writing – but it is an act strangely overdetermined. Following some initial coaching by Pandarus to write a letter that is decisive yet not too rhetorically overwrought, Troilus ends up attempting to authenticate his letter by spilling his tears on the exterior of the letter, rather than on the sealed-up lines of inscription constituting the letter's inner, i.e., communicational surface. Whereas Pandarus suggests that Troilus "biblotte" his script with "teris ek a lite" (2.1027), the hero instead "with his salte teris gan … bathe / The ruby in his signet, and it sette / Upon the wex deliveriche and rathe" (1.1086–88). Following the now conventionalized gender analysis of male suffering in the poem – Louise Fradenburg's distinction, for instance, between the heroic nature of Chaucerian masculinity evidenced in immersion in violence coupled with public suffering and the nonheroic nature of Chaucerian femininity evidenced as mere survival[1] – we can conclude that the altered or botched hydraulic scenario of the tears applied to the signet and in turn to the sealing wax signifies the occultation of male suffering. If male suffering is to be celebrated, made public, it must find clear expression in any number of readable and visible forms – not just in the pageantry of the histrionized, heroic self bedecked with wounds, arrows, and bashed-up armor, but precisely too in this situation concerning the staining of preexistent writing, making for a mutated, but still visible and readable writing of the body's internal and invisible suffering. The tear-blotted wax fails to do that, chalking up for Troilus yet another moment of deferred masculinity and, as gender-theorized or feminist criticism has often found, a kind of feminized status as a failed masculine romance hero.

And yet this strangely charged moment of gender semiosis – where the masculine act of suffering's decisive self-representation as the double spilling of inscriptional liquids (ink, then tears) gives way to the feminine shedding of "mere" or evanescent tears that will be shortly lost – has a counterpart in

---

[1] Louise Fradenburg, "'Our owen wo to drynke': Loss, Gender and Chivalry in *Troilus and Criseyde*," *CTC*, 88–106.

the poem concerning another allegorical system lodged on the same image, that of masculinity's expression as a kind of "hydraulic" action in which an occulted interior emerges upward and outward. I refer to the heretofore critically neglected set-piece, in Book 3 of *Troilus and Criseyde*, in which the hero emerges through a gutter in Pandarus's house to seduce Criseyde. I will show how that action, regarding too the architecture of Pandarus's house, invokes the allegory of biblical typology to represent an expressly masculine action: the welling up of the hero into the physical presence of his beloved to successfully consummate his desire.[2]

*

Under Pandarus's guidance and aggressive prompting – the hero finds comparison with a mouse (3.736) among Pandarus's scornful urgings – Troilus prepares to secretly find his way to Criseyde's chamber. It is difficult to determine an exact picture of the tricky architecture in Pandarus's house; it seems partly constituted by the gothic trappings of secret passageways and concealed entrances here and there, all effective enough to have Troilus seem to suddenly appear kneeling at the head of his beloved's bed (3.953). The sequence of Troilus's physical incursion into Criseyde's chamber begins with Pandarus leading Troilus from the hero's own tiny room (his "stuwe" [3.698]) through a concealed door ("And with that word he gan undon a trappe" [3.741]) and into the very passageway – under a floor, behind a wall? – that must connect with Criseyde's room via another concealed door out of which Pandarus himself emerged before his niece and to her astonishment ("'What, which wey be ye comen, benedicitee? / ... And how unwist of hem alle?'/ 'Here at this secre trappe-dore,' quod he," [3.757–59]). Lying between and connecting the two trapdoors is the conduit in which Troilus awaits, as Pandarus prepares Criseyde:

> "Now stant it thus . . .
> This Troilus, right platly for to seyn,
> Is thorugh a goter, by a pryve wente,
> Into my chaumbre come in al this reyn,
> Unwist of every manere wight" (3.785–88).

---

2   The most extensive study of Pandarus's house is Saul Brody, "Making a Play for Criseyde: The Staging of Pandarus' House in Chaucer's *Troilus and Criseyde*," *Speculum* 73 (1998): 115–40. Following H. M. Smyser, "The Domestic Background of *Troilus and Criseyde*," *Speculum* 31 (1956): 297–315, Brody devotes much of his analysis to the demonstration (even using speculative diagrams) that Chaucer's Pandarian spaces represent actual and realistic architectural details in a contemporary London townhouse. However, and after demolishing a Robertsonian idea about Pandarus-as-devil and Troilus-as-lost-soul traversing the nether regions of the world symbolized in spatially subjacent Pandarian hydrological passageways (p. 133), Brody's main point is that Pandarian architecture represents stagecraft settings reminiscent of the mystery plays with their two-tiered cosmic settings (heavens/hells) – an unacknowledged "typological" resolution which, however, itself marks a staged (Pandarian) fiction intended to render Criseyde as a kind of sophisticated playgoer (pp. 138–39). The "goter" for Brody is therefore merely a metaphorical or euphemistic referent in a social play of seduction (i.e., Pandarus was simply "lying" to Criseyde about the sequestered Troilus safely tucked away in that concealing conduit), one replete with the self-reflexive dramaturgical language of deception.

Oddly, Pandarus declares that Troilus entered his own private chamber using the secret "gutter," whereas we have seen how Pandarus tacitly "unpinned" the door of Troilus's "stuwe" prior to his leading the hero "by the lappe" into the conduit, where he presently waits. At a very whimsical level, Troilus indeed becomes a kind of "mouse," one relegated to negotiating the spaces of his friend's house behind walls and under floors.

But the symbolic significance of this fleeting and practically ephemeral sequence having to do with Pandarian architecture bears an allegorical weight far from the realm of the whimsical. I suggest that we have at this point an instance of what Chauncey Wood once classified as an encrypted sort of biblical allusion constitutive of Chaucer's poetics that is designed to be "deliberately disguised for artistic effect."[3] The machinery of biblical allusion, more so in terms of Troilus's and Criseyde's self-realization of biblical typology or the imagery of figura, stands, in Lawrence Besserman's analysis, in a very peculiar light to begin with;[4] and this extremely encrypted, vaguely apparent biblical allusion hinges on the loaded though proleptically active word "goter." The word is loaded in that, as an allusion, it points the reader to one of the most momentous occurrences in biblical salvation history: the secret emergence of King David via the *tzinor* to surprise the Jebusites, conquering their city of Jebus – later Jerusalem – in 2 Samuel. The word is "proleptical" in that Chaucer's word "gutter" uncannily prefigures the Early Modern English translation of that channel or conduit discovered and exploited by the conquering David (recall that the Vulgate rendering of the concept is *fistula*) as expressed in the words of the King James Version of scripture: "And David said on that day, Whosoever getteth up to the gutter, and smiteth the Jebusites ... he shall be chief and captain" (2 Sam. 5:8). If this node of biblical-typological allusion does indeed configure the allegorical contouring of another conquest – the taking of Criseyde by a now allegorically active and effective Troilus – then the hero has passed through an incident that valorizes him as a hypermasculine figural type, for no biblical type more effective as a masculine model than the Old Testament member of the fabled Nine Worthies, King David himself, could be secured in Chaucerian typological poetics.

As I have long held and shown elsewhere, biblical typology rarely functions in apodictic and unidimensional ways.[5] It is often a self-compromising system in which types, antitypes, and their "countertypes" get layered onto each other in secular medieval texts, such as Chaucer's great romance, in semiotically complex ways.[6] If the singular and fugitive typological allusion to the conquest of Jerusalem hinges on the sole word "gutter," a corollary image of the holy city appears slightly earlier in Pandarus's discourse when the arch-mediator helps

3   Chauncey Wood, "Artistic Intention and Chaucer's Uses of Scriptural Allusion," *Chaucer and Scriptural Tradition*, ed. David Jeffrey (Ottawa: University of Ottawa Press, 1984), 35–61, at p. 36.
4   Lawrence Besserman, *Chaucer's Biblical Poetics* (Norman: University of Oklahoma Press, 1998), pp. 164–65. For a comprehensive catalog of all direct biblical citations and allusions in *Troilus and Criseyde*, see Besserman, *Chaucer and the Bible* (New York: Garland, 1988), pp. 253–76.
5   See my "A Theory of Biblical Typology in the Middle Ages," *Exemplaria* 3 (1991): 359–83.
6   James Paxson, "Theory of Biblical Typology," pp. 368–69.

stage the seduction that is to come during the storm. Once again, only a vague-looking though potentially disguised or encrypted allusion to the architecture of Solomon's First Temple organizes the description made by Pandarus of his house's architecture in regard to the layout of rooms, the disposition of his sleeping guests and, of course, the sequestered Criseyde awaiting her lover and his helpful coach:

> "And nece, woot ye wher I wol yow leye,
> For that we shul nat liggen far asonder,
> And for ye neither shullen, dar I seye,
> Heren noyse of reynes nor of thonder?
> By God, right in my litel closet yonder.
> And I wol in that outer hous allone
> Be wardein of youre wommen everichone.
>
> "And in this myddel chambre that ye se
> Shal youre wommen slepen, wel and softe;
> And there I seyde shal youreselven be."
> …
> Tho Pandarus, hire em, right as hym oughte,
> With wommen swiche as were hire most aboute,
> Ful glad unto hire beddes syde hire broughte,
> And took his leve, and gan ful lowe loute,
> And seyde, "Here at this closet dore withoute,
> Right overthwart, youre wommen liggen alle,
> That whom yow list of hem ye may here calle." (3.659–68, 680–86)

Again, we must work to extract a general architectural picture of the arrangement in Pandarus's house, but it seems reasonably clear that Criseyde (as would all noble guests or relatives) gets her own "closet" (like Troilus's "stuwe") to herself. Outside of that private locale lie, in a "middle" room, her attendant women, and beyond that, in the "outer" part of the house, will lie Pandarus, guardian or watchman of the layered precincts of women within.

Here too, I suggest, is another of Chaucer's disguised typological allusions: the mere tripartitism of potentially symbolic architecture – outer/inner/innermost – calls up the construction of Solomon's First Temple, built not just as the Israelites' religious center and treasury but out of respect to the desires of David for such a sacred place, as it is famously described as a structure of three chambers (1 Kings 6:6). The nested, tricameral architecture, enclosing ever-more sacred and increasingly restricted spaces within, would not have been lost on the typological potential of the medieval imagination as it is expressed in subtle Chaucerian poetics: the "outer house" may suggest the so-called Porch or vestibulum (Hebrew, *ulam*) of the Temple; the "middle chamber" could be either the interior Holy Place (Hebrew, *hekhal*) or, indeed, the so-called Middle Chamber attached to the southern side of Solomon's Temple that was lodged on an elevated platform and used for storage purposes. Criseyde's closet might allude to the Holy of Holies, the nethermost or innermost *sanctum sanctorum* (Hebrew, *debir*) that housed the Ark of the Covenant, was sealed by the sacred veil, and was accessible only once a year to the High Priest alone.[7] That most impenetrable and off-limits of spaces, locus of the divine, thus equates cleverly to the locality of the beloved that must be aggressively transgressed by the lover – a semiotic equation by now commonplace in the historical understanding of medieval thought (desire for the female, or for the desiring female = sacred and ineffable act of theophany in Christian theology), as Alexandre Leupin has so convincingly demonstrated.[8]

Above all, the typological allegory of Jerusalem (on the verge of its possession by the Israelites) and the sacred architecture of Solomon's Temple (representing the consummation of the Israelites' presence and power in the holy city) rest on the decisive action of the heroic male, first the conquering David and then the builder Solomon. This allegorical underpinning to the heroic lover of Chaucer's romance moves to obviate, or at least to modify and realign, the demasculinized status that Troilus has undergone through the poem's many moments of indecisive activity on the hero's part in general, and in particular through the odd but overdetermined episode of the love letter's composition, a minor monument to the text's gendered "hydraulic semiotics." Now, the allegorical reflection of Solomon's Temple in the architecture of Pandarus's house does not per se involve the other, dialectical aspect of Chaucer's hydraulic semiotics; I have gone into the detail of uncovering that typological allusion to show that typology involves the layering of a sacred allegorical referent – here, Jerusalem, representable as its soon-to-be-transformed precursor, Jebus, and as its architectural synecdoche, the holy Temple of Solomon – across, in this case, two prior temporal horizons.[9]

But the "hydraulic"[10] or hydrological aspect of David's *tzinor*, or *fistula*, or gutter, ensures the pulsive, or explosive, aspect of masculine symbolic action – the emergence upward and inward (to the object of desire and incursion) – that enables the realigning of the hero's gendered status in *Troilus and Criseyde*. It remains in this brief essay to therefore give this typological-allegorical sketch

---

7   Paul Achtemeier, gen. ed., *Harper's Bible Dictionary* (San Francisco: Harper & Row, 1985), pp. 1022–25.

8   Alexandre Leupin, *Barbarolexis: Medieval Writing and Sexuality*, trans. Kate Cooper (Cambridge, MA: Harvard University Press, 1989), pp. 6–7, 13–16.

9   James Paxson, "Theory of Biblical Typology," p. 370.

10 I admit to having some fun with this markedly anachronistic word out of modern physics, which technically refers to the eruptive or explosive power of any fluid which, since it cannot be put under compression, must force a way out of a cavity or conduit or be harnessed to the effect of multiplying initial energy or effort put upon said fluid. The sexual and genital version of masculine hydraulics goes without saying; but the implication in my essay's vocabulary that Chaucer's water-and-conduit imagery prefigures the actual "hydraulics" of modern liquid-state physics gains more credence in the context of Chaucer's neo-Aristotelian wave-motion physics as voiced by the Golden Eagle of the *House of Fame*. Although Chaucer's take on fluid mechanics freely and erroneously likens the wave-form expansion of disturbed (or compressed) air to the wave-form of disturbed water, i.e., the growing set of concentric circles constituting the ripple effect caused by a stone thrown into water, the poet does get absolutely correct the fluid mechanics of water alone and in itself. Chaucer's physics of rippling, expanding water waves involves a precise sense of hydraulic action in an age far, far before our own with its only recently and painfully developed apprehension of the deadly effects of a tsunami – a further implication that lies below in my claims about Chaucer, the FEMA engineer before the fact! See *House of Fame*, 2.789–822.

more depth by pinning that intertextual system of allusion and resignification on some historical foundations involving the anthropological apprehension of David's gutter regarding ancient practices, and involving the contemporaneous historical value of urban spaces and water conduiting for the English fourteenth century.

*

It bears mentioning that the *tzinor* of Jebus has been a matter of some debate for archeologists and geologists studying the environs of the city of Jerusalem. To be sure, the concept of the secret water-supply channel invokes the still-current practice throughout the Middle East of the construction and mainte- nance of underground water tunnels that are tapped into through vertical surface wells at regular geographic intervals. The so-named *qanat* (in Arabic), in fact, is a construction of ancient heritage that might have served as another model for David's gutter. The *qanat* even serves current anthropological wisdom as a material sign of the social creation and solidification of urban life itself in that long-inhabited region, and in turn (in the context of Middle-Eastern prehistorical development), of the passage from nomadic culture to civilized life – likewise as it had been allegorically represented in scriptural narrative by the settling of Jerusalem by David's previously nomadic people; or by the earlier conquest of Jericho by Joshua and his people seeking to settle down in the grain-rich cities of Syro-Palestine.[11] Whether the *tzinor* or gutter of 2 Samuel 5:8 was an entirely artificial construction still incurs debate;[12] likewise, there has long been an impulse in archeological thought to assimilate it to the secret conduit built by King Hezekiah – and presumably located in 1868 by Charles Warren – in order to tap the pool of Siloa (and help Jerusalem resist the attacking Assyrians) as recorded too in the Old Testament.[13]

Of importance to this discussion of typology and gender semiotics, however, is the emphasis in all such pictures – anthropological, archeological, and scrip- tural proper – upon the link between the value of the conduits of life-saving water and the decisiveness of male action in socially or societally dynamic situations.[14] We could wonder, then, if this chain of associations had further, and personal, historical value in the life of Chaucer.

If there is one biographical fact about the historical Chaucer as a "maker" other than of his poetic body of production, it involves his successful accom-

---

[11] For a lucid discussion of the value of the *qanat* and of the settling of the Holy Land by the nomadic Israelites, see Jacob Bronowski, *The Ascent of Man* (Boston: Little, Brown, 1973), pp. 60, 68–72, 77.

[12] See D. Gill, "Subterranean Waterworks of Biblical Jerusalem: Adaptation of a Karst System," *Science* 254 (1991): 1467–71, for description of such structures as modified through the sculpting of preex- istent caves in a limestone topography.

[13] Ibid. See too 2 Kings 20:20; Isaiah 22:9,11; 2 Chronicles 32:2–4; 2 Chronicles 32:30; Ecclesiasticus 48:17.

[14] Either the construction and maintenance or the seizing of such structures would have appealed at least to Chaucer's classical sensibilities; classical and medieval readers would have marveled, for instance, at Herodotus's description of the famous, mile-long water-supply tunnel engineered by one Eupalinus on the island of Samos. See *The Histories*, trans. Aubrey de Selincourt (New York: Penguin, 1954), p. 228.

plishment, marked by technical virtuosity as well as considerable administrative skill, as Clerk of the Works during the early 1390s. Nothing less could be said than that the poet himself implemented the hydraulic or hydrological salvaging of his native land! The terrifying gale of March 5, 1390, required the special construction of a form of "gutter" under the direction of a man who was taken as an expert in the inspection, upkeep, and repair of special marine or hydraulic structures including wharves, bridges, walls, drains, watergates, and other waterworks.[15] Chaucer's job included not just the planning and ordering of actual repairs, but the granting of summonses to landowners held negligent in the upkeep of waterworks adjudged faulty once storm conditions damaged the land with battering and flooding.[16] As such legalistic duty would have been getting under way in the wake of the storm of 1390, the truly imposing test of skill – to a man holding a post not unlike a director of the US Federal Emergency Management Agency well before the fact – was in actual design and construction of channels to drain flooded (and thus useless) farmland along the Thames and in the marshes of Kent.[17] As Donald Howard relates, the channels "or ditches were drainage canals, sometimes as much as 15 feet deep and 48 feet wide, that could serve as waterways for boats; they were called 'sewers' (the modern meaning of the word was not to develop for two hundred years), whence the mistaken notion that Chaucer served on a sanitation commission."[18] The more modern semantic narrowing of "sewer" to mean an enclosed tunnel or channel underground for conveying rainwater or waste echoes with the "goter" used by Troilus; but it more emphatically connects Chaucer's skill as a director of engineered waterway projects with the urban instantiation of such hydraulic technologies in the fourteenth and fifteenth centuries. The changing identification of London as a New Troy, in both the Chaucerian and Lydgatean perspectives, centered often on the city's impressively reengineered water supply, storm drainage, and wastewater systems.[19] If the "gutter" of Pandarus's house bears a typological connection to the Old Testament image of David's secret incursion into Jerusalem, as I have argued so far; and if that typological and scriptural

[15] John Gardner, *The Life and Times of Chaucer* (New York: Knopf, 1977), pp. 282–83.

[16] John Gardner, *The Life and Times of Chaucer*, p. 283.

[17] Such floods had long plagued the southeast coast of the isle of Britain. The Laud Chronicle records a fatal flood blown in by a great gale in 1125; see G. N. Garmonsway, ed. and trans., *The Anglo-Saxon Chronicle* (London: Dutton, 1953), pp. 255–56. Accordingly, severe flood zones in Kent had already undergone maritime and hydraulic engineering of considerable sophistication by the twelfth and thirteenth centuries; see "Early Medieval Romney Marsh" at www.liv.ac.uk/geography/RomneyMarsh.

[18] Donald Howard, *Chaucer: His Life, His Works, His World* (New York: Fawcett Columbine, 1987), p. 458.

[19] For a splendid study of "New Troy's" representation in literary texts as a model city possessed of well-engineered water-supply and waste-management systems, see David DeVries, "And Away Go Troubles Down the Drain: Late Medieval London and the Poetics of Urban Renewal," *Exemplaria* 8 (1996): 401–18, at pp. 410–11. See too John Ganim's interesting comparison of William Fitz Stephen's description of twelfth-century London and John Stow's sixteenth-century *Survey of London*, again with special focus on water-delivery, waste-management, and flood-control systems, in "The Experience of Modernity in Late Medieval Literature: Urbanism, Experience and Rhetoric in Some Early Descriptions of London," *The Performance of Middle English Culture: Essays on Chaucer and the Drama in Honor of Martin Stevens*, eds. James J. Paxson, Lawrence Clopper, and Sylvia Tomasch (Cambridge: D. S. Brewer, 1998), pp. 77–96.

legacy can find counterbalancing in some general anthropological knowledge we now possess about water supply in ancient cities and tablelands of the Middle East, the scene of the hydraulic architecture of Pandarus's house may well amount to one of the few literary and symbolic moments that hold a charge of biographical value to the technical interests of the public Chaucer roughly at the time of the poem's completion and that must have resonated for him at a personal and professional level. That biographical and personal resonance, it must be further conjectured, enables a sustained parallel between the gendered structure of Troilus's own bifurcated personality constituting the internal semiotics of the poem: heroic acts such as draining the land through hydraulic engineering are the physical and cultural work in the real world of working men like Chaucer. Chaucer, the private writer of love poetry, one often expressing self-doubt and inefficacy, must yield to the public Chaucer, Clerk of the Works, who saves the land for his king and people – an act no less heroic and masculine than the military use of secret tunnels for incursional or intrusive purposes into conquered regions of the heart, of the polis.

*

In a recent essay on the scene of Troilus's coached letter-writing, I took a turn somewhat different from the findings made in this short study: I argued that the upsurging of fluid, signaled finally as the spilled tears of the poem's hero, signified as well the Platonic desire – and ironically so – for pure presence, for the non-mediated proof that the lover was suffering with yearning for his beloved and that the physical act of inscription on parchment short-circuited or obviated the temporal and metaphysical distancing characteristically symbolized by writing in the grand Platonic scheme, in which writing (*graphē*) derives from speech (*lexis*) which derives from thought (*dianoia*) which derives from/as apprehension of the material world (*hylē*) which derives or emanates from the Real or ideal world (*morphē*). In the scene of Troilus's tear-blotting of the letter, the internal and prelexial, doubly pregraphic experience of pure interiority usurps writing's tertiary position.[20] But I also tempered this abstractly semiological finding with other historical data about the actual imaging of water-blotted documentation in the context of late fourteenth-century thought. In the chronicle writings of Chaucer's contemporary writer, Thomas Burton of Meaux, we find imagery that should remind us of Chaucer's role in the March 1390 storm aftermath: Burton regularly obsessed over the damage done to documents kept in the storage chambers of his Yorkshire abbey – damage done not just because of the dilapidated condition of the old buildings into which rainwater always seemed to work its way, but from the notorious and regular floods from the Humber and Hull Rivers.[21] The best Thomas could do was retrieve and rescue

---

20 James Paxson, "Triform Chaucer: Deconstruction, Historicism, Psychoanalysis, and *Troilus and Criseyde*," *Approaches to Teaching Chaucer's* Troilus and Criseyde *and the Shorter Poems*, eds. Tison Pugh and Angela Jane Weisl (New York: MLA, 2007), pp. 127–32, at p. 128.

21 James Paxson, "Triform Chaucer," pp. 131–32; and see Antonia Gransden, *Historical Writing in England*, vol. 2 (Ithaca, NY: Cornell University Press, 1982), pp. 351–61.

old charters, deeds and chronicles. But that too takes us round a circle and back to the masculine doings of the active man – conqueror, aggressive and seducing lover, great builder, public servant of the king, and rescuer of the objects of the historical past. The at-first loose connections plausibly linking all these actions – and via typological, semiological, philosophical, anthropological, and historical threads – enrich the picture of Chaucer's complex protagonist. And I hope I have begun to show, if even tendentiously, how the gender semiotics of *Troilus and Criseyde* "constructs" the poem's ill-fated hero, Troilus, using a peculiarly hydraulic imagery.

6

Masochism, Masculinity, and the Pleasures of Troilus

HOLLY A. CROCKER and TISON PUGH

With a title that is simultaneously declarative and descriptive, one might think we would have a confident answer to the guiding question of this essay: what are the pleasures of Chaucer's *Troilus and Criseyde*? This question remains difficult to answer, for reasons that pertain to the poem's construction of Troilus's masculinity out of the fracturing experience of suffering. At its basic level of plot and character, the tale of an arrogant and sulky bachelor who wins the fleeting love of a morally inscrutable widow through the oily machinations of her lascivious uncle seems an unlikely source of literary pleasure. With its formulaic structure, featuring love's debilitating desire, its momentary reward, and its inevitable loss, *Troilus and Criseyde* seems almost deliberately unappealing. For instance, Gretchen Mieszkowski argues in her feminist analysis of the text that "Male Chaucerians may be surprised to learn that reading *Troilus and Criseyde* for the first time is almost invariably a disappointment for a woman."[1] Of course, there arises no inherent discrepancy between a pleasureless narrative and a pleasurable reading experience, since, as Roland Barthes observes, "The text of pleasure is not necessarily the text that recounts pleasures."[2] If the same could be said for depictions of pain, then we might readily agree that Troilus's suffering potentially provides a source of pleasure in the poem. Taking pleasure from another's pain, however, is often regarded as socially suspect and ethically corrupt. Even if religious practice recuperated this "sacramental theatre" in the late Middle Ages, the pleasures involved in contemplating the agonies of another continue to be fraught with a deep antagonism about what it means to be moved by the spectacle of another's pain.[3]

As Chaucer's *Troilus and Criseyde* insistently demonstrates, the tension at issue here is the power of passivity, particularly the ways in which a painful sight can move a viewer beyond the limits of volition. Although pain reduces an individual agent to a helpless state, Chaucer explores the power of suffering to affect

---

[1] Gretchen Mieszkowski, "Chaucer's Much Loved Criseyde," *ChauR* 26.2 (1991): 109–32, at p. 109.
[2] Roland Barthes, *The Pleasure of the Text*, trans. Richard Miller (New York: Hill and Wang, 1975), p. 55.
[3] Sarah Beckwith, *Signifying God: Social Relation and Symbolic Act in the York Corpus Christi Plays* (Chicago: University of Chicago Press, 2001), pp. 59–71.

others. Because Troilus's passivity achieves the effects of agency, moving others through his stasis, Chaucer's poem demonstrates the fundamental transformation that occurs within scenes of suffering. Commenting on Georges Bataille's fascination with sacrifice, Susan Sontag affirms the sacralizing power of pain in terms that pertain to Chaucer's depiction of Troilus: "It is a view of suffering, of the pain of others, that is rooted in religious thinking, which links pain to sacrifice, sacrifice to exaltation."[4] As a result of his suffering, Troilus achieves an elevated position, and through Troilus's sacrifice, Chaucer converts a helpless condition into an empowered spectacle. It should also be emphasized, however, that transforming Troilus into an exalted figure concomitantly requires a process of unmaking to unlock the pleasures promised by the poem's sacrificial poetics. As Elaine Scarry so memorably argues, pain at once entails destruction and creation.[5] Even as Troilus's suffering creates an exalted form of identity, the poem allows readers to witness the deconstruction of a culturally empowered model of masculinity.

In other words, one of the pleasures of Troilus's pain derives from the ways in which a form of masculine privilege is denied. Troilus's presumptuous desire to remain immune to the pull of amorous affection is defeated by the power of one look. As he roams freely about the temple, his roving gaze is stopped short. The sight of Criseyde penetrates Troilus, reducing him to astonishment and remaking him into a lover. The process of his transformation dismantles an elite model of manhood, for it is in contrast to his suffering that Diomede's prevailing methods of courtship appear as predatory exercises of masculine aggression. This is not to say, however, that the identity Troilus vivifies is of a more culturally common variety. Rather, his suffering refines even more delicately an elite model of masculinity. Troilus's suffering consolidates a rarefied formulation of masculinity in which his endurance of pain is identified as a defining experience for the culturally privileged male. By considering the readerly pleasures that ensue from this spectacle of suffering, we suggest that Troilus's pain creates a fantasy of elite masculinity, which undermines and even challenges the culturally enabled model of manhood that a figure like Diomede exemplifies. In sum, Troilus's stasis, helplessness, and loss are exalted because they separate privileged masculinity from the agency, domination, and possession that a Trojan prince otherwise might claim.

Troilus's Masochism: Beyond Courtly Love

Because we are interested in the gendered dynamics of exaltation involved in Chaucer's erotic theater of pain, much of what follows engages recent theoretical interest in the relation between courtly love and masochism. Slavoj Žižek's now-

---

4 Susan Sontag, *Regarding the Pain of Others* (New York: Farrar, Straus, Giroux, 2002), p. 99. See also Georges Bataille, *Tears of Eros* (San Francisco: City Lights, 1989), pp. 79–82; 204–7.
5 Elaine Scarry, *The Body in Pain: The Making and Unmaking of the World* (Oxford: Oxford University Press, 1985).

familiar suggestion, that "it is only with the emergence of masochism, of the masochist couple, towards the end of the last century that we can now grasp the libidinal economy of courtly love," unites medieval and modern cultures through a structure of desire and disavowal.[6] Drawing on Jacques Lacan's discussions in his *Ethics of Psychoanalysis*, Žižek transforms the limitations of masculine heterosexual desire into a straight scene of male empowerment.[7] Because the courtly lady is imagined as an "inhuman partner," the *finamen* stages his identity through a series of responses that display his suffering as a willing act of his own volition.[8] Troilus would appear to be the poster-boy for this suffering, to the extent that his individuated pain promises a general expression of courtly love's captivating passions. Despite his representative status, however, Troilus is uniquely alone in his experience of sorrow. Troilus's suffering is placed so excessively at the narrative's forefront that it is easy to overlook the exclusive singularity of the position he occupies. Yet Chaucer goes further than the familiar romance narrative of courtly masculine suffering, for Troilus does not endure his suffering on behalf or at the behest of Criseyde.

Unlike the traditional masculine subject, whose ability to act in relation to others situates his identity, Troilus is defined more extremely by his immuring passivity. Indeed, as Winthrop Wetherbee observes, passivity structures the character of Troilus more than any other feature: "The most striking feature of Troilus's role as lover is his extraordinary passivity. From the moment Criseyde's image enters his heart, he is virtually powerless to act."[9] Gregory Sadlek likewise notes the exceptional nature of Troilus's passivity: "All courtly lovers suffer from fear, melancholia, and even despair, but Troilus suffers from these and from passivity to an extreme degree."[10] Troilus's stasis reaches the point of negation, so that one striking example serves to indicate his general mood throughout the narrative:

> For mannes hed ymagynen ne kan,
> N'entendement considere, ne tonge telle
> The cruele peynes of this sorwful man,
> That passen every torment down in helle. (4.1695–98)

The excess of these lines – no mere human could imagine or describe Troilus's pains, because Troilus's sufferings are worse than the torments of hell – typifies the hyperbole running throughout descriptions of Troilus. Certainly, love hurts in *Troilus and Criseyde*, but Troilus is repeatedly pierced and penetrated by its implements of desire. Pandarus asks Criseyde if she will take pity on Troilus's

---

6   Slavoj Žižek, *The Metastases of Enjoyment: Six Essays on Women and Causality* (London: Verso, 1994), p. 89.

7   Jacques Lacan, *The Ethics of Psychoanalysis, 1959–60: The Seminar of Jacques Lacan*, Book VII, ed. Jacques-Alain Miller, trans. Dennis Porter (New York: Norton, 1992), pp. 149–50.

8   Slavoj Žižek, *Metastases*, p. 91. A particularly fine exploration of courtly love's relation to masochism in medieval literature is Jeffrey Jerome Cohen's chapter, "Masoch/Lancelotism," in his *Medieval Identity Machines* (Minneapolis: University of Minnesota Press, 2003), pp. 78–115.

9   Winthrop Wetherbee, *Chaucer and the Poets* (Ithaca, NY: Cornell University Press, 1984), p. 65.

10   Gregory Sadlek, "Love, Labor, and Sloth in Chaucer's *Troilus and Criseyde*," *ChauR* 26 (1992): 350–68, at p. 351.

suffering: "'Yee, nece, wol ye pullen out the thorn / That stiketh in his herte?'" (3.1104–5), and Troilus laments that "'fro my soule shal Criseydes darte / Out nevere mo'" (4.472–73).[11] This imagery establishes Troilus's incapacity to assert himself erotically, making him the most helpless member of the poem's amorous community.

If Troilus experiences an extreme state of passivity within the poem, he is not altogether powerless in his love affair. In her reading of the lyric counterplots of *Troilus and Criseyde*, Clare Kinney characterizes the first *Canticus Troili* as expressing "male complaint in the absence of an object of desire, expressed by way of the apostrophizing and interrogation of external forces against which one is powerless."[12] This type of powerlessness takes work, requiring an active form of submission to desire. For instance, in the first *Canticus Troili*, the young lover intimates that this condition of powerlessness confers pleasure: "'If harm agree me, wherto pleyne I thenne?'" (1.409). Given that the bulk of the narrative (Books 1, 4, and 5) focuses in large measure on Troilus's laments, this line of the *Canticus Troili* reinscribes the crippling pains of lovesickness. Here as elsewhere, Troilus perpetuates his pain through affirmative consent. As Mervin Glasser acknowledges, masochism invariably involves such a transmutation: "it can be seen that there is always an element of deception in masochism, always an arrogant contempt and assertion of control hidden behind the humiliation and submission."[13] If Troilus prolongs his agony because it gives him claim to love's experience, the pleasure he derives from suffering suggests his ultimate mastery of desire.

In such a manner, Troilus acknowledges his control over the masochistic ordeal that paralyzes him: "'O quike deth, O swete harm so queynte, / How may of the in me swich quantite, / But if that I consente that it be?'" (1.411–13). Envisioning death and harm invading his body, Troilus constructs himself as conquered in love, creating his identity through his abnegating declarations. Troilus, in effect, agrees to be conscripted into the service of love as its powerless agent. Through the exercise of this powerlessness, moreover, he experiences pleasure. Thus, as much as the narrator foregrounds Troilus's pain, it is also critical to realize that his suffering is a performance of self-possession that produces pleasure. Following Pandarus's advice to simulate the role of a suffering lover, Troilus feigns sorrow as a means to gain erotic fulfillment:

> Therwith it semed as he wepte almost.
> "Ha, a" quod Troilus so reufully,
> "Wher me be wo, O myghty God, thow woost!
> Who is al ther? I se nought trewely." (3.64–67)

---

11 Criseyde's love is constructed as a penetrating dart and thorn, but these images are ultimately gendered in an ambiguous fashion, since the narrator reports that she is also penetrated by love's thorn: "To God hope I, she hath now kaught a thorn, / She shal nat pulle it out this nexte wyke. / God sende mo swich thornes on to pike!" (2.1272–74).

12 Clare Kinney, "'Who made this song?': The Engendering of Lyric Counterplots in *Troilus and Criseyde,*" *SP* 89.3 (1992): 272–92, at p. 285.

13 Mervin Glasser, "Aggression and Sadism in the Perversions," *Sexual Deviation*, 3rd edn., ed. Ismond Rosen (Oxford: Oxford University Press, 1996), pp. 279–99, at p. 292.

This sorrowful display, similar to the tears with which Troilus bedews his letter to Criseyde, indicates the pleasures of his agony. Troilus's performance of pain signifies through a contradictory semiotics, which suggests deep suffering and the boundaries of that suffering at once. Limiting his anguish to the boundaries of himself, pain offers Troilus a way to locate and refine his masculinity.

In short, Troilus suffers for himself, as a means to define and secure his identity in relation to himself alone. Before the *Canticus Troili* of Book 5, Troilus cultivates sorrow as a private rehearsal that eludes all other audiences:

> For which hym likede in his songes shewe
> Th'enchesoun of his wo, as he best myghte;
> And made a song of wordes but a fewe,
> Somwhat his woful herte for to lighte. (5.631–34)

Expressive anguish lightens Troilus's mood, showing the self-indulgent strain of pain he affirms within himself. Troilus does not submit himself to the will of another, but instead, sings of his own death as the culmination of the identity he fashions for his pleasure: "'Toward my deth with wynd in steere I saille'" (5.641). Accordingly, Troilus's narrative trajectory entails realizing the perfect pleasure, or the ultimate sacrifice, through his own death. With his wish for death, Troilus fits the classic definition of masochism envisioned by Freud.[14] Yet Troilus's culminating stasis resists absolute negation, making it more similar to the ecstatic "shattering" of subjectivity that Leo Bersani finds in masochism than the eviscerating termination that Freud connects to this so-called "perversion."[15]

Passive Productions: Troilus's Moving "Manhed"

Even so, Troilus's desire for death is ultimately constitutive of his identity, galvanizing an idealizing process of consolidation that achieves fixity through the radical fracture of traditional masculine identity.[16] Troilus's passivity, paired with the ennobling autonomy of endurance that he manifests in suffering, unmakes the heroic ideal of male power. Yet this process of fragmentation also creates a

---

14   For Sigmund Freud's discussions of masochism, see "A Child Is Being Beaten," *The Standard Edition of the Complete Psychological Works*, trans. James Strachey (London: Hogarth Press, 1953–66), vol. 17, pp. 177–204; *Three Essays on the Theory of Sexuality*, *Standard Edition*, vol. 7, pp. 125–248; and, relevant to the specular dynamics of masochism pursued in this essay, see "Instincts and Their Vicissitudes," *Standard Edition*, vol. 14, pp. 111–40.

15   Leo Bersani, *The Freudian Body* (New York: Columbia University Press, 1986), pp. 29–50.

16   Leo Bersani, *Freudian Body*, p. 39–41, affirms and expands Jean Laplanche's argument, *Life and Death in Psychoanalysis* (Baltimore, MD: Johns Hopkins University Press, 1976), that sexuality is fundamentally masochistic. Kaja Silverman, *Male Subjectivity at the Margins* (New York: Routledge, 1992), explores this "shattering" of the self as a constitutive feature of masculinity in modern representations. Michael Uebel, "Masochism in America," *American Literary History* (2002), pp. 389–411, gives an invaluable theoretical and cultural reading of masochism's relation to masculinities, and Jeffrey Cohen, *Medieval Identity Machines*, pp. 78–79, begins his analysis of courtly love by connecting masochism to dominant forms of male identity.

new model of manhood, which is based on sacrifice and forbearance rather than aggression and authority. Highly visible in the fourteenth century, this type of "manhed" potentially signals something of a departure from courtly narratives of erotic service.[17] Or rather, it demonstrates the ways in which secular and religious stories of sacrificial desire interanimate during this period. In Chaucer's tragic romance, Christ as much as Lancelot lends heroic intelligibility to Troilus's pain.[18] As Aranye Fradenburg points out, the elevation of the penalized body was informed by the visual sacralization of Christ's pain in the lay economy of religious desire in the late Middle Ages.[19] This cultural valorization of suffering provides a valuable commentary on masochism's connection to courtly love, for in this rendering of loving sacrifice, it is the bleeding, broken body of the divine that is sublimated. If courtly love raises woman to the status of the Thing, an unapproachable and even untenable object, her position is comparatively powerless in the theatrical economy of elite desire.[20]

The ornamental agency of the courtly lady is implicitly acknowledged in modern theorizations, for Lacan then Žižek similarly characterize the lady's capricious demands as extraneous exercises of inconsequential power. In other words, because the courtly lady submits her long-suffering lover to gratuitous feats of strength, courage, and suffering, her agency is effectively affirmed as insignificant, insensible, and unnecessary.[21] By contrast, the anguish, patience, and humility of Christ's sacrifice converts passivity into a potentially salvific power. Because Christ's suffering is undertaken to preserve those transcendent principles of love, compassion, and redemption that his "manhed" incarnated, Christ's sacrifice promises to recover an entire community through his self-fulfilling agony. A Christic economy of suffering thus accesses a completely different register of desire than those of long-suffering knights who serve demanding ladies. Although deliberate submission can reform any identity's relation to agency, converting weakness into strength through a managed display, for Troilus, this process of subjection is a way to assert his privileged detach-

---

17 See the *MED*, s.v. "manhed(e)," 1–3, pp. 134–36, for numerous examples suggesting the three senses of this term: (1) the human condition; (2) Manly virtues; (3) Belonging to the race, age, or occupation of men.

18 See Jeffrey Cohen, *Medieval Identity Machines*, pp. 79–115, for a meditation on masochism's relation to Lancelot's submission to Guinevere; Robert Mills, "'Whatever You Do Is a Delight to Me!': Masculinity, Masochism, and Queer Play in Representations of Male Martyrdom," *Exemplaria* 13 (2001): 1–37, connects exaltation to suffering in religious literatures; and Stephen Barney, "Troilus Bound," *CTC*, 1–16, traces the religious register of elevation that Chaucer uses to define Troilus's heroism.

19 L. O. Aranye Fradenburg, *Sacrifice Your Love: Psychoanalysis, Historicism, Chaucer* (Minneapolis: University of Minnesota Press, 2002), pp. 32–41. Also see Miri Rubin, *Corpus Christi: The Eucharist in Late Medieval Culture* (Cambridge: Cambridge University Press, 1991), pp. 131–34; and Sara Beckwith, *Christ's Body: Identity, Culture and Society in Late Medieval Writings* (New York: Routledge, 1993), p. 23, for the importance of the visible elevation of the host as a representation of Christ's broken yet exalted body.

20 Jacques Lacan, *The Ethics of Psychoanalysis*, pp. 149–51.

21 Jacques Lacan, *The Ethics of Psychoanalysis*, pp. 149–51; also see Slavoj Žižek, *Metastases*, pp. 89–94.

ment from a transactional economy of mutable desire.[22] From his interactions with Pandarus, it is clear that Troilus embraces his stricken stasis, even though Pandarus advises the young knight not to fall into this amatory trap:

> "Delyte nat in wo thi wo to seche,
> As don thise foles that hire sorwes eche
> With sorwe, whan thei han mysaventure,
> And listen naught to seche hem other cure." (1.704–7)

Nevertheless, Troilus ignores Pandarus's suggestions to act in an aggressive fashion, revealing that Troilus's only attachment is to his own suffering. Even as he frets over love's power to destroy him, Troilus repeatedly asserts his immunity to circumstantial change by relating to love only as an experience of personal anguish.

As Troilus achieves greater success in love, it becomes clear that his identity emerges from inaction, for it is his lack of doing that establishes his relation to amorous passion. Criseyde's intervention in the bedroom scene, when she revives her lover from his famous swoon, is surprising more for the action it subsequently inspires, since at no point has Troilus shown the capacity to be a vivacious lover. The poem's compensatory characterization of Troilus's domination, "This Troilus in armes gan hire streyne" (3.1205), is a marked departure from his fearful dealings with Criseyde at other points in their courtship. During their first meeting, when Criseyde asks for Troilus's "lordshipe" as a defense against her enemies (3.76), Troilus may only gather himself enough to beg " 'Mercy, mercy, swete herte!' " (3.98), before dropping back into awed silence. To compensate for Troilus's lack of action, Pandarus constantly moves, working to inspire Troilus out of a listless state through his relentless agitations. Worn out with his hero's trepidations, Pandarus finally asks, " 'Artow agast so that she wol the bite?' " (3.737). It is a fair question, because after Pandarus gets Troilus into bed, Criseyde must work to arouse her suitor: "She ofte hym kiste; and shortly for to seyne, / Hym to revoken she did al hire peyne" (3.1117–18). Only after his dominance is secured by the interventions of others does Troilus assume a position of amorous agency: " 'Now yeldeth yow, for other bote is non!' " (3.1208).

Troilus's desire to please Criseyde, therefore, appears only as a product of his efforts to gain relief for his emotional pain. Accordingly, their sexual encounter prioritizes Troilus's romantic desire, since Criseyde's erotic power is carefully directed to consolidate his privileged position. Troilus's faltering hesitation as a lover suggests his sincerity, yet the bedroom scene has more troubling consequences, because his private passivity is matched by his public posture of renunciation. Criseyde's playful question, " 'Is this a mannes game?' " (3.1126), could

---

[22] Gilles Deleuze, "Coldness and Cruelty," *Masochism: Coldness and Cruelty / Venus in Furs* (New York: Zone Books, 1989), 9–138, esp. pp. 77–78, elaborates the contractual basis of masochism. Thus, although such a process of collaboration and negotiation is explicitly transactional (elsewhere, pp. 10–20, Deleuze suggests the masochist's aim is to find, produce, and persuade his ultimate tormentor), there is always a privileged fantasy of detachment that accompanies masochism.

easily be transferred from bedchamber to parliament, for Troilus's performance of passivity signifies his entitlement in this arena as well. In both cases, Troilus protects his desire, refusing to expose his feelings to the vulnerabilities of trans-action. As a result, he allows others to settle the parameters of exchange that inform his desire without his participation. While Pandarus secures Troilus's bliss, the parliament ensures his woe. These instances are similar in their capacity to fix Troilus's relation to Criseyde without his intervention. Because the status of his erotic desire is settled externally, Troilus retains a position of detach-ment that allows him to gain pleasure from suffering, honor from endurance. Although Troilus's fear demonstrates his reverence for Criseyde, his worries over offending her effectively prevent him from acting on her behalf.

Unsurprisingly, the power derived from Troilus's renunciation resonates with the tale's Boethian imperatives, recording the ways in which personal autonomy emerges from the phenomenology of suffering. Mark Miller's recognition of the connection between masochism's productive investments in disavowal and an antinomy of the will inherent to human subjectivity is crucially instructive in thinking about the identity that Troilus consolidates through his experience of loss.[23] As Miller suggests through his readings of *The Consolation of Philos-ophy* and *Le Roman de la Rose*, masochism pinpoints a volitional investment in suffering, refining what he characterizes as the "aporetic" dynamic of agency.[24] Yet Miller's attempt to expand masochism, so that "a drive to self-violation and a willing investment in suffering ... does not reduce to *any* set of empirical instances of it ... but is rather a constitutive condition of agency as such," evacu-ates the particularized contours of identity his account otherwise explains.[25] Like Chaucer's romance of Troy, Miller accepts masculinity as the standard for humanity more generally. Such an equation is problematic, Chaucer's poem demonstrates, because it overlooks the ways in which masculinity is produced as masochistic to secure its privileged position.

Masochism must remain relational to retain intelligibility, but its concentra-tion on the subjection of one partner entitles a singular form of suffering, which, in Chaucer's poem, confers masculine privilege. As the masochistic subject directs his attention inwards, focusing on the ways in which pain refines his rela-tion to the principles he values within himself, the worth of his suffering only emerges in relation to that which has been jettisoned. Thus, although suffering requires a spectator, the shattering experience of pain allows the masochistic

---

[23] Mark Miller, *Philosophical Chaucer: Love, Sex, and Agency in the* Canterbury Tales (Cambridge: Cambridge University Press, 2004), pp. 4–26.

[24] Mark Miller, *Philosophical Chaucer*, pp. 111–90.

[25] Mark Miller, *Philosophical Chaucer*, p. 140. In a series of puzzling disavowals, Miller seeks to disconnect his use of masochism from studies of sexuality, despite the fact that often he uses the idiom of sexuality to discuss the gendered erotics of the texts he addresses. Despite his insistence that "masochism in this further sense is thus not an aberration, and not even something that picks out one group of people with a distinctive kind of desire," only a paragraph before he suggests that masochism "allegorizes a split in romance masculinity of which Chaucer and the writers of the *Rose* were very much aware" (p. 140).

subject to leave that bond behind.[26] In *Troilus and Criseyde*, the exclusive privilege of this position is affirmed through Troilus's unwillingness to speak in Criseyde's defense when she is to be traded for Antenor. Through his silence, Troilus consolidates his masochistic identity, entitling a masculinity staked on loss rather than possession. Some readers find this scene unsettling because it reveals Troilus's lack of investment in Criseyde. In what turns out to be an uncannily familiar scene of gender differentiation, Troilus affirms renunciation, specifically of a feminine Other, as the most powerful masculine position in this domain. As Troilus's inaction demonstrates, passivity becomes powerful through its disavowals of anything outside or unlike the self that is subject to pain.

Regendering Agency:
Domination, Submission and the "Slydinge of Corage"

Chaucer's poem thus challenges traditional renderings of gendered agency, though by doing so, it does not topple masculinity's claims to cultural empowerment.[27] Instead, it constructs a unique form of masculinity, which is superior to other forms of gender identity – masculine or feminine – through its radical passivity. This remaking of masculine power stands in particular contrast to models of masculinity staked on externalized agency. Indeed, it is worth noting that in a poem set within the theater of war, traditional exercises of masculine agency are largely ineffectual. Despite oaths of protection from some of the most powerful men in Troy (Hector, Deiphebus, and Troilus), Criseyde remains vulnerable within the walls of this city. Most notably, Hector's protests are summarily set aside by the larger parliamentary body. The contrast between Hector's attempt to defend Criseyde and Troilus's mute acceptance of her exchange is a pivotal moment, which empties out the connection between masculine agency and cultural power. It is true, as Rosanne Gasse argues, that Troilus has no plausible reason for maintaining his silence: "But if Prince Hector's verbal defense does not stir up scandalous rumors of an illicit liaison between himself and Criseyde, why should any reader believe that a similar, supportive speech by *Prince* Troilus would?"[28] Yet the parliament's wholesale disregard

---

26 Of course, this separation is an illusion, a fantasy affirming the subject's supposed ability to reject relational forms of desire. As Bersani argues (in answer to those who might see "self-shattering" as a means to escape relational styles of sexuality), "Masochism is not a viable alternative to mastery, either practically or theoretically. The defeat of the self belongs to the same relational system, the same relational imagination, as the self's exercise of power; it is merely the transgressive version of that exercise" ("Sociality and Sexuality," *Critical Inquiry* 26 [2000]: 641–56, at p. 648).

27 Jill Mann, *Geoffrey Chaucer* (Atlantic Highlands, NJ: Humanities Press, 1991), pp. 165–71, recognizes the ways in which Chaucer valorizes passivity through Troilus's conduct, but she calls such exaltation a "feminization" of the hero. Because the poem still preserves gender difference through Criseyde's actions, however, it seems more accurate to suggest that masculinity has been restyled in this poem. As Kaja Silverman, *Male Subjectivity at the Margins*, p. 65, suggests of modern representations of masculinity, recognizing lack as a masculine attribute can also be empowering in a possessive formulation. Because a man *has* lack, he is a man.

28 Rosanne Gasse, "Deiphebus, Hector, and Troilus in Chaucer's *Troilus and Criseyde*," *ChauR* 32 (1998): 423–39, at p. 435; her italics.

for Hector's objections suggests that the outcome of this debate would remain unchanged, regardless of Troilus's (in)action.

Troilus, then, at least preserves the integrity of his desire, prioritizing passivity as an organizing feature of elite masculinity. Although his focus on personal suffering illustrates the self-centeredness of this form of masochism, the poem valorizes this centering of the masculine self to prevent the kinds of exploitation and domination that define other men in this poem. Hector's example reveals that masculine agency is ultimately helpless in the service of others, an ornamental display that makes no difference to the conditions of the culturally dispossessed, such as Criseyde. Even so, Hector's variety of masculine agency is certainly preferable to its malevolent double, which is depicted as manipulative in the best of circumstances, exploitative in the worst. Pandarus's machinations are crucial to the poem's union of lovers, yet his schemes are troubling for the instrumental use he makes of Criseyde. Urging Troilus to "ravysshe" Criseyde takes on a less benign cast in the context of the Trojan war, since, as Diomede explains, this transgression dooms the city, and the lovers at its heart: "'And men shul drede, unto the worldes ende, / From hennesforth to ravysshen any queene'" (5.894–95). Furthermore, it becomes clear that Pandarus views Criseyde as disposable, a placeholder in the drama of desire that engrosses Troilus. With his pithy platitude, "'The newe love out chaceth ofte the olde'" (4.415), Pandarus reveals his disregard for Criseyde's well-being.

Moreover, when Pandarus asks Troilus to protect Criseyde's reputation, he acknowledges that he has potentially abused his position as Criseyde's uncle and guardian: "'But wo is me, that I, that cause al this, / May thynken that she is my nece deere, / And I hire em, and traitour ek yfeere!'" (3.271–73). Nevertheless, the exercise of such influence over women is expected of men in this culture, as Troilus recognizes: "'youre fader shal yow glose / To ben a wif'" (4.1471–72). When Troilus laments the control her father wields, however, he differentiates his masculinity from the structure of domination that defines the power of other men. His lack of agency distinguishes him from men such as Pandarus and Calkas, who use women to further collectivized masculine interests. More importantly, Troilus's passivity separates him from men like Diomede, who acquire women to mark their supremacy, primarily over other men. When the prologue to Book 4 introduces Diomede, it marks him as the beneficiary of Troilus's suffering. Although the mechanical rotation of Fortune's wheel diminishes the volitional power of both men – "And on hire whiel she sette up Diomede" (4.11) – this image nevertheless suggests that Troilus's loss amounts to Diomede's gain. An entire book before his first appearance, Diomede is aligned with a masculinity defined by its domination of others.

Diomede's entry into the poem affirms his predatory agency, because when Criseyde is handed over to the Greeks, Diomede views her exchange as an opportunity to extend his mastery. Perceiving Criseyde's amorous attachment, Diomede decides to wedge himself into her erotic life, because to him, the ability to part Criseyde from her lover will establish his power. When he takes the reins of her horse, it is a forbidding sign of his amorous designs upon Criseyde. Moreover, with his avowal, "'Al my labour shal nat ben on ydel'" (5.94), Diomede reveals a significant difference between the masculinities that this poem associates with traditional heroic culture and the gender identity it creates for Troilus. Similar to Pandarus, Calchas, and Hector, Diomede's masculinity is defined by its agency. Unlike these other men, Diomede does not act in relation to or on behalf of others; instead, he acts upon others, showing his masculinity through aggression. Because his agency is completely externalized, Diomede's identity is written upon the bodies of those around him. As his conduct in courtship illustrates, his ability to affect Criseyde and then Troilus establishes the Greek warrior's masculinity. When he presents his suit to Criseyde, moreover, he catalogues his own features in a manner that simulates the perspective of distanced appraisal. With his aggressive form of detachment, which is devoid of personal reflection, Diomede provides the ultimate contrast to Troilus's insular form of masculinity.

Hence, even if they both enjoy the affections of Criseyde, Troilus and Diomede are differentiated by their contrasting relations to her. While Troilus endures the refining pains of loss, Diomede enjoys the enthralling pleasures of possession. Diomede's possession, moreover, is an aggressive strategy of homosocial conquest, for he only views Criseyde as a weapon he may use to wound his Trojan enemy: "'But whoso myghte wynnen swich a flour / From hym for whom she morneth nyght and day, / He myghte seyn he were a conquerour'" (5.792–94). Diomede's success, particularly in regard to his quest to win Criseyde's affection, does not ultimately affirm his ascendancy in this masculine contest. On the contrary, Diomede's efforts further distinguish Troilus, allowing the namesake prince of this legendarily besieged city to emerge as a hero who is valorized through suffering. Troilus's triumph, despite his loss, emerges from the poem's continual focus on Criseyde as the primary agent of Troilus's destruction. Despite Diomede's attempts to recast this love affair as a contest between men, Criseyde herself acknowledges her priority in Troilus's demise: "'For I have falsed oon the gentileste / That evere was, and oon the worthieste'" (5.1056–57). Criseyde's recognition that she made the wrong choice when she traded Troilus for Diomede prevents this affair from becoming a homosocial struggle over a passive object of desire.

Criseyde's agency, then, short-circuits the contest that might otherwise exist between Diomede and Troilus. This is not to say that there is not a clearly drawn contrast between masculinities; indeed, the differences that emerge between these men repeatedly affirm the superiority of Troilus's position. Diomede may finish this narrative as Criseyde's lover, but her famous "slydynge" (5.825) reveals how little he wins in his conquest. Her changing affections, therefore, affirm renunciation as the superior masculine disposition. In other words, Troilus's passivity, both in love and in loss, affords him a type of detachment that prevents Criseyde's mutability from altering the constancy of his character. Troilus stays true to Criseyde, as she acknowledges in her final letter: "'I kan nat in yow gesse / But alle trouthe and alle gentilesse'" (5.1616–17). By so doing, he stays true to those components of character he distills through his suffering. Due to his steadfast endurance of pain, therefore, Troilus is elevated to a position from which he can see the shifting contests of others. Perched in the immutable eighth sphere, Troilus rises above the petty struggles that negotiate flows of agency in everyday transactions of desire. Ultimately, then, if there is no masculine contest between Diomede and Troilus, it is because Troilus never competes, but uses masochism's self-centering power to affirm the immutable qualities that pain refines within him.

While Troilus's demise corresponds to the profile of the masochist as June Rathbone articulates it, "The masochist ... systematically ruins his chances of happiness and success," his downfall secures his character in a fashion that can only be regarded as self-fulfilling.[29] Troilus thus embraces the singularity of the masochistic body, in which "everything is sealed tight."[30] The immuring isolation of avowed pain, therefore, creates a masochistic subject immune to the powers of others. At least in theoretical terms, it is certainly possible for women to experience this subjective suffering, especially in the religious mystical culture of the late Middle Ages.[31] Nevertheless, this form of masochism is overwhelmingly imagined as a privileged formation of masculine identity, particularly in later theoretical treatments that use courtly love as an apparatus to understand erotic desire or the Middle Ages. Indeed, viewing Chaucer's tale through the lens of courtly love simultaneously captures and distorts the gendered dynamics of agonistic desire between Troilus and Criseyde. Even as Troilus is allowed the singularity that is elsewhere the preserve of the mystic, Criseyde is bound to the social arrangements that construct femininity as an iconic production of community values.[32] Indeed, the cultural circumstances that produce feminine identity make it difficult to imagine that a woman such as Criseyde would be allowed to inhabit this space of cultural privilege, where she might refine the isolable self through the reflexively refining experience of pain.

Thus, although Criseyde is granted a degree of autonomy over her erotic attachments, she is not allowed to occupy a place of immured suffering, because her widowed status fully integrates her into the fabric of her patriarchal community. Her involvement in this culture's amorous alignments gives her a degree of agency, but her erotic detachment further problematizes agency as it operates more broadly in this poem's gendered distributions of power. Criseyde's ability to direct herself in matters of love, it turns out, simply reveals her inability to remain constant to one lover when she is faced with changing cultural circumstances. With Criseyde's betrayal, all forms of relational agency – including submission, protection, and domination – are thereby associated with the

---

29 June Rathbone, *Anatomy of Masochism* (New York: Kluwer/Plenum, 2001), p. 302.
30 Gilles Deleuze and Felix Guattari, *A Thousand Plateaus: Capitalism and Schizophrenia*, trans. Brian Massumi (Minneapolis: University of Minnesota Press, 1987), p. 150.
31 Richard Kieckhefer, *Unquiet Souls: Fourteenth-Century Saints and Their Religious Milieu* (Chicago: University of Chicago Press, 1984), p. 147, suggests that late medieval female mystics are "sado-masochistic" in their devotional practices.
32 Richard of St. Victor, *De quatuor gradibus violentae caritatis*, ed. G. Dumeige (Paris: Vrin, 1955), p. 177, in his classification of the four levels of mystical experience (insuperable, inseparable, singular, and insatiable), suggests that the "singular" state is that in which the soul passes into God [*transit in Deum*]; David Aers, *Chaucer, Langland, and the Creative Imagination* (London: Routledge, 1980), pp. 128–35, remains the most eloquent account of the social forces that construct and restrict Criseyde.

shifting, mutable, and sliding inconstancy of transactional desire. Agency is thereby "feminized" in the poem, since such volitional gestures are associated with Criseyde as a frangible, unreliable, and translatable locus of desire. From Hector to Pandarus to Diomede to Criseyde herself: these characters act in relation to the mutable circumstances that constitute human community.

Troilus, who stands outside this differential fray, is insulated by his passivity, which is markedly different than Criseyde's submission because her surrender involves subjecting herself to another. It is fundamentally, and problematically according to the poem, a process of opening the self relationally. Troilus's subjection is quite the opposite, for he closes himself to others as a means to refine the self through the isolated endurance of pain. Troilus's refusal to engage in transactions of desire is therefore the refusal to submit to any other besides that self he defines for and within himself. His radical autonomy thereby associates passivity with masculinity, creating a privileged space of selfhood where suffering becomes an expression of the self's internal fulfillment. Since Christ's sacrifice is often aligned with this form of passivity, we might suppose that such agonistic self-definition is also reserved for religious celibates, whose alienation from normative models of gender and sexuality contribute to their spiritually refining suffering. Instead, through poems such as *Troilus and Criseyde*, this isolated form of pain is sexually and socially incorporated into elite masculine culture. Troilus's debilitating bouts of amorous suffering are not represented as estranging flights from sexual desire; rather, as instances of erotic suspense, they become sustaining examples of desire's function in the "properly" socialized masculine subject.

Troilus's death is the predictable, if extreme, result of this deferential logic. The masculinity that emerges from Troilus's demise, however, is somewhat more surprising: by rendering passivity as subjection, this poem rewrites masculinity in terms of static principles rather than stirring actions. In other words, Troilus's death marks his steadfastness more than his prowess, for his passive refinement is more important than his martial feats. The poem's hyperbolic rendering of Troilus's prowess illustrates how little his deeds matter in defining the man he is already revealed to be: "For thousandes his hondes maden deye, / As he that was withouten any peere, / Save Ector, in his tyme, as I kan here" (5.1802–4). Almost ostentatiously, death on the battlefield only serves as an engine of elevation, releasing Troilus from any remaining entanglements of desire. Furthermore, Criseyde does not merit an afterthought in Troilus's reflection, showing that masculine desire, not its feminine object, is distilled through the experience of suffering. Although his misfortunes in love might occasion their revelation, the poem suggests that the defining qualities of Troilus's masculinity, including fortitude, steadfastness, and endurance, are antecedent and immutable characteristics. As a consequence, Troilus maintains a degree of control over his suffering, taking pleasure from the pain he bears in service to his self-fulfilling principles. Troilus is therefore a willing victim, whose subjection is of his own design, if not fully of his own making.

Readerly Desires: The Pleasures of Troilus and Criseyde

Despite his overwhelming isolation, the self-centering circuit of Troilus's desire is never completely closed. Like other forms of masochism, Troilus's experience of pain is deeply connected to relations of spectatorship.[33] Yet Troilus's masochism differs from other performative forms of passivity for the ways in which he relates to his audiences. By refining himself through the experience of pain, Troilus displays his visible separation from those immediate others who might bear witness to his anguish. This is particularly true with regard to Criseyde, for Troilus continually affirms his distance from her, even when he asks for her favor: " 'That with the stremes of youre eyen cleere / Ye wolde somtyme frendly on me see'" (3.129–30). Pandarus, by contrast, refuses a spectatorial relation to Troilus's agony, even when Troilus encourages Pandarus to find pleasure in his imminent death: " 'For harmes myghten folwen mo than two / If [Troilus's love] were wist – but be thow in gladnesse, / And lat me sterve, unknowe, of my destresse'" (1.614–16). Through alternating refusals, it might seem that Troilus has trouble finding an audience for his agony. Yet the narrative's obsessive attention to his pain obviates any such possibility. Instead, it becomes obvious that the audience for Troilus's suffering does not reside within the poem, but is constructed through the tissued relations connecting the poem to its receivers.

Most famously, the poem's narrator functions as a go-between in the poem, situating readers as witnesses to the sufferings this story reveals. By giving readers what Evan Carton calls a "share of the responsibility" for the poem's meaning, the narrator simultaneously licenses and regulates readers' responses.[34] In petitioning "moral Gower … [and] philosophical Strode / To vouchen sauf, ther nede is, to correcte, / Of youre benignites and zeles goode" (5.1856–59), the poem acknowledges the inventive autonomy that individual readers exercise. But the famous directive, "Go litel bok, go, litel myn tragedye" (5.1786), attempts to control the ways in which broader audiences respond. In order to balance these forces, the poem imagines pleasure as both a moral and a philosophical response to Troilus's pain. The poem thus transforms a spectacular relation to pain into an experience of readerly pleasure by positing its inherent moral content. In other words, watching Troilus suffer is not simply an indulgent exercise in voyeuristic fascination. Instead, the act of reading expresses profound commitment to the philosophical principles Troilus affirms. Ultimately, then, we are supposed to enjoy watching Troilus suffer because he merits elevation.

In turning to the Fury Thesiphone's assistance to pen "Thise woful vers, that wepen as I write" (1.7), the poem becomes a "sorwful instrument / That helpeth loveres … to pleyne" (1.10–11). Forging a memorial identification with the poem's readers, the narrator reveals the power of passivity galvanizing this

---

[33] Michael Uebel also points out that postmodern theorists of masochism usually downplay its specularity, focusing instead on its potential as a form of withdrawal, and thus self-improvement, in ways that we believe are uncannily Troilan ("Masochism in America," pp. 394–97).

[34] Evan Carton, "Complicity and Responsibility in Pandarus' Bed and Chaucer's Art," *PMLA* 94 (1979): 47–61, at p. 53.

poem's sacrificial poetics. Being moved by the pain of another, Chaucer's poem insists, is a condition of passivity that affirms moral quality and philosophical depth. The condition of suffering, furthermore, is a state of helplessness with redemptive power. Offering up Christ as a model of perfect suffering, the poem's conclusion stresses the sacrificial exaltation of this divine love: "And loveth hym the which that right for love / Upon a crois, oure soules for to beye" (5.1842–43). As Stephen Barney observes,

> To be true is to be vulnerable to death; Chaucer directs our attention at the end of the poem to the other man, bound to a cross, "that sothefaste Crist, that starf on rode," who rose and redeemed. This is the archetype of the bondage that frees.[35]

As Barney argues, there is a redemptive cast to suffering in *Troilus and Criseyde* because all of Troilus's suffering teaches valuable moral truths. Leaving behind only the transcendent principles refined through pain, the pleasures of Troilus ultimately derive from the ability to exceed those differential categories that moderate everyday human interactions, including gender.

As the critical tradition of sacrificial exaltation would have it, then, *Troilus and Criseyde* is not about the ways in which one elite form of masculinity eclipses another. Rather, its philosophical impetus focuses on transcendence in a way that frees human relations from their transactional particularity. At the end of the poem, however, we are left with the spectacle of an exalted Trojan prince. The position Troilus occupies is exclusive, a moral reflection of his elevated gender-status in Troy. But his masculinity is more powerful than any heroic depiction, since Troilus gains a redemptive power from the experience of suffering. It should be noted, moreover, that Troilus's deliverance is reserved for himself, and for readers of the poem who assent to a transmutation of pain into pleasure. The power of passivity in the poem, then, is fully vested in Troilus's ability to move readers to accept an idealized narrative of his erotic suffering. The solemn power that would seemingly accrue from enjoying Troilus's stasis, pain, and death ultimately affirms the stability, pleasure, and permanence of his privileged position. By identifying masculinity with sacrifice, Chaucer's poem elevates Troilus's identity beyond courtly representations of masochistic suffering. The pleasures of Troilus, as his "celestial laughter" suggests, are the ecstatic joys that result from inhabiting a masculine position whose transcendence erases the cultural traces of its literary production.[36]

---

[35] Stephen Barney, "Troilus Bound," p. 15.
[36] This phrase is from Alfred David, "Chaucerian Comedy and Criseyde," *ETC*, 90–104, at p. 90, who suggests that Troilus's satisfaction prevents any readerly desire to see this poem as tragic.

7

"The Dreams in Which I'm Dying": Sublimation and Unstable Masculinities in *Troilus and Criseyde*

KATE KOPPELMAN

In his reading of Charlie Chaplin's *City Lights*, Slavoj Žižek argues that "In the network of intersubjective relations, every one of us is identified with, pinned down to, a certain fantasy place in the other's symbolic structure."[1] For Chaucer's Criseyde, this fantasy place is the place of the courtly lady, the sublime object of courtly order, male desire, and homosocial associations. However, instead of silently accepting her pinning, Criseyde speaks. Further, Criseyde dreams. She dreams of disintegration and bodily annihilation. Of course, Troilus dreams of dying as well – and in fact, the poem grants him his dreams while denying Criseyde hers. The voice of Criseyde gives us not just an image of a subject suffering who wants to be free from that suffering (this is what we see in Troilus), but instead, a subject suffering who chooses to remain in the world, who chooses the ethical path, rather than the path of pure solipsism. Chaucer's poem is not only about courtly love, but also about ethical relationality – of what a full awareness of and compassion for the other might actually look like. The subject position that chooses this fullness of subjectivity – the reality of being pinned down – is the female one while the primary male position in the poem (and the representative of the male symbolic structure that pins down those within it) chooses a path of significantly less ethical awareness.

This essay investigates Criseyde's particular relationship to the creation and maintenance of masculine identity throughout Chaucer's poem. I argue that Troilus uses Criseyde as a focus for his own masculine desires – thus, he sublimates her, making her the locus of his sense of identity through and beyond homosociality and war. However, I am further interested in how Criseyde's own voice, speaking from the position of sublimation – a position she ultimately refuses – simultaneously establishes her own fully aware subjectivity while highlighting the dependent and less fully aware subjectivity of Troilus. She is asked to be The Courtly Lady, the source of divine salvation, the marker of

[1] Slavoj Žižek, *Enjoy Your Symptom!: Jacques Lacan in Hollywood and Out* (New York: Routledge, 1992), p. 5.

nationality, and a martyr to both love and history. However, she rarely accepts such positions with confidence and assurance – instead she expresses dread, doubt, self-loathing, and confusion about those roles into which she has been (or might be) thrust. Appearing in a collection of essays on masculinity and maleness, this essay might seem out of place – my primary object of investigation is, indeed, the character of Criseyde in Chaucer's poem. However, I follow the lead of many notable critics of the poem, most recently Holly Crocker, who argue that we cannot read Troilus, or maleness, in the poem without attending to Criseyde, or femaleness, almost simultaneously.[2] This essay's intent is not to prove that Troilus's masculinity is somehow failed or passive, but to demonstrate how very much it relies upon an assumed secure role for Criseyde, the object of his affection. She must be a sublime object; she must reflect his sublimated desires. But if and when she challenges that role, if and when the object speaks as subject, her speech reveals the constructed nature of masculinity in the poem – producing masculine posturing that is shifting, uncertain, and lacking in compassionate awareness for others. Chaucer shows us how unstable and unintelligible gender roles are when those upon whom such roles are forced are shown to resist. Criseyde's resistance marks her constructedness and the interdependent constructedness of Troilus. Her resistance creates the confused anxiety of Troilus – his hesitation and uncertainty that have been variously read by modern critics. Far from being "punished" for such resistance (a fate Criseyde herself would welcome), she is rewarded by being, ultimately, the fullest subjectivity in the poem.

"Who woot in soth thus what thei signifie?" (5.371)

Chaucer's poem begins with an ethical injunction – a command that the sorrows and adversities described in the poem be remembered by later lovers and, presumably, by later readers:

> But ye loveres, that bathen in gladnesse,
> If any drope of pyte in yow be,
> Remembreth yow on passed hevynesse
> That ye han felt, and on the adversite
> Of othere folk. (1.22–26)

By calling attention to "othere folk," who may have suffered "adversite," a word that means both misfortune and hostility, the poem suggests that Troilus's particular sorrow and suffering (his famous "double sorwe" [1.1]) is only one that the poem will present. While Troilus is mentioned by name throughout the poem's beginning, he also shares this stage of woe and travail with others who are unnamed but who also suffer unavenged:

---

2   Holly Crocker, "How the Woman Makes the Man: Chaucer's Reciprocal Fictions in *Troilus and Criseyde*," *NPC*, pp. 139–64.

> And biddeth ek for hem that ben despeired
> In love, that nevere nyl recovered be,
> And ek for hem that falsly ben apeired
> Thorugh wikked tonges, be it he or she. (1.36–39)

According to the narrator, the poem is intended to generate an ethical feeling in its readers – to make them "biddeth," plead for or pray for, those who are suffering from love, but also those who have been "apeired," or harmed through speech, be they men or women.

Chaucer's poem asks us to consider the position of the other when we experience our own pleasures or pains: "and thynketh how that ye / Han felt that Love dorste yow displese, / Or ye han wonne hym with to gret an ese" (1.26–28). Given this imperative, we must attend to Troilus's almost total lack of ethical concern throughout the poem. We are to feel with those who suffer, and it is Criseyde who both suffers and who acknowledges the suffering of others. Her confusion in response to this position (her "slydynge") is evidence neither of her fault nor of her failure in loving; instead, this evidences her subjectivity, her fullness of self, what Winthrop Wetherbee has recently called "an assertion of [Criseyde's] essential humanity."[3] Wetherbee compares the ways in which Troilus and Criseyde deal differently with the pressures of their love, their fates, and their worlds in a poem he calls "an inexhaustible lesson in how seriously to take oneself and one's world." He further notes: "[Criseyde] nonetheless possesses a maturity, a capacity for taking life seriously and an appreciation of what is at stake in pursuing the pleasure it offers, which is lacking in Troilus and which he fails to appreciate in her."[4] Such maturity is, according to the narrator, due our admiration and our commiseration because we are fellow subjects – we are, like Troilus, Pandarus, and Criseyde, fellows who are subjects to and subjects of. But we are also, like Criseyde alone in the poem, struggling to understand how such subjectivity (and subjectedness) can be reconciled, rather than finding consolation in a poetic ending that removes us from the conflict entirely.

From this perspective, Chaucer's poem does not simply turn into a medieval self-help guide – a courtly-love confessional or memoir of a courtly lady. It retains its status as and interest in the role of fantasy – fantasy as a generic concept (the poem as romance and as a time-tripping combination of medieval and classical concerns), but also fantasy as a shaper of identity and interrelations. Holly Crocker argues that "Troilus wants to use Criseyde to capture what Jacques Lacan calls the subject's 'Ideal-I'; he needs a mirror that will reflect his fantasy of himself for that fiction to obtain the appearance of reality."[5] In many readings of the poem, Criseyde's status as a fantastic figure (an object of worship) retains a central place. But if, as Cindy Vitto and Marcia Marzec suggest, we have begun to read Criseyde's movement "along the spectrum of agency from object to subject," we must also consider how her fantasies struc-

---

3 Winthrop Wetherbee, "Criseyde Alone," *NPC*, 299–332, at p. 299.
4 Winthrop Wetherbee, "Criseyde Alone," pp. 300, 304.
5 Holly Crocker, "How the Woman," p. 140.

ture her reality – or how they serve to react against elements of that reality, as the case may be.[6] According to Žižek, fantasy "bears witness to (and tries to cope with) the fact that I am originally decentered, part of an opaque network whose meaning and logic elude my control."[7] Further, Bruce Fink notes that, "The choice of submission is necessary *if* one is to come to be as a subject, but it maintains its status as choice since it is nevertheless possible to refuse subjectivity."[8] Criseyde voices the paradox of such a choice when she sorrowfully reacts to Pandarus's news about Troilus's love for her:

> "Of harmes two, the lesse is for to chese;
> … … … … … … …
> "Now wel," quod she, "and I wol doon my peyne;
> I shal myn herte ayeins my lust constreyne." (2.470, 475–76)

Subjectivity, for Criseyde, involves choosing "peyne" and constraint (to "constreyne" indicates force, domination, and oppression). She chooses to be subject to the desires and demands of others – other subjects, but also other cultural and social expectations. In Chaucer's poem, being a subject involves being subject to signifiers – Lacan repeatedly refers to the subject as "suffer[ing] from the signifier" – responding to the call from others (to be niece, widow, lover, prisoner, daughter).[9] In the context of Chaucer's initial injunction, suffering from signifiers (or from signification – becoming culturally readable) is a form of "hevynesse" (1.24), a word indicating, again, oppressiveness. The narrator of the poem suggests that we acknowledge the weight and the arbitrary nature of such signification, and its limits, at the beginning of Book 2, not surprisingly the book that also introduces us most directly to Criseyde: "Ye knowe ek that in forme of speche is chaunge / Withinne a thousand yeer, and wordes tho / That hadden pris, now wonder nyce and straunge" (2.22–24). Signifiers change and can produce "wonder," both amazement and, possibly, fear. Rather than an apology for mistranslation, this is Chaucer's plea that we attend to how words that are "now wonder nyce and straunge" affect those who are subject to them.

Chaucer's poem presents to us a drama about subjects, signifying orders, and their limits. As a narrative of courtly love, the poem demonstrates the attempted mastering of such limits through the figure of the courtly lady – it is a poem about the relationship between men and women in love. Julia Kristeva's *Tales of Love* speaks about the ways in which the history of western love has affected those women caught up in its own particular modes of signification. In speaking about the Shulamite in the Song of Songs, Kristeva explains how participation in a patriarchal system of love produces a certain sort of female subjectivity:

6   Cindy Vitto and Marcia Smith Marzec, "Introduction," *NPC*, 1–10, at p. 5.
7   Slavoj Žižek, *The Plague of Fantasies* (London: Verso, 1997), p. 9.
8   Bruce Fink, *The Lacanian Subject: Between Language and Jouissance* (Princeton, NJ: Princeton University Press, 1995), p. 50.
9   Jacques Lacan, *The Seminar of Jacques Lacan, Book VII: The Ethics of Psychoanalysis, 1959–1960*, ed. Jacques-Alain Miller, trans. Dennis Porter (New York: Norton, 1992), p. 143.

if not partial. As such, she shows us that the very nature of courtly fantasy (and the identities it produces, substantiates, and sanctions) is based upon partiality. My reading highlights moments in the poem that serve multiple functions. First, the moments that mark Criseyde as the elected sublime object, the courtly lady, also show us her own reactions to that marking, her awareness of both her own position in the signifying network and the position of others in that same network. Secondly, the same moments demonstrate Criseyde's fantasies about bodily destruction – her dreams of dying – while also showing us her attempts to reconcile those dreams with the reality of which she is a part. Finally, such moments in the poem are often followed by (or are preceded immediately by) demonstrations of Troilus's ethical blindness – his recurring self-absorption, his failure to respond to the ethical injunction of the narrator, to think "on the adverste / Of othere folk" (1.25–26).

In describing his interest in medieval courtly love and specifically the place of the medieval courtly lady, Lacan begins with a statement of astonishment:

> With courtly love things are all the more surprising because they emerge at a time when the historical circumstances are such that nothing seems to point to what might be called the advancement of women or indeed their emancipation ... [the courtly lady] is essentially identified with a social function that leaves no room for her person or her own liberty.[18]

What for Lacan is a surprise – that a woman could be granted representational power without being granted agency – is not such for Criseyde or, I would argue, for the sorts of readers Chaucer wants to encourage (readers who are ethically aware). Lacan sees "the poetic field" of courtly love denying "the feminine object ... all real substance," assuming that all courtly ladies are, unfailingly, "strange," "terrifying ... inhuman partner[s]."[19] Additionally, Kristeva argues that "courtly songs neither describe nor relate ... They have no object – the lady is seldom defined ... she simply is an imaginary addressee, the pretext for the incantation." However, for Kristeva, and it would seem for Chaucer's Criseyde, such a representational expectation can and does often produce "a strong reaction on the part of women who were unwilling to bear ... the representation [itself]."[20] Criseyde, as courtly lady, confirms to certain generic traditions: she is idealized, worshipped, and described as being capable of both anger and healing. But she also confronts those traditions directly: she puzzles over what is expected of her, she dreams of bodily fragmentation that might exempt her from the economy of courtly desire, she praises and prematurely nostalgizes her self-governance. Criseyde refuses the inhumanity and emptiness of sublimation. In fact, even during the moments when we might see Criseyde as traditionally fulfilling the expectations of courtly love, we also see her questioning those expectations or turning them against themselves – producing a figure of split

---

[18] Jacques Lacan, *Ethics*, p. 147.
[19] Jacques Lacan, *Ethics*, pp. 52, 149, 150.
[20] Julia Kristeva, *Tales of Love*, pp. 287, 374.

subjectivity that simultaneously causes us to see the male characters in the poem as the ones who are more appropriately "mere" in their poetic presence.

We know that Criseyde is a sublime object for a number of reasons. She is "strange" when her materiality is questioned: is she a woman or a goddess, is she a saint or a person, is she a whole being or just "special" pieces (her lips, her arms, her eyes)? She is hostile when she is granted the power to withhold her healing balm: Troilus fears Criseyde's wrath, and Pandarus grants her the power to save but also to kill by not granting her "cure." She is absent when her motives, her thoughts, her words are unknown. Finally, for Lacan, the sublime object is beautiful, but its beauty stands as a guardian against a destructive ugliness, against death:

> The true barrier that holds the subject back in front of the unspeakable field of radical desire that is the field of absolute destruction, of destruction beyond putrefaction, is properly speaking the aesthetic phenomenon where it is identified with the experience of beauty. ... It is obviously because truth is not pretty to look at that beauty is, if not its splendor, then at least its envelope.[21]

When Criseyde's beauty no longer serves its function in the poem – when she leaves Troilus and accepts her position in relation to Diomede, Troilus confronts "the field of absolute destruction" and chooses its relative freedom in death. Although not a suicide, Troilus has previously demonstrated his willingness to avoid the battlefield, or to approach it as a vehicle for increasing his reputation in the eyes of Criseyde. In choosing to fight, Troilus knows (and hopes) for a violent death, but one that will ultimately be ennobled by the gleam of chivalric heroism. But for Criseyde, truth is never veiled by a false beauty, by a fantasy of romance or salvation. Criseyde refuses, through her voice, to become inhuman, merely an envelope. Thus, she chooses to stay in the world, to face the putrefaction that is subjectivity in a signifying network of male desire and war.

Chaucer establishes Criseyde's position as courtly and sublime lady in three primary ways: he suggests that she may be divine, he highlights her powers over life and death, and he depicts her as at least partially veiled (as unknowable at certain moments in the poem). Like Emelye in the *Knight's Tale*, Criseyde's status as more than "simply" human is immediately highlighted by both the narrator and Troilus himself:

> So aungelik was hir natif beaute,
> That lik a thing inmortal semed she,
> As doth an hevenyssh perfit creature
> That down were sent in scornynge of nature. (1.102–5)

Before readers meet Criseyde – before even hearing her voice – we learn of her position on the margins of humanity. Her beauty is angelic, like an immortal thing, perfect, but also "in scornynge," in contempt, of nature – all of these things "semed" to be associated with her, but we are never sure of her full

---

[21] Jacques Lacan, *Ethics*, p. 217.

identity. We should also note that Troilus first sees Criseyde in the space of the temple – in the face of other relics, other objects of devotion that are, like Criseyde herself, "trist aboven everichon" (1.154). It is during the festival of the object that Criseyde appears to Troilus: "In beaute first so stood she, makeles" (1.172). She is exceptional, she is special, she is to be worshipped.

At the same time that the narrator establishes Criseyde's status as nearly divine, he also establishes her power over life and death. After we are told of her position as "an hevenyssh perfit creature," we are also, along with Criseyde herself, made aware of her position as healing object not only within the economy of her relationship with Troilus, but more broadly, in the economy of this particularly masculine symbolic network – of war, of prisoner exchange, of vengeance. Hector assures Criseyde that "youre body shal men save" (1.122), meaning, in the context of his speech, that Criseyde will be granted protection by the Trojans, even though her father has betrayed them and left her to absorb their possible vengeance ("he and al his kyn at-ones / Ben worthi for to brennen, fel and bones" [1.90–91]). However, this promise cannot be read without consideration of how the poem increasingly puts Criseyde in the position of sublime object. Thus, while men will protect her body, we learn that she will also save the bodies of men, Troilus and Pandarus most specifically. Of course, this is the power that Pandarus repeatedly reminds her of throughout the poem:

> "The noble Troilus, so loveth the,
> That, but ye helpe, it wol his bane be.
> Lo, here is al! What sholde I moore seye?
> Doth what yow lest to make hym lyve or deye." (2.319–22)

Unless she helps him, she will be Troilus's "bane," his slayer. This is, according to Pandarus, "al" there is to say about her position in relation to Troilus. Further, as is the case with her beauty in the temple, Criseyde's powers over life and death are associated with a divine power that can grant life, but only through a violent death, as she is repeatedly associated with saints. Toward the end of the poem, when Criseyde's "betrayal" begins in earnest, her association with sainthood is highlighted by Troilus. He and Pandarus pass by her house and Troilus calls out, "'And farwel shryne, of which the seynt is oute!'" (5.553).

Finally, Criseyde is continuously veiled throughout the poem – most notably through the narrator's expressions of unknowing in relation to her thoughts and actions. While we are allowed to hear certain of her deliberations at length ("'Is this youre reed? Is this my blissful cas?'" [2.422]), other aspects of her thought processes are denied to the narrator and thus, to us: "But how it was, certeyn, kan I nat seye, / If that his lady understood nat this, / Or feynede hire she nyste, oon of the tweye" (1.492–94). To "understonden" means to comprehend, but it also means to signify – thus, the narrator does not know if Criseyde understands or if she signifies what is expected of her.

As is appropriate for a sublime object, Criseyde retains the mark of the unknown. However, the poem complicates these positions of sublimity by simultaneously showing us Criseyde's reactions to many of them. This voice expresses both her ethical compassion for others and her fantasies of self-destruction – fantasies she ultimately does not fulfill.

> *"But he that departed is in everi place / Is nowher hol,*
> *as writen clerkes wyse"* (1.960–61)

When, at the start of Book 2, we finally hear Criseyde's own voice, it is saturated with an awareness of her position within this masculine signifying network while also being aware of her position among others who are a part of the reality that pins her down. Her reactions to the demands placed upon her by Pandarus and Troilus show us that she submits to the subject positions thrust upon her. However, these reactions also reveal a confusion on her part – a confusion about what the effects of such submission will be upon her, and a confusion about how her desires might harm others around her. Her reactions, in others words, mark her as possessing the sort of ethical awareness called for by the narrator of the poem. They also mark her as split, as ambivalent, as other-to-herself in a way never matched by Troilus. Her disembodied presence in the poem haunts Book 1, although even at this point, we are given an image of Criseyde that is both singular (exceptional) and other-centered. In the space of the temple, Criseyde is "Among thise othere folk" (1.169), a place she remembers and retains throughout the poem. Certainly, she is among others when she begs Hector for his help, she is among others when we see her flanked by her female attendants, she is among others when she is dragged to Deiphebus's house by Pandarus, and she is most fully among others when she submits to the prisoner exchange and enters the Greek camp – as a foreigner, but also, at the same time, as a newly admitted member of that group (through her association with her father). Even at the moments when Criseyde sets herself apart from others, she does so within the context of others and especially within the context of the suffering of herself and those others. Such ethical positioning happens at three main moments in the poem: Criseyde's reaction to Pandarus's announcement in Book 2, her insistence in Book 3 that the love she shares with Troilus provides for both her honor and Troilus's pleasure, and her reaction to the news of the prisoner exchange in Book 4. In these cases, Criseyde demonstrates both her own dreams of fragmentation and her ultimate decision to stay within the world and serve the needs not only of herself but also of others. These moments contrast with those poetic scenes that show Troilus's reaction to suffering and tribulation: his enactment of love in Book 3, his reaction to the prisoner exchange in Book 4, and his reading of his own prophetic dream in Book 5.

David Aers points out that it is important that we remember that the love affair takes place in the midst of a deadly war.[22] In the case of reading the varying degrees of ethical concern displayed by Criseyde and Troilus, this contextual detail becomes particularly valuable. Upon seeing Criseyde and falling in love

---

[22] David Aers, "Chaucer's Criseyde," p. 195.

with her, Troilus reacts by abandoning all other responsibilities: "So muche, day by day, his owene thought, / For lust to hire, gan quiken and encresse, / That every other charge he sette at nought" (1.442–44). Troilus's "charge[s]," his burdens but also his obligations, betoken a dense network of chivalric duties – all of which he "sette[s] at nought" in favor of his inward lusts. Further, for Troilus, "Alle other dredes weren from him fledde, / Both of th'assege and his savacioun" (1.463–64). In a poem that sets its action amid a war and that closes with an apparently salvific ending, such fleeing seems troublesome. For, while we might initially read this as a "typical" courtly response to love (one that Chaucer highlights as well in the *Knight's Tale*), when compared to Criseyde's responses that follow, and when read in light of the poem's interest in compassion and an awareness of the suffering of others, this sort of reaction becomes increasingly close to irresponsibility and solipsism. When, previous to the sections quoted above, Troilus makes "a mirour of his mynde," he does so not to examine his own feelings and judge their place in a world of war or of love with another, but only to gaze further at the image (ever partial) of a woman he has yet to meet: "he saugh al holly hire figure, / And that he wel koude in his herte fynde" (1.366–67). In contrast, Criseyde is first presented to us – when she is presented as a speaking voice – as one fully aware of and concerned about the war being waged around her. We find her, famously, reading out loud with others "Of the siege of Thebes" (2.84). Her reaction to Pandarus, when he tells her that he has some news, is to proclaim, "'For Goddes love; is than th'assege aweye?'" (2.123). Although she has told her uncle that she would rather be "'ay in a cave / To bidde and rede on holy seyntes lyves,'" she chooses to remain focused on the world at hand, on the war and her place within it (2.117–18). Her fantasy is to be shut away in a cave, reading stories of saints whose bodies were rent and torn apart, but she instead surrounds herself with the bodies and voices of others and focuses not on tales of courtly love – the sort of stories her uncle assumes she would be reading – but on stories of war and suffering.

Book 2 presents Criseyde as a figure confronted by multiple expectations: she is a widow, a niece, a female friend, and now an object of love. It shows us her confusion in reaction to those expectations ("'As help me God, I not nat what ye meene'" [2.133]), but it also shows us how she deals with such confusions – not by denying her place or by following through on her fantasies of separation and disintegration, but by consideration and commiseration. After proclaiming to her uncle that she does not know what he means by his teasing words and after being told that the news relates to Hector and Troilus, Criseyde prays: "'In good feith, em,' quod she, 'that liketh me / Thei faren wel; God save hem bothe two!'" (2.162–63). Additionally, after being told not only that she is the object of unrequested admiration and that she has the power to either kill or save Troilus, she prays again, this time in a most Boethian fashion:

> "What, is this al the joye and al the feste?
> Is this youre reed? Is this my blisful cas?
> Is this the verray mede of youre byheeste?
> Is this paynted proces seyd – allas! –

> Right for this fyn? O lady myn, Pallas!
> Thow in this dredful cas for me purveye,
> For so astoned am I that I deye." (2.421–27).

As Boethius does, Criseyde seems uncertain about the "paynted process," the deception, that is her "cas," her situation, which is "purveien," foreseen but also ordained, by others. Her uncertainty makes her "astoned" (a word that signifies surprise but also a physical smash or blow) almost to death. This prayer, however, is followed not by additional scenes of Criseyde's lamentations, but by her thoughts on the larger nature of suffering and on how she might save both her reputation and the life of a knight whom she has not met. Without the assistance of a figure such as Philosophy, she reasons: "'As men ben cruel in himself and wikke; / And if this man sle here himself – allas! – / In my presence, it wol be no solas'" (2.458–60). Humanity is, according to Criseyde, capable of such cruelty and wickedness, but she cannot add another death, more suffering, to the rolls. Thus, she decides,

> "For myn estat lith in a jupartie,
> And ek myn emes lif is in balaunce;
> But natheles, with Goddes governaunce
> I shal so doon, myn honour shal I kepe,
> And ek his life" – and stynte for to wepe. (2.465–69)

Criseyde's own suffering and her own threatened position (her "estat" that is in "jupartie") become one with the suffering of others (in this case, her uncle and Troilus), and she acts in a way that might serve the needs and desires of all three. Book 2 also includes Criseyde's dream of the exchange of hearts – an image of violent bodily destruction that, in the space of Criseyde's position in the poem, betokens not her death, but her willingness to sacrifice her wholeness to become part of another. Such a dream, variously read by critics, demonstrates the unique position Criseyde occupies in the poem – as a sublime object who speaks and who considers the ways in which her own fear might be supplanted by a compassion (a shared feeling).

When Book 3 brings Troilus and Criseyde together, the differing reactions of the two lovers to the presence of the other speak directly to the injunction with which the poem began. Although Criseyde comes to the meeting under false pretenses, threats, and fear, she maintains her consideration for the feelings of others. Accepting her position as divine love object, she provides the balm required to save herself, her uncle, and Troilus. The book begins with Criseyde again asking for clarification from her uncle: "'telle me the fyn of his entente. / Yet wiste I nevere wel what that he mente'" (3.125–26). But it also stresses that what Criseyde wants from the love affair is to benefit everyone involved: "'And myn honour with wit and bisynesse / Ay kepe; and if I may don hym gladnesse, / From hennesforth, iwys, I nyl nought feyne'" (3.165–67). Such a double attention, to preserve her "honour" and his "gladnesse," two potentially adverse concerns, continues in the more immediate presence of Troilus himself when Criseyde says to Pandarus, "'So werketh now in so discret a wise / That

I honour may have, and he plesaunce'" (3.943–44). Finally, we are told that in loving Troilus, Criseyde puts an end to her own fear and gives herself to Troilus: "Right so Criseyde, whan hire drede stente, / Opned hire herte and tolde hym hire entente" (3.1238–39). The image of Criseyde's heart "opned" should remind us of her earlier dream of the eagle, emphasizing the nature of the "drede" she has put aside in speaking to Troilus of her "entente," her desire, but also her purpose – something that the narrator has earlier told us remained veiled in his understanding of Criseyde.

All of this is contrasted starkly with the way Troilus responds to the affair in Book 3, suggesting that Criseyde's willingness to interrogate her position and to speak from it, provides her with a fuller subjectivity – a subjectivity more acutely aware of the others with whom it shares the world – than Troilus's. Troilus confirms Criseyde's position as divine *object* with, "'O mercy, God, what thyng is this?'" (3.1124), and he then confirms such a lack of subjectivity by comparing their love-making to a lark being caught by a sparrowhawk and by stroking her partial and bound body.[23] As Criseyde "as an aspes leef ... gan to quake" in his arms, Troilus turns his thanks and prayers to the gods and promises Criseyde not ease, but more constraint: "'O swete, as evere mot I gon, / Now be ye kaught; now is ther but we tweyne! / Now yeldeth yow, for other bote is non!'" (3.1206–8). She is caught and must yield to him – there is, for Criseyde, no other relief or salvation ("bote"). When Troilus collapses, his last words bespeak his lack of compassion and his singular concern for his own well-being:

> Than seyde he thus, "God woot that of this game,
> Whan al is wist, than am I nought to blame."
> Therwith the sorwe so his herte shette
> That from his eyen fil there nought a tere. (3.1084–87)

In a swoon, Troilus insists that God knows him to be blameless – for what, we are not told. Where Criseyde's heart has previously opened, Troilus's notably closes ("shette"), and he does not even weep. While Criseyde laments that she was born, she remains attentive, alert to the suffering of this fellow being, and she promises the swooning Troilus that she is "nought wroth" and that she will offer "my trouthe" to save him (3.1110–11).

Such contrasting reactions to suffering are given to us again in Book 4, when the lovers face the realities of war: the prisoner exchange that sends Criseyde to

---

[23] This sort of synecdochal identification is common, of course, in courtly love literature. In this case, Criseyde's body is described:
> Hire armes smale, hire streghte bak and softe,
> Hire sides longe, flesshly, smothe, and white
> He gan to stroke, and good thrift bad ful ofte
> Hire snowissh throte, hire brestes rounde and lite.
> Thus in this hevene he gan hym to delite. (3.1247–51)
What is notable about this, however, is the way it is contrasted with Criseyde's own voice and her own acknowledgment of the role to which she has submitted, an acknowledgement that Troilus seems not to have heard.

the Greeks and returns the soon-to-be-traitor, Antenor, to Troy. Not surprisingly, both lovers mourn such a turn of events. However, their reactions and responses to the "necessite" are starkly different. Towards the beginning of Book 4, Troilus enacts his lovesickness in an extreme manner. Although he has previously wished for his own death – to save him from the pain of loving Criseyde – at this point in the poem, Chaucer extends Troilus's masochistic imaginings, allowing us, like Pandarus, to watch the "woodnesse" of sorrowful Troilus from a safe narrative distance (4.238). Troilus locks himself in his room, throws himself on his bed, beats his chest, thumps his head against the wall, and asks for salvation through death: "'O deth, allas, why nyltow do me deye? / Acorsed be that day which that Nature / Shop me to ben a lyves creature!'" (4.250–52). In terms of the narrative of the poem, this behavior is fitting – Troilus has, after all, just learned that Criseyde, his "swete fo" (1.874), will be exchanged for Antenor, the future traitor to the Trojans. However, in terms of character, Troilus's grief seems excessive and not fully sincere. In part, this reaction comes from the way in which Chaucer has previously – for three books of poetry – presented us with a different sort of bodily grief and mental confusion through the character of Criseyde. In her reading of Criseyde, Gayle Margherita points out that "the poet's first mention of the romance's heroine refers to an event that in fact never occurs within the narrative itself: her death."[24] Indeed, in terms of fantasies of death and dismemberment, Criseyde trumps Troilus's meltdown in Book 4. Criseyde repeatedly imagines – through dreams and anxieties about rape – her body breaking into pieces. Chaucer often describes Criseyde only synecdochically – referring to her heart, her hand, her eyes. Additionally, Chaucer aligns Criseyde with images of violent bodily destruction throughout the poem – associating her with Procne and Philomela, with Proserpine, with Daphne but, oddly, denying her direct association with that Ovidian tale of mutual bodily destruction, Pyramus and Thisbe. Given this constant narrative attention to Criseyde's particularly female version of a death drive, Troilus's relatively temporary bodily self-loathing (his most hyperbolic mourning lasts for under 300 of this over 8,000-line poem) lacks a certain weight. More significantly though, what we see in comparing these two scenes of mourning is one figure's lack of acceptance of his own subjectivity (as divided and as dependent upon others): Troilus, in shock, exclaims, "'Is ther no grace, and shal I thus be spilt?'" (4.263). Troilus's lament for a selfhood that is not yet "spilt" follows closely upon his self-isolation and precedes Pandarus's attempts to soothe Troilus by suggesting that Criseyde is replaceable. Again, it is not Troilus's mourning that is notable here, but it is how that mourning, and the place it occupies in the larger narrative construct of the poem, differs from the mourning of Criseyde – described immediately after Troilus's reminder that he awaits the balm of death ("'O deth, that endere art of sorwes alle, / Com now, syn I so ofte after the calle'" [4.501–2]).

After hearing the news of her impending exchange, Criseyde practices her

---

24   Gayle Margherita, "Criseyde's Remains," *Exemplaria* 12.2 (2000): 257–92, at p. 257.

mourning in ways starkly different from Troilus's laments. First, we see Criseyde again among others:

> And thus she brenneth both in love and drede,
> So that she nyste what was best to reede.
> But as men seen in towne and al aboute
> That wommen usen frendes to visite,
> So to Criseyde of wommen com a route. (4.677–81)

In love and in fear, Criseyde first considers what is best, what guide ("reede") she should follow – considering others (men in the town, but also the women friends she used to visit) before deciding to act. And while what follows shows us that Criseyde must hide the reasons for her sadness from the women she visits, it is clear that for Criseyde, an element of commiseration is integral to her place within the Trojan city. Once she leaves Troy, Criseyde laments her loss of a speaking community, "Ther was no wight to whom she dorste hir pleyne" (5.728). Even though the women with whom she visits misunderstand the source of her tears ("Wenden that she wepte and siked sore / Bycause that she sholde out of that route / Departe, and nevere pleye with hem more" [4.716–18]), in the space of a poem that has been repeatedly concerned with reputation, this is not a surprising misrecognition. In a poem that is concerned with coming to feel for others, this acknowledgement of what it means to "know" another is particularly poignant.

After this interaction, Criseyde, like Troilus before her, returns to her room to suffer alone. We find her there in the midst of self-mutilation – literally tearing her body apart, making it into something new, unsublime, undivine, ugly. When Pandarus arrives, he finds her blushing for shame at her behavior and, notably,

> Hire face, lik of Paradys the ymage,
> Was al ychaunged in another kynde.
> The pleye, the laughter, men was wont to fynde
> On hire, and ek hire joies everichone,
> Ben fled; and thus lith now Criseyde allone. (4.864–68)

In this scene, we see Criseyde's closest acceptance of the role of sublime object – that is, at the moment when we are allowed to see her beauty turn to ugliness, changed to another "kynde" (another sort, but also another essential nature, again linking Criseyde's sublimity with otherness), we are also allowed to see her "truth," her function as a veil for the discontents of her culture, her society, her self. Notably, this must be undertaken "allone." At this point of the limit – of the turning from beauty to ugliness – Criseyde speaks again as an ethical creature. Acknowledging what Troilus never does, Criseyde bemoans:

> "Gret is my wo," quod she, and sighte soore
> As she that feleth dedly sharp distresse;
> "But yit to me his sorwe is muchel more,
> That love hym bet than he himself, I gesse.
> Allas, for me hath he swich hevynesse?

> Kan he for me so pitously compleyne?
> Iwis, his sorwe doubleth al my peyne." (4.897–903)

Her suffering is great, but in only two lines she turns to the suffering of her lover, the thought of his pain causing her more grief than does her own. This lament expresses Criseyde's concern for the suffering of her lover – not simply a concern for her own suffering and a pleading to be released through grace. Additionally, it suggests that Criseyde is touched by the "hevynesse" being experienced by Troilus for her. But the poem puts such reactions in the form of questions – does he have such heaviness for me? can he complain so piteously? – suggesting that there is doubt whether Troilus's suffering really is for another. Based upon what we have already seen of that suffering, the answer seems likely to be, no. As a representative of Troilus and his particular form of fellow-feeling, Pandarus turns away from Criseyde's pain and forcefully reminds her of Troilus's pain – suggesting that at the very least, Troilus should not have to find her in this state of unbeauty, " 'That he yow nat bywopen thus ne fynde'" (4.916), and further suggesting that Criseyde leave behind her own feelings and turn to "som wisdom" (4.928) to solve the problem at hand. Thus we find that even after being denied her own legitimate feelings of sorrow and loss, Criseyde, once again, accepts the call of the signifying network and constructs a plan that, she hopes, will serve all those involved. She tells both Troilus and Pandarus, " 'For ther is art ynough for to redresse / That yet is mys, and slen this hevynesse'" (4.1266–67). Additionally, we should remember that the "hevynesse" to which Criseyde refers in this scene is the same weight to which the narrator calls our attention at the beginning of the poem – a weight that we, as lovers, as readers, and as fellow subjects, should attend to and not ignore.

Although Criseyde's plan, on a practical level, might seem unlikely, it is a plan that considers the larger situation in which the two lovers find themselves. She acknowledges the law to which they must submit and for which, it should be noted, Troilus is meant to be a representative as a knight and Trojan:

> "Now herkneth this: ye han wel understonde
> My goyng graunted is by parlement
> So ferforth that it may nat be withstonde
> For al this world, as by my jugement.
> And syn ther helpeth non avisement
> To letten it, lat it passe out of mynde,
> And lat us shape a bettre wey to fynde." (4.1296–302)

She submits to the law, to the decision of parliament, most certainly ("Now herkneth this" serves as a proclamation of her decision), she abandons pointless whining, and she proposes action in the face of the fate that has been dealt to her and her lover ("lat us shape a bettre way"). Her lover, on the other hand, chooses to flee rather than to face the situation, " 'And go we anon; for as in myn entente, / This is the beste, if that ye wole assente'" (4.1525–26). Criseyde must remind Troilus that not only is such a plan built around a certain mistrust of her loyalty, it would also abandon others who will be affected by its outcome:

> "But that ye speke, awey thus for to go
> And leten alle youre frendes, God forbede
> For any womman that ye sholden so,
> And namely syn Troie hath now swich need
> Of help. And ek of o thing taketh hede:
> If this were wist, my lif lay in balaunce,
> And youre honour; God shilde us fro meschaunce!" (4.1555–61)

How can the two lovers run away when others need them and when doing so would threaten not only those unnamed "frendes," but also their health and reputation as well? They cannot abandon friends and Troy itself – reminding us, again, of Criseyde's awareness of the larger scope and effects of war. Criseyde's final word decides the case and reminds us of her very particular position in the poem:

> "And forthi sle with resoun al this hete!
> Men seyn, 'The suffrant overcomith,' parde;
> Ek 'Whoso wol han lief, he lief moot lete.'
> Thus maketh vertu of necessite." (4.1583–86)

She knows better than Troilus what it means to make virtue of necessity, and what the "suffrant" can overcome because she has already done both – as a widow, as the daughter of a traitor, as that to which a hero, dying for love, has come for salvation and healing. Unfortunately for Troilus, he cannot learn this lesson during his material life, leaving him, again, isolated from others at the very end of the poem.

Book 5 of Chaucer's poem moves relatively quickly as compared to the rest of the story of these two lovers. The narrator returns the unknown element to Criseyde – "But trewely, how longe it was bytwene / That she forsook hym for this Diomede, / Ther is non auctour telleth it" (5.1086–88) – even as he describes Diomede's courting and Criseyde's confused reactions to this new demand by the signifying network. In terms of scenes, we should note that where Criseyde is shown to us almost constantly surrounded by others (and reacting to them even in the midst of her own sorrow and confusion), Troilus is again shown as seeking out solitude: "To chaumbre he wente." He abandons any other responsibilities – "of nothyng took he hede" (5.202). In his solitary space, he thinks upon Criseyde not as a whole person, but as a collection of body parts ("'Wher is hire white brest? Wher is it, where? / Wher ben hire armes and hire eyen cleere / That yesternyght this tyme with me were?'" [5.219–21]). He is concerned not for her well-being, but for his own alone.

The most telling demonstration of Troilus's solipsism comes in response to his dream of Criseyde and the boar. The dream is simple: Troilus sees himself walking alone in a forest "to wepe / For love of here that hym these peynes wroughte" (5.1235–36) when he comes upon a boar with huge tusks. The boar lies kissing Criseyde, who is folded in the creature's arms "faste" (5.1240). On a practical level, Troilus's reaction is correct because Criseyde has "bytrayed" him with Diomede (5.1247). But, on the level of ethical concern, his response does not adhere to what the narrator has told us our reaction should be to the suffering of others. Why does Troilus not fear for Criseyde's own safety upon having such a dream? Why does he not, as his dream-self, fight the boar to wrest Criseyde from its grasp? Why does he not awaken in horror at what she must be going through in the camp of the enemy? Although the poem does not ask these questions of its male protagonist, the narrative framework established in Book 1 allows its readers the space for these sorts of concerns.

Winthrop Wetherbee argues that one of the functions of Criseyde is to point out "the blind spots and contradictions of Trojan chivalry." Further, Wetherbee claims that

> The inability of the male figures in the poem to recognize Criseyde as a person in her own right, or acknowledge the peculiar difficulty of her situation in Troy, is symptomatic of the profound limitations of the chivalric view of life, limitations which it is one of the major projects of Chaucer's poetry to expose and criticize.[25]

According to Lacan, "The poetry of courtly love [addresses] certain discontents of the culture."[26] An acknowledgement of Criseyde's voice allows us to see not only discontents having to do with being a woman in the Middle Ages, but those having to do with being a male as well. Wetherbee notes that "Criseyde's destiny has been defined by her relation to Troilus, whose life is a series of idealized male roles."[27] Of course, Criseyde's own life has been a series of idealized female roles, revealing to us the differing ways in which both characters have responded to those ideals – ideals that are, as Jacqueline Murray describes medieval masculinity, "not always coherent: they may be competing, contradictory, and mutually undermining."[28] Unlike the other characters in Chaucer's poem – characters like Troilus who, despite some complaining, accept without question all the roles presented to them as medieval subjects – Criseyde shows us those moments when the signifying order oppresses to the point of driving us towards our own destruction. While Criseyde laments this movement, she also, concomitantly, desires it. For, were it to play out to its fullness, she would be relieved of the responsibility of being a subject, of being subjected. Peter Beidler asks, "is it any surprise that [Criseyde] wants out, either by stopping time at the moment of her temporary protection by Troilus or by suicide?"[29] That she does not cross the limit to accept fantasies of dissolution is heroic in the extreme. Like us, Criseyde is left a part of her "opaque network" – and this is what is fascinating about her. Approaching the poem from this perspective forces us to reconsider the way that Criseyde imagines death, life, and how both function in relation to others.

---

25 Winthrop Wetherbee, "Criseyde Alone," p. 318.
26 Jacques Lacan, *Ethics*, p. 150.
27 Winthrop Wetherbee, "Criseyde Alone," p. 299.
28 Jacqueline Murray, "Introduction," p. x.
29 Peter Beidler, "'That I was born, allas': Criseyde's Weary Dawn Song," *NPC*, 255–76, at p. 276.

8

"A Mannes Game":
Criseyde's Masculinity in *Troilus and Criseyde*

ANGELA JANE WEISL

In her provocative work *Female Masculinity*, Judith Halberstam suggests that,

> far from being an imitation of maleness, female masculinity actually affords
> a glimpse of how masculinity is constructed as masculinity. In other words,
> female masculinities are framed as the rejected scraps of dominant mascu-
> linity in order that male masculinity may appear to be the real thing."[1]

In *Troilus and Criseyde*, Criseyde performs both traditionally defined femininity
– located primarily in her anxiety, her beauty, and her inconstancy – and a female
masculinity that shows itself in a series of moves that attempt self-preservation
in a world defined by male masculinity's "real thing." Suggesting that a "widespread indifference to female masculinity ... has sustained the complex social
structures that wed masculinity to maleness and to power and domination,"
Halberstam offers an explanation for the hesitation on critics' part to identify
and interrogate Criseyde's masculinity except in light of a perceived "unmanning" of her counterpart Troilus within the contexts of courtly and sexual love.[2]
Yet doing so shows Chaucer to anticipate two assumptions of contemporary
criticism: that gender is not tied exclusively to sex, and that masculinity (and
femininity, of course) is performed multiply as characters move through the
contexts he provides. If these multiple performances are ultimately constrained
by a normalizing force that concludes his works, Chaucer's own resistance to
conclusion suggests an anxiety about the very act of gender restriction required
by narrative closure, while simultaneously showing it to be, in Carolyn Dinshaw's
words, "a set of assumptions, a catalogue of postures" located not in sex but in
a rhetoric of performances and "impersonations."[3]

Chaucer's hesitation to define masculinity leaves the critic searching for small
shreds of evidence. Some are found in the consummation scene of Book 3, a

---

[1] Judith Halberstam, *Female Masculinity* (Durham, NC; Duke University Press, 1998), p. 1.
[2] Judith Halberstam, *Female Masculinity*, p. 2.
[3] Carolyn Dinshaw, *Chaucer's Sexual Poetics* (Madison: University of Wisconsin Press, 1989), p. 30.
    Dinshaw speaks in particular of the *Canterbury Tales* here, yet her concept of gender as impersona-
    tion made up of a variety of postures serves an understanding of *Troilus and Criseyde* equally effec-
    tively.

common element of romance, whether narrated explicitly as it is here or implied as it is in many of Chaucer's contemporaries' works in the same genre. Finally together after two books of Troilus's immobilizing desire, Criseyde's internal debate, and Pandarus's *bisynesse*, the lovers find themselves together in Pandarus's "litel closet" (3.662). As Trolius faints and sighs, Criseyde demands, "'Is this a mannes game? / What, Troilus, wol ye do thus for shame?'" (3.1126–27). This inquiry follows Pandarus's earlier demand upon throwing Troilus into bed with Criseyde: "'Is this a mannes herte?'" (3.1098). This scene is suggestive for many reasons, yet it shows particularly the difficulties of determining what masculinity might be in *Troilus and Criseyde*. If in the poem's larger context, its engagement of multiple generic conventions is bound to create gender confusion, here readers come face to face with gender complexity, even within this fairly contained moment of the poem's romance plot.

That said, from the consummation scene, it is possible to determine some elements of Chaucer's understanding of masculinity by Pandarus's and Criseyde's questions. Chaucer does not provide extensive discourse on masculinity, although in making fun of Troilus for his inaction in romance, he suggests a contrast between men's public activity in war and their private passivity in love. Troilus as lover is contrasted to his more traditionally masculine warrior self, as well as to both Hector and Diomede. The latter, who like Troilus is both warrior and lover, is shown to be more active in both guises; instead of rendering him immobile, his desire for Criseyde causes him to act. The values of war – honor, prowess, activity, and, indeed violence – may be understood as masculine concerns, for as Halberstam notes, "masculinity in society inevitably conjures up notions of power and legitimacy and privilege; it often symbolically refers to the power of the state and to uneven distributions of wealth."[4] Chaucer adds to these some suggestions about what may be masculine in love – or at least in love-making.

For a start, anyone with a "mannes herte" does not faint in bed, and he should be able to get himself there. Although Gretchen Mieszkowski argues that fainting is not unmasculine in medieval literature, as it is an act assigned to men in love, it is hard not to read Criseyde's and Pandarus's questioning of Troilus's manhood in light of this swoon.[5] Indeed, Alcuin Blamires suggests that, "despite traditional misogynist cant about female lust and insatiability, the female sexual drive was generally characterized as passive."[6] Thus a reading of passive sexuality as feminine works in the context of Chaucer's language. In addition, the scene also suggests that love is, in some respects, a "mannes game," constructed by and for men, in which they have an inherent advantage.

---

4   Judith Halberstam, *Female Masculinity*, p. 2.
5   Gretchen Mieszkowski, "Troilus's Faint and the Fainting Heroes of Romance," International Congress on Medieval Studies, Kalamazoo, MI, Saturday, May 6, 2006. Although this talk began Mieszkowski's discussion of this issue, she has realized it more fully in her essay in this volume that considers Troilus's faint as a performed act of masculinity, as one in an extended series of fainting medieval lovers. Using Judith Butler's sense of performed gender as a starting point, she notes that because fainting in medieval romance is essentially a male activity, it is thus a badge of masculinity.
6   Alcuin Blamires, *Chaucer, Ethics, and Gender* (Oxford: Oxford University Press, 2006), p. 85.

However, these quasi-definitions do not rest particularly on the story's ostensible hero, but on the ambiguous figure of Pandarus and the complex character of Criseyde, who, in showing herself profoundly aware of both "mannes hertes" and "mannes games," occupies one of many masculine positions within the perpetually shifting narrative. Stephanie Dietrich notes "how much gender slippage the language of Chaucer's *Troilus and Criseyde* reveals" and adds that

> in his construction of Troilus's masculinity, Chaucer both conforms to expected literary conventions for the characterization of the male hero and invents details that resist essentialized models of gender. The result is a double-edged and culturally complex approach to characterization in which Chaucer undermines gender expectations in his presentation of Troilus's "masculinity."[7]

It is Criseyde who is called "slydyng" in Chaucer's text (5.825), and it is equally important to see the double-edged and complex characterization of her as a figure simultaneously feminized and masculinized.

Many readings of *Troilus and Criseyde* suggest that Criseyde occupies a masculine space in the narrative that is vacated by Troilus through his courtly love behavior – certainly in the first three books of the poem, and perhaps the fourth as well, since there, Troilus is rendered passive in the parliament, in the bedroom, and in his inability to affect any change of circumstance, or even to change Criseyde's mind. Perhaps more useful, however, is recognizing Criseyde as offering up an alternative, female masculinity. Speaking of the Wife of Bath, Karma Lochrie implies that Chaucer challenges ideas of masculinity, noting "by placing masculinity, with its ties to authority, commerce, violent mastery, social mobility, and publicity, 'up for grabs,' the Wife performs an alternative masculinity."[8] Given that Criseyde is already, to misquote Chaucer's *Franklin's Tale*, "lord in love" (5.793), the possibilities for her offering up an alternative masculinity that extends beyond the boundaries of the romance plot into the epic and thus bring her into what Lochrie calls the "world of marital rivalry, textual contestation, and sexual struggle" come to the fore.[9]

Criseyde's authority in romance is unsurprising: the lady is conventionally constructed as the locus of power against the vulnerability created by the male lover's desire. For all her seeming anxiety about the love affair, Criseyde appears to be the far more experienced, active lover, another function of her widowhood. If Troilus's inactivity prevents him from showing a "mannes herte," Criseyde's composure suggests that she possesses one. The overarching narrative conventions of romance render her masculine in these first books, provided readers proceed from the shreds of definitions of masculinity that Chaucer offers up. However, once the war reasserts itself within the narrative, and epic takes over from romance, the reading of Criseyde as "tendre-herted, slydynge of corage"

7 Stephanie Dietrich, "'Slydyng' Masculinity in the Four Portraits of Troilus," *MC*, 205–20, at p. 205.
8 Karma Lochrie, *Heterosyncrasies: Female Sexuality When Normal Wasn't* (Minneapolis: University of Minnesota Press, 2005), p. 98.
9 Karma Lochrie, *Heterosyncrasies*, p. 97.

(5.825) tends to dominate readers' understanding and thus becomes the source for both condemnation and sympathy. The image of her "with women fewe, among the Grekis stronge" (5.688), with all its implicit threat, becomes a symbol of a reclaimed feminine isolation and vulnerability.

This reading ultimately negates Criseyde, rendering her formless and passive, which the poem quietly but steadily refuses to do. Understanding Criseyde as entirely vulnerable and useless, unable to escape her father and prey to the dangerous advances of powerful men, is to make her, in Mary Behrman's words, "much less interesting. Stripped of any motives of her own, Criseyde becomes a mere automaton, and the readers' interests switch to the men who manipulate her." Criseyde is either "the tale's victim or its villain."[10] She can be read as a simple traitor to love, who should have chosen death over dishonor (or Diomede) when circumstances refused to allow her to return to Troy, but while many readers have done so, the poem suggests a more complex course: it reveals her as condemned not because she is "slydynge of corage," but because she acts in self-protection, choosing the most powerful figure around as her protector in Greece as she had in Troy, denying certain elements of her own desires to do so. Thus, Criseyde's failure in *Troilus and Criseyde* comes not from her rejection of her position as the masculinized lady created by the romance genre, but in her at least partially successful attempt to preserve it, even within the epic narrative of war. Halberstam's definition of masculinity is essentially epic. Noting that it seems to "extend outward to patriarchy and inward into the family"; that it "represents the power of inheritance, the consequences of the traffic in women, and the promise of social privilege"; that it inevitably "conjures up notions of power and legitimacy and privilege"; and that it "refers to the power of the state," she could be describing the gendered dynamics of *Troilus and Criseyde.*[11] By maintaining her active, self-determining position within the war, instead of accepting the feminine vulnerability that brought about her trade in the first place, Criseyde attempts to save herself, if not her reputation.

Throughout the poem, Criseyde's portrayal creates a tension between passive construction and self-determined action; she is pulled between the roles that the text's genres create for her and the contradictory actions the poet allows her to take, which, to increase confusion, are often a product of the very roles they seem to countermand. Part of the difficulty arises from the ways that Criseyde is defined by the passive femininity conveyed by her status as solitary widow and romance lady. Indeed, Gretchen Mieszkowski views her as "substanceless, ... a lack" in her position of the "lady of courtly love" and adds that "she responds to others; she does not act herself. She stands for no independent values. She is Western woman: supportiveness without content, and absence of being, the Other, sheer responsiveness, no one at all."[12] Chaucer certainly opens up the possibility of reading Criseyde as passive femininity through the emphasis on her solitude, although this, too, is ultimately ambiguous. Her fear, which by

---

10   Mary Behrman, "Heroic Criseyde," *ChauR* 38.4 (2004): 314–36, at p. 315.
11   Judith Halberstam, *Female Masculinity*, p. 2.
12   Gretchen Mieszkowski, "Chaucer's Much Loved Criseyde," *ChauR* 26.2 (1991): 109–32, at p. 126.

Book 5 comes to be an essential texture of her portrait, makes her vulnerable, while her role as desired object also renders her passive and observed, tied to the conventions of love. Yet ironically, her fear causes her to act as much in Book 5 as in Book 1, and it is her position as romance heroine that provides her with a kind of subjectivity and authority in the love relationship that does not completely vanish at the point of consummation but continues to inform her actions – and Troilus's expectations – in Book 4. Even her widowhood is an ambiguous symbol of passivity and activity. Widowhood is a kind of solitude, as we see in Chaucer's repeated use of the word "alone" to describe Criseyde, but it also provides an opportunity for women to be free of male control, a status she later calls to the reader's attention.

Chaucer builds these contrasts and tensions between Criseyde's two positions throughout the poem. She is first introduced in a state of abandonment and vulnerability, because Calkas has left her:

> Of hire lif she was ful sore in drede,
> As she that nyste what was best to rede;
> For bothe a widewe was she and allone
> Of any frend to whom she dorste hir mone. (1.95–98)

She is also introduced as a potential romance heroine, as the narrator dwells on her beauty:

> So aungelik was hir natif beaute
> That lik a thing inmortal semed she,
> As doth an hevenyssh perfit creature,
> That down were sent in scornynge of nature. (1.102–5)

This picture is further complicated by the reintroduction of her anxiety; she is "Wel neigh out of hir wit for sorwe and fere" (1.108). Yet this very fear, which would seem to render her inert, does the opposite; taking control of her situation, she allies herself with the most powerful, most masculine figure the poem offers, Hector, the prince of Troy. Always a warrior, never a lover (his wife, Andromache, never enters the text), Hector occupies one of the few uncompromised spaces. Edward Condren sees Criseyde's plea here as an attempt at seduction; in abandoning "her passivity to lay her helplessness before Hector," she aims to cast him as her lover.[13] Although this argument is somewhat unconvincing, Condren's analysis remains suggestive: if Criseyde is indeed making this ploy, she is casting herself in the male role. After all, Blamires reminds us, "that, since men 'do' the deed in sex and pursue women, then women are recipients not agents where sexual activity is concerned."[14] Readers of Chaucer are aware from the *Book of the Duchess* that the male lover casts himself at the lady's feet crying "Merci"; of course, *Troilus and Criseyde* offers this formula

---

[13] Edward Condren, "The Disappointments of Criseyde," *Chaucer and the Challenges of Medievalism*, eds. Donka Minkova and Theresa Tinkle (Frankfurt: Peter Lang, 2003), p. 195.
[14] Alcuin Blamires, *Chaucer, Ethics, and Gender*, p. 85.

as well. So in her mixture of passivity and activity – Condren agrees that "this sequence ... remains the only act planned and executed by Criseyde herself"[15] – she mirrors two male activities.

Of the two, however, her active choice to connect herself to Hector bears greater implications for understanding Criseyde's masculinity in the poem. Berhman points out that Criseyde "admires men of action, men like heroic Hector who value their individuality and refuse to let challenges daunt them."[16] Her vision of Troilus as war hero causes her to fall in love with him, not any admiration for the passive lover who writes the letter and whom Pandarus represents. The Troilus she sees is "a knyghtly sighte" (2.628). To look on him is "to loke on Mars, that god is of bataille" (2.630); he is further described as "so like a man of armes and a knight / He was to seen, fulfilled of heigh prowesse" (2.631–32). Troilus here appears at his most Hector-like, which the people's cry, "'Here cometh oure joye / And, next his brother, holder up of Troye!'" (2.643–44), firmly cements in Criseyde's mind.

The scene in which Criseyde sees Troilus takes place in another ambiguous context: Troilus's desire, as presented by Pandarus's "paynted proces" (2.424), causes Criseyde to feel "wel neigh starf for feere / So as she was the ferfulleste wight / That myghte be" (2.449–51); she worries that "for myn estat lith now in juparte" (2.465) due to Troilus's promise to die (and Pandarus's promise to die with him) should she not capitulate. However, she also maintains an active sense of her own responsibility, saying that she "'love a man ne kan I naught, ne may / Ayeins my wyl'" (2.478–79). That she ends up loving Troilus does not negate her acknowledgment of her own active will in her choice; she is not simply the objectified lady of romance. Even when the romance constitutes her as passive and desired, the immobile object of her dream of the eagle in Book 2, Criseyde "certainly does not view herself as a passive person" on whom meaning is imposed.[17] Again, the reader is confronted with a tension between Criseyde's fear and her self-determining force. At this moment, her understanding of her widowhood as a complex position is also revealed. The role of modest widow suggests a kind of isolation, if only a social one that allows singing and reading with her ladies, and Criseyde's dark clothing "evokes both the idea of Criseyde's vulnerability and the visual sign of her personal loss" and testifies "to the reality of human mortality and mutability," while emphasizing her "state of being alone and vulnerable."[18] It also suggests a possible availability: "the role [of modest widow] is not compatible with a sexual relationship, but it is compatible with the platonic segment of the *lady-role*, which Pandarus bullies Criseyde into accepting."[19] Yet in her widowhood, Criseyde sees her own freedom:

---

[15]   Edward Condren, "The Disappointments of Criseyde," p. 195.

[16]   Mary Behrman, "Heroic Criseyde," p. 315.

[17]   Mary Behrman, "Heroic Criseyde," p. 315.

[18]   Laura Hodges, "Sartorial Signs in *Troilus and Criseyde*," *ChauR* 35.3 (2001): 223–59, at pp. 225–26.

[19]   Florian Schleburg, "Role Conformity and Role-Playing in Troilus, Pandarus, and Criseyde," *Of Remembraunce the Keye: Medieval Literature and Its Impact through the Ages*, ed. Uwe Boker (Frankfurt: Peter Lang, 2004), 79–93, at p. 97. See also Laura Hodges, "Sartorial Signs," p. 226.

> "I am myn owene womman, wel at ese,
> I thank it God – as after myn estat,
> Right yong, and stonde unteyd in lusty leese,
> Withouten jalousie or swich debat.
> Shal noon housbonde seyn to me 'Chek mat!'
> For either they ben ful of jalousie,
> Or maisterfull, or loven novelrie." (2.750–56)

Her recognition that widowhood provides self determination because it frees women from the hierarchies of the sexual economy causes Criseyde to ask "'Sholde I now love, and put in jupartie / My sikernesse, and thrallen libertee?'" (2.773–74), noting that in love, "'we wrecched women nothing konne'" (2.781). In contrast to the earlier presentation of widowhood as fearful solitude, here it becomes an active, powerful position that allows for self-determination and self-construction. Criseyde's chess metaphor reveals her masculine agency again: while "Criseyde's allusion to chess also reveals that she thinks of herself in martial terms," allying herself with the powerfully masculine figures of Hector and Troilus in their warrior guise that has just been presented to her, it also shows the potential for the female to take on masculine traits of mobility, power, and central importance.[20] Or, as Jenny Adams comments, "a reader/player, who sees himself or herself as a piece on the board, must take responsibility for his or her own ethical conduct"; therefore, the player becomes responsible for her own actions rather than perceiving herself as acted upon.[21] In chess, the queen is the most versatile piece, able to move in all directions and any number of squares, while the king is limited to a single square's movement, and his capture loses the game. Indeed, the king is a quite feminized figure in chess; he runs and hides behind the castle, and if he must start moving around, the player is in trouble.[22] If widowhood allows Criseyde to assume the metaphoric position of a chess queen, it also allows her to win within a metaphor equally suited to love and to war, the two worlds of Chaucer's poem.

In the romance world, Criseyde claims the power available to romance heroines. This power may ultimately be a conventional fiction providing no real autonomy, but it remains inscribed in the story as a given. Criseyde is aware of and seems to enjoy some of these elements of power while understanding the difference between them and the more "real" autonomy of her widowhood. Criseyde adds to the powers of romance a self-determining factor. The contrast between the two lovers' decisions are striking; "while Troilus performs his unconditional surrender in a soliloquy, Criseyde negotiates a contract in front

---

[20] Mary Behrman, "Heroic Criseyde," p. 319.

[21] Jenny Adams, "'Longene to the Playe': Caxton, Chess, and the Boundaries of Political Order," *Essays in Medieval Studies* 21 (2005): 151–66, at p. 155. Adams has written more fully on chess in the medieval mindset in *Power Play: The Literature and Politics of Chess in the Late Middle Ages* (Philadelphia: University of Pennsylvania Press, 2006).

[22] I am grateful to Robert Squillace for instruction on the different moves chess pieces make on the board.

of a witness, fixing the rights and duties of both parties."[23] Blamires calls this a radical disruption of the "passive/active assumption in the scenes of courtship of Criseyde," and in so doing alerts readers to the shifting nature of gender within the love narrative.[24] In establishing the terms under which she will agree to love Troilus – that her honor and reputation will be protected – Criseyde again defines the terms of her consent – and does so publicly, thus in the masculine realm.[25] That these guarantees ultimately fail does not detract from Criseyde's self-determination, but from its ability to function within the assumptions of the genres of the narrative. The irony of her desires – the protection of her honor and reputation – given the ending of the poem only serves to create greater tension between the roles Criseyde attempts to play and the boundaries the worlds of Troy and the Greek camp (as well as the boundaries of epic and romance) impose.

To return to the romance, Troilus (with the help of Pandarus) constructs the traditional "love me or I will die and my death will be on your hands" equation; his promise to die for her, as reported by Pandarus, causes Criseyde's fear in Book 2. Yet at Deiphebus's house, Criseyde is amused by the power she wields over Troilus's health, thinking "Best koud I yet ben his leche" (2.1582). Criseyde knows what is going on: she is no innocent virgin – as I argue elsewhere, "the power she claims over Troilus during their courtship actually comes from more than convention – she has more experience with love (or at least sex) than he does."[26] But the rest of her mental response is also interesting; Criseyde "with sobre cheere hire herte lough. / For who is that ne wolde hire glorifie, / To mowen swich a knyght don lyve or dye?" (2.1592–94). Criseyde's awareness of her power within the love game shows a familiarity with "mannes games," as well as an ability to play them. After all, when Troilus finally gives up his swooning at the consummation scene and demands "'Now yeldeth yow, for other bote is non!'" (3.1208), she again shows her control, saying "'Ne hadde I er now, my swete herte deere, / Ben yold, ywis, I were now nought heere!'" (3.1210–11). For all the ways that the sex scene remasculinizes Troilus, casting him as the eagle of her dream and her as the "sely larke" caught in the claws of the "sperhawk" (3.1191–92), Criseyde establishes her presence in an active way. Declaring, as she does, that "this wouldn't be happening if I didn't want it to" implies that her own desires are the "bottom line," not Troilus's. Indeed, this moment separates Criseyde as experienced widow able to control her sexual circumstances from the innocent virgin and provides an image of sexuality neither delicate nor restrained. It is her presence, her desire, that makes the consummation possible. After all, Troilus, not she, is thrown into bed; if he lacks

---

[23] Florian Schleburg, "Role Conformity," p. 87.

[24] Alcuin Blamires, *Chaucer, Ethics, and Gender*, p. 85.

[25] Karma Lochrie's previously quoted ideas on masculinity's ties to "authority, commerce, violent mastery, social mobility, and publicity" seem particularly vital for understanding why the public world of *Troilus and Criseyde* appears to be rendered masculine in contrast to the feminized, private world of love. See *Heterosyncrasies*, p. 98.

[26] Angela Jane Weisl, *Conquering the Reign of Femeny: Gender and Genre in Chaucer's Romance* (Cambridge: D. S. Brewer, 1995), p. 31.

the "mannes herte" in this scene, she does not. The bliss that follows is as much her doing as Troilus's or Pandarus's.

The larger question of Criseyde's masculinity arises outside the boundaries of the romance, as the poem begins its descent "out of joie" in Book 4. Given how often Criseyde is considered the poem's betrayer, and given that in the proem to Book 4 the narrator laments that he must explain "how Criseyde Troilus forsook – / Or at the leeste, how that she was unkynde" (4.15–16), it is useful to note the multiple betrayals and lessons of the parliament scene and its aftermath. As Laura Howes points out, Criseyde is a victim of a series of betrayals that begins with Calkas's desertion: they "continue through the decision of the Trojan parliament to trade her, are evident in Pandarus's abandonment of his role as her helpmate once the trade has been set, and culminate in the narrator's telling of her side of the story in the later books."[27]

At this point in the story, war is revealed to be the poem's most profound "mannes game," and this game operates by a set of rules that, far more than the rules of love, renders women passive objects. Hector insists that Criseyde "'nys no prisonere'" (4.179) and that "'we usen here no women for to selle'" (4.182), but the "noyse of peple" (4.183) drowns out his protests, insisting that he "lat tho fantasies be!" (4.193). In reading this moment, Diane Steinberg suggests that the feminine spaces of Troy come up against the masculine spaces of Greece in their complex ideas "of women's status as objects that can be owned and thus subjected to commodification and exchange."[28] For the purposes of this discussion, Troy is thus figured as the locus of courtly romance, while the Greeks wage war upon sexuality and desire (Helen's desire in particular). Whether Hector's fantasies are of Criseyde's freedom or of Troy's refusal to engage in the traffic in women (ironic, given Helen's presence and role in the war), they are overcome; in the game of war, Antenor appears a more valuable player than Criseyde. Chaucer calls the audience's attention to the inherent irony of this assumption, noting:

> For cloude of errour let hem to discerne
> What best is. And lo, here ensample as yerne:
> This folk desiren now deliveraunce
> Of Antenor, that brought hem to meschaunce,
>
> For he was after traitour to the town
> Of Troye. (4.200–5)

The very act of the Trojan parliament that casts Criseyde as traitor causes their own betrayal, serving as a macrocosm of Troilus's fate.

The aftermath of the parliament scene continues to cast Criseyde in masculine positions just as it attempts again to render her passive, making her a pawn

---

[27] Laura Howes, "Chaucer's Criseyde: The Betrayer Betrayed," *Reading Medieval Culture*, eds. Robert Stein and Sandra Prior (Notre Dame, IN: University of Notre Dame Press, 2005), 324–43, at p. 324.

[28] Diane Steinberg, "'We do usen here no wommen for to selle': Embodiment of Social Practices in *Troilus and Criseyde*," *ChauR* 29.3 (1995): 259–73, at p. 259.

in yet another martial game of chess. After Criseyde and Troilus lament and faint, enacting and parodying the Pyramus and Thisbe story, she takes responsibility for constructing a plan of action. Accepting the situation, she declares "'ye han wel understonde, / My goyng graunted is by parlement / So ferforth that it may nat be withstonde / For al this world, as by my jugement'" (4.1296–99). In recognizing the strength of Parliament's decree as a part of the rules of war, in which running away constitutes cowardice and evasion, and in using her own judgment to assess the situation, she again shows a strong awareness of the force of "mannes games" and their necessities, urging Troilus to view the positive possibility of double success, saying "'have ye both Antenore ywonne / And me also'" (4.1315–16). If these words drip with irony, it is only in retrospect. She promises that she will return "er dayes ten" (4.1320) and anticipates peace and the joint restorations of Helen and herself. In this sense, Criseyde (perhaps unrealistically) imagines a conclusion to war and to love that does not involve destruction or betrayal. Should that not come to pass, she proposes alternative plans that will bring her back to Troy as well, and as Behrman suggests, "unlike Troilus, she displays great confidence in her own abilities and plots to bring about her safe return to Troy without her lover's help."[29] Her self-reliance is not surprising given Troilus's and Pandarus's failure to protect her; even Pandarus suggests as Laura Howes points out, that if Criseyde "cannot come up with a plan she will 'for do' – destroy – herself. ... [T]he onus for coming up with a plan sits squarely with Criseyde. Her womanly 'wit' is somehow considered equal to this task."[30] Once again, Criseyde's vulnerable circumstances lead her to a kind of masculine action; for all readers' knowledge that her plans will fail, it is hard not to admire her for rising from her faint and making them.

With the change in genre comes a change in rules, and Cassandra's interpretation of Troilus's dream shows the narrator's awareness of these transformations. As Mary Sanok notes, "[Cassandra] suggests that in leaving Troy, Criseyde has become part of a different narrative, a narrative that continues the Theban story that Criseyde had left off at the commencement of her affair with Troilus."[31] Sanok's contention that the *Thebaid* is really the story of the poem, for Criseyde at least, is suggestive. By noting Pandarus's disappointed reaction to Criseyde's reading, she shows that "Criseyde's text is not the vernacular romance" but the epic itself; because she chooses this narrative over the "soft headed romantic fiction that might make her more susceptible to [Pandarus's] plans," the romance narrative of *Troilus and Criseyde* interrupts her real story.[32] This story, then, operates by a different series of terms and expectations, not that Criseyde entirely abides by those either.

In the Greek camp, Criseyde's fear emerges again, and the pattern established by the earlier books – that for her, fear is a motivation to action, not to vulner-

---

29 Mary Behrman, "Heroic Criseyde," pp. 315–16.

30 Laura Howes, "Chaucer's Criseyde," p. 326.

31 Mary Sanok, "Criseyde, Cassandre, and the *Thebaid*: Women and the Theban Subtext of Chaucer's *Troilus and Criseyde*," *SAC* 20 (1998): 41–71, at p. 55.

32 Mary Sanok, "Criseyde, Cassandre," p. 47.

able isolation – plays itself out. Shifting from a discussion of Troilus's anxious waiting, the narrator describes Criseyde: "Upon that other side ek was Criseyde, / With wommen fewe, among the Grekis stronge" (5.687–88). Adding that " 'My fader nyl for nothyng do me grace / To gon ayeyn, for naught I kan hym queme' " (5.694–95), she sees the possibility that " 'My Troilus shal in his herte deme / That I am fals' " (5.697–98); furthermore, realizing that if she runs away she will likely be caught and held as a spy, she nearly gives in to her distress. In a sense she has already written her ending: Troilus will deem her false, and she will be held (at least by tradition) as a traitor to love. The demands of war clearly inform this section; despite Troilus's demands in his letter that Criseyde return to Troy, we increasingly see its impossibility. Behrman offers the suggestion that "Troilus does not really expect Criseyde to reunite with him; rather he expects her to behave like a proper lady and die for her love," and in response to Troilus's earlier passivity at the parliament, she notes that "when Troilus fails to make even the slightest attempt to rescue his ill-fated lover, Criseyde realizes that she must bring about her own salvation. As she spins out her plan, she gains more confidence in her abilities to effect her own rescue."[33] In a choice between following the expectations of romance to placate a lover who has hardly done his "knight in shining armor" part to rescue her, Criseyde opts for activity over passive acceptance to save herself.

Many readers have rendered Criseyde "a terrifying, power-hungry figure" who "emerges as less a woman than a monstrous, near-masculine, abomination, the incarnation of the Medusa Myth," as Behrman notes.[34] However, these understandings of her seem as much an overreading of her self-determination as viewing her as an entirely passive victim does. Either reading fails to find what is most interesting and engaging in the creation of Criseyde, and what may ultimately exonerate her from either set of charges. Given that the narratives of love and of war must both conclude – Chaucer reminds us that "Aprochen gan the fatal destinie" (5.1) – Criseyde is once again caught between two possible solutions, both narratively impossible. She must either return to Troilus, which the poem makes increasingly unlikely, or she must kill herself, which given her character, seems equally untenable.

Laura Howes comments that "one of the tragedies of this poem is that Criseyde believes she has free will when in fact she does not."[35] What ultimately separates Criseyde's masculine behavior from the behavior of men in the poem is the range of choices she has, and their difference from those she thinks she has. In a sense, this may represent the methodology of Chaucer's attempts to

---

[33] Mary Behrman, "Heroic Criseyde," pp. 330, 326.

[34] Mary Behrman, "Heroic Criseyde," p. 314. See, for example, D. W. Robertson, "Medieval Doctrines of Love," *A Preface to Chaucer* (Princeton, NJ: Princeton University Press, 1962) and Winthrop Wetherbee, *Chaucer and the Poets: An Essay on* Troilus and Criseyde (Ithaca, NY: Cornell University Press, 1984) among many others. In early readings of the poem, E. Talbot Donaldson was distinct in his sense that the author did not condemn nor demonize Criseyde, although he attributed this to his being in love with her. See "Criseyde and Her Narrator," *Speaking of Chaucer* (New York: Norton, 1970), pp. 65–83.

[35] Laura Howes, "Chaucer's Criseyde," p. 334.

determine what masculinity is, for as Halberstam demonstrates, "masculinity ... becomes legible as masculinity when it leaves the white, male, middle-class, body."[36] Criseyde's attempts to make use of masculinized power and privilege, and her inability to maintain her own reputation while doing so, point out both the limitations of and access to masculinity within the poem.

In Winthrop Wetherbee's view, what [Criseyde] cannot understand is the severe limitations her status as a woman has placed on her freedom to choose her course. In a world where her security has depended on her ability to effectively mirror male expectations and desires, she has never really seen the possibility for autonomy.[37]

At each attempt, Criseyde's self-determining actions have turned out to be contingent. Because she is a woman, she cannot act alone; she must rely on the protection, and thus the decisions of men. Each move towards action is thwarted; she calls upon Hector, but he cannot save her from being traded; her father's will to bring her to Greece and keep her there cannot be changed by her plotting; her need for safety in the Greek camp leads her to Diomede, which destroys her long-preserved and valued reputation. The generic conventions in which she finds herself also thwart her attempts; confined and defined by the expectations of epic and romance, she pays the price for challenging them.

Diomede is presented in a much less courtly light than Troilus. He and Hector are the only overtly and unambiguously masculine figures in the poem. Ironically, he and Criseyde share a philosophy of activity; in Book 2, Criseyde declares "'he which that nothing undertaketh, / Nothyng n'acheveth'" (2.807–8), while Diomede echoes her sentiments later, saying "'for he that naught n'asaieth, naught n'acheveth'" (5.784). Given Criseyde's continuing quest for action in masculine terms, it is not surprising that she once again is allied with a man of action and confidence. Neither of them believes that achievement is possible without action, and if Criseyde's actions are somewhat limited by her gender, they become comprehensible in this context.

Diomede himself is "prest and courageous" (5.800) in his needs, "with sterne vois and mighty lymes square, / Hardy, testif, strong, and chivalrous / Of dedes" (5.801–3). Free with his tongue, and envisioned in Troilus's dream as a boar, he appears distinct from the threatening "Grekis stronge" only by his desire for Criseyde and his method of getting her. His metaphor for love is fishing. As he imagines winning Criseyde, he thinks

> How he may best, with shortest taryinge,
> Into his net Criseydes herte brynge.
> To this entent he koude nevere fyne;
> To fisshen hire he leyde out hook and lyne. (5.774–77)

---

36 Judith Halberstam, *Female Masculinity*, p. 2. Halberstam adds that "the shapes and forms of modern masculinity are best showcased within female masculinity" (p. 2), and the failures of Criseyde's attempts at choice and self-determination highlight the privileges of masculinity within Chaucer's poem.
37 Winthrop Wetherbee, "Criseyde Alone," *NPC*, 299–332, at p. 325.

More predatory than elevated, Diomede is clearly not planning the romantic course that Troilus took to gain her. Behrman sees Criseyde as a "self-determined, desiring woman" who yearns for a relationship "not tainted by the artifice of courtly conventions,"[38] and with Diomede that is certainly what she gets. Although he nods in the direction of courtly language, the speed of their "courtship" belies any *fin amors* methodology, if not intentions. Secure in his actions and understanding, both of how love works and of how the Trojan war will end, he suggests that Criseyde ally herself with the winning side, noting that "'ye shal in Grekis fynde / A moore parfit love'" (5.918–19) than she did among the Trojans and suggests "'I wol ben he to serven yow myselve'" (5.923). Although Criseyde defends the worth of the Trojans and mentions her dead husband, she ultimately calls her situation to the fore in light of Diomede's remarks. The result is that Diomede "refte hire of the grete of al hire peyne" (5.1034). Criseyde's choice becomes less difficult to understand in light of her previous actions. She is once again alone, and once again afraid; she once again risks being the abandoned woman, a Trojan among Greeks. If they win the war, she may well be among their spoils. Past evidence suggests a single workable solution: she must ally herself with the most powerful man around to protect herself. Only her own alliances work; even if Hector could not ultimately prevent her trade, at least he, unlike the others, made an effort. The relationships of family are not salutary for Criseyde: neither her father Calkas nor her surrogate father Pandarus is ever shown to work for her protection or on her behalf. Thus once again Criseyde uses her passive situation as a source of self-sustaining action. Although she is often considered to have fallen to Diomede's pressure, her consideration of her circumstances suggests greater intention in taking a preemptive role in her own life, rather than passively being overcome by circumstances. After all, Diomede is right: the Greeks do win the war, and Criseyde cannot return to Troy. Her choice once again is death or dishonor, and she makes this choice with open eyes.

However, she is aware of the consequences of her decision. Indeed she declares them:

> "Allas, of me, unto the worldes ende,
> Shal neyther ben ywriten nor ysonge
> No good word, for thise bokes wol me shende.
> O, rolled shal I ben on many a tonge!
> Thoroughout the world my belle shal be ronge!
> And wommen moost wol haten me of alle.
> Allas, that swich a cas me sholde falle!" (5.1058–64)

Despite her comment about women readers, Criseyde experiences a kind of emasculation; as Judith Fetterley defines it, "women are taught to think as men, to identify with the male point of view, and to accept as normal and legitimate

---

[38]   Mary Behrman, "Heroic Criseyde," p. 316.

a male system of values, one of whose central principles is misogyny."[39] This process turns women away from women, forcing them, in Dinshaw's terms, to "read like men." The problem with "reading like a man," she notes, is "that it totalizes, that it not only insists on a unified reading but construes as feminine and consequently excludes whatever does not accord with that whole."[40] The female masculinity that has driven Criseyde's activity throughout the work is a victim of this exclusion; everything that has rendered her autonomous and heroic is negated through this projected totalizing reading.

Criseyde's anxiety about how she will be read is well founded, although the narrator himself sees room for pity. Even if her name "is publysshed so wide, / That for hire gilt it oughte ynough suffise" (5.1095–96), he suggests that if "I myghte excuse hire any wyse, / For she so sory was for hire untrouthe, / Iwis, I wolde excuse hire yet for routhe" (5.1097–99). Although Howes includes the narrator among Criseyde's betrayers for his "neglect in telling her side of the story in the later books," and accuses him of turning "the fascinating character we have come to know in books two and three, full of nuance and humor and life, into the kind of female character we see represented practically everywhere else in late medieval literature: an inconstant woman who seduces men, tricks them, and leads them unfailingly into a state of sorrow and woe,"[41] it seems that the narrator may, indeed, offer the possibility of much more complex under-standings of his poem's heroine. For as Blamires suggests, the poem ultimately rejects these potentially totalizing readings, noting that "Chaucer's narratives show creative awareness of ragged seams, and of overlaps where the nap of each cloth does not run in quite the same direction."[42]

Criseyde's concern that "women moost wol haten me of alle" has ramifica-tions for an exploration of her masculine behavior. Interestingly, in the two most overt responses to *Troilus and Criseyde*, it is women who condemn her. In Henryson's *Testament of Cressid*, Cynthia condemns Criseyde by punishing her with leprosy and destroying her beauty: "'Fra heil of body I thee now depryve, / And to thy seiknes sal be na recure, / But in dolour thy dayis to indure'" (337–39).[43] Chaucer also has Criseyde condemned by a woman – or at least has himself condemned for writing about her. In the *Legend of Good Women*, Alceste declares:

> "Hast thow nat mad in Englysh ek the bok
> How that Crisseyde Troylus forsok,
> In shewynge how that wemen han don mis?
> ... ...

---

[39] Judith Fetterley, *The Resisting Reader: A Feminist Approach to American Fiction* (Bloomington: Indiana University Press, 1978), p. xx.
[40] Carolyn Dinshaw, *Chaucer's Sexual Poetics*, p. 54.
[41] Laura Howes, "Chaucer's Criseyde," p. 324.
[42] Alcuin Blamires, *Chaucer, Ethics, and Gender*, p. 19.
[43] Robert Henryson, "The Testament of Cressid," *The Story of Troilus*, ed. R. K. Gordon (Toronto: University of Toronto Press, 1978), pp. 351–67.

Why noldest thow as wel [han] seyd goodnesse
Of wemen, as thow hast seyd wikednesse?"

(*LGW*, G 264–66; 268–69)

Alceste's accusation – with all the good women in the world, why write about the bad one? – puts Criseyde firmly in the negative camp. But Alceste and Cynthia are not, in fact, real women; they are female impersonators at the service of their male authors. More vitally, in having Criseyde address her own reputation in the guise of female readership, Chaucer "produces an extended meditation on what happens to the female reader's sense of self when she encounters a textual representation of a woman."[44] Turning to a contemporary female reader and writer, it is useful to consider Christine de Pizan as a model for challenging Criseyde's assumption. Christine herself is no stranger to a self-defining female masculinity; in the *Mutacion de Fortune* she undergoes a metaphorical sex-change, casting off her female body and becoming a "real man" in the face of adversity, an image so potent for her that she returns to it in *L'Avision Christine*, written in the same year as she explores literary women in the *Livre de la Cité des Dames*.[45]

If Christine "offers the female reader a potential version of herself, a mindset or self-image she could adopt as her own," Chaucer offers a woman with whom it is hard to identify, in part because of the ways she is written out of the poem, and in part because of the ways that her condemnation is inscribed within it. Christine challenges the "damaging effect of alignment with a nega-tive female literary figure, and demonstrates how that damage can be repaired," unlike Chaucer who "never offers his imaginary male audience, or by proxy the female audience, the option to identify with [Criseyde]."[46] In rewriting the lives of female literary figures in a revised context, Christine offers a reclamation of

---

[44] Kara Doyle, "Criseyde Reading, Reading Criseyde," *NPC*, 75–110, at p. 76.
[45] In the *Livre de la Mutacion de Fortune*, Christine says:

Estoit muee ed enforcie
Et ma voix forment engrossie
Et coprs plus dur et plus isnel
Mais choit de mon doy fu l'anel
Qu'Ymenetis donné m'avoit
Foit et hardi cuer me trouvay
Dont'esbahi, mais j'espouvay
Que vray home fus devenu.

(My appearance was altered and made stronger,
My voice became deeper,
My body, harder and more agile.
But the ring that Hymen had given me
Fell from my finger
I found within myself a strong and hardy spirit,
Which amazed me,
And proved that I
Had become a real man.)

Christine de Pizan, *Le Livre de la Mutacion de Fortune*, ed. Susan Solente. 4 vols. (Paris: Picard, 1959–66), vol. I, pp. 51–53. The English translation is taken from Diane Bornstein, *Ideals for Women in the Works of Christine de Pizan* (Detroit, MI: Wayne State University Press, 1981), pp. 13–14.
[46] Kara Doyle, "Criseyde Reading," pp. 77, 92.

women's literary history. She does not touch Criseyde, and in praising figures like Lucretia who choose death over dishonor, she implies the reading Criseyde anticipates. However, in addressing women's inconstancy, Christine suggests that the accusation is a product of men, who fall into equal and greater fickleness, despite claiming a stronger character and condition for themselves.[47] Although she praises constant women like Griselda, she decries cheating men, and finally has Rectitude point out, against the charge that women are deceitful, that

> the common good of a city or land or any community of people is nothing other than the profit or general good in which all members, women and men, take part. But whatever is done with the intention of benefiting some and not others is a matter of private and not public welfare.

She adds that men "never address women, nor warn them against men's traps even though it is certain that men frequently deceive women with their fast tricks and duplicity."[48] Suggesting that ladies who killed themselves for love, such as Dido and Medea, died because of the fault of loving too much, Christine's logic, if not her examples, suggests an understanding of Criseyde's choices and their causes, as well as her attempt to function within the duplicitous rules of a man's game.

It is significant in this formula that the narrator condemns Criseyde's female readers to a much less rich reading of the poem than Chaucer ultimately offers. Indeed, feminist critics have sought to redeem Criseyde, understanding the complex nexus of her fear, her desire for free will and action, and her attempts to offer an alternative masculinity. One last possibility of Criseyde's choice of a self-determined role comes at the end of the story. Holly Crocker points out that Troilus "dies because the feminine image he creates to reflect his own elevated status does not remain an icon signifying his singular noble masculinity,"[49] and thus Criseyde fails to occupy the place designed for her and has chosen, like the few others in the poem who act on their own will, the path of action. She may receive the blame for the poem's movement "fro wo to wele and after out of joie" (1.4), but even this imposed definition that attempts to render her meaning must grow out of her resistance to inhabiting the passive spheres of romance and epic ideals. Whether Criseyde is ultimately a victim of her fears, or of patriarchal society and its traffic in women, or of romance; whether she is a schemer, or a virago, or a pragmatist, or a traitor, one thing is apparent – in choosing dishonor over death, in choosing Diomede's protection, Criseyde, within a feminized context, plays a "mannes game" with a "mannes herte."

Karma Lochrie suggests that "authority itself, then, provides the cultural capital for masculinity regardless of its different registers for clerical and bourgeois men"; she adds that the claiming of that authority "represents a floata-

---

47   Christine de Pisan, *The Book of the City of Ladies*, ed. and trans. Earl Jeffrey Richards (New York: Persea, 1982), 2.47.1.
48   Christine de Pisan, *The Book of the City of Ladies*, 2.54.1.
49   Holly Crocker, "How the Woman Makes the Man: Chaucer's Reciprocal Fictions," *NPC*, 139–64, at p. 140.

tion, if you will, of the primary medieval masculine signifier and an exercise in imagining female masculinity."[50] If the authority Criseyde attempts to claim is subjectivity, we are offered in her another exercise of exactly this kind of imagining. If this is received, as Halberstam suggests, "as a pathological sign of misidentification and maladjustment, as a longing to be and have a power that is always just out of reach,"[51] it nonetheless allows readers to challenge the totalizing "reading like a man" that Dinshaw characterizes as excluding "whatever does not accord with that whole."[52] The poem itself, in its continual challenging of normativity through Criseyde's attempts to claim masculinity for herself, persistently destabilizes gender as it attempts to control it.

[50] Karma Lochrie, *Heterosyncracies*, p. 98.
[51] Judith Halberstam, *Female Masculinity*, p. 9.
[52] Carolyn Dinshaw, *Chaucer's Sexual Poetics*, p. 54.

9

Troilus's Gaze and the Collapse of Masculinity in Romance

MOLLY A. MARTIN

In creating his version of Boccaccio's *Il Filostrato*, Chaucer emphasizes the visual tropes of the romance genre and of the courtly lover throughout the work. The visual narrative, read through the lenses of courtly love, medieval optics, and modern theories of gazing and seeing, illuminates the interconnectivity of gender and genre in the text. The crucial moments of sight, in which Troilus loses masculine control over his gaze, force Chaucer away from both the romance genre and his source text. By juxtaposing romance and other genres, and through a metanarrative insistence on naming other genres, Chaucer attempts to solve the visual incompatibility of masculinity and romance. Plotting together vision, gender, and genre, the romance of *Troilus and Criseyde* avoids and negates the inherent, generically encoded problem of a gaze that emasculates its subject.

Visual studies have occupied an ever-increasing space on the critical landscape in recent decades. However, most theorists still assume the gaze exerts a systematic patriarchal dominance, transcending sensory boundaries such as the eyes. Consequently, they discuss the gaze unilaterally, neglecting the multiple movements between eye and image. This approach derives from feminist film criticism of the 1970s, which focuses on the male gaze's production and manipulation of the female figure. In her foundational essay, "Visual Pleasure and Narrative Cinema," Laura Mulvey uses Freud and Lacan to examine the position of the female film star, an image for the (male) audience's gaze. The scopophilic cinema experience assigns pleasure and power to the viewer, culminating in a gendered bifurcation of the roles in the visual experience:

> [P]leasure in looking has been split between active/male and passive/female. The determining male gaze projects its fantasy onto the female figure, which is styled accordingly. In their traditional exhibitionist role women are simultaneously looked at and displayed, with their appearance coded for strong visual and erotic impact so that they can be said to connote *to-be-looked-at-ness*.[1]

---

[1] Laura Mulvey, "Visual Pleasure and Narrative Cinema," *Visual and Other Pleasures* (Bloomington: University of Indiana Press, 1989), 14–26, at p. 19.

The male forces the female to produce this stereotypical and erotically charged image. Mulvey underscores the "determining" power of the masculine position: only the male has access to visual power. He "projects," and she is "displayed." Mulvey's unidirectional gaze parallels theories of voyeurism. Christian Metz, for instance, emphasizes the distance between the subject and object in the cinematic, and thus voyeuristic, gaze. He notes a contrast between "senses at a distance (sight and hearing)" and "senses of contact," which demand that the organ and the sensed object touch. Metz explains the necessity of a "gulf, an empty space, between the object and the eye," a separation from the object resulting in lack of contact.[2] Because this distance prevents contact, it facilitates the power that Mulvey argues only men access.

Mulvey's stance provides the foundation of a shifting critical understanding of the gaze.[3] However, Ann Kaplan claims that while the strict categories of "male" and "female" may change, the social distinction between "masculine" and "feminine" remains intact.[4] This tendency to consider the gaze primarily as a tool of mastery, particularly a gendered mastery, perseveres, with few dissenting critics. Only recently has Todd McGowan discussed the multidirectional nature of gazing and seeing, claiming that the gaze reflects back from the object to the viewer and thus assumes mastery.[5] The essentialized gaze theory of Mulvey and her followers generates complex readings of medieval narrative and psychology, but despite this complexity, a unilateral and "male" gaze continues to dominate criticism.[6] However, the nature of vision, particularly as understood in the Middle Ages, does not reflect this singularity of direction; medieval optical theorists believed in a physical movement from the object seen to the viewing eye. The gaze results in an image projected back upon the viewer, and this image is beyond the control of the (male) gazer at that moment. This powerful gaze, voyeuristic and fetishistic as it may be, leaves a space for the

---

2   Christian Metz, "The Imaginary Signifier," trans. Ben Brewster, *Screen* 16.2 (1973): 14–76, at pp. 60–61.

3   See Mary Ann Doane, Patricia Mellencamp, and Linda Williams, eds., *Re-vision: Essays in Feminist Film Criticism* (Frederick, MD: University Publications of America, 1984); Lorraine Gamman and Margaret Marshment, eds., *The Female Gaze: Women as Viewers of Popular Culture* (Seattle: Real Comet, 1989); and Mary Ann Doane, "Film and the Masquerade: Theorizing the Female Spectator," *Screen* 23.3–4 (1982): 74–87.

4   Ann Kaplan, "Is the Gaze Male?" *Desire: The Politics of Sexuality*, eds. Ann Barr Snitow, Christine Stansell, and Sharon Thompson (New York: Monthly Review, 1984), 321–38, at p. 331. Mulvey's own "Afterthoughts on 'Visual Pleasure and Narrative Cinema' Inspired by King Vidor's *Duel in the Sun*," first published in 1981 and reprinted in *Visual Pleasures*, pp. 29–38, rethinks but basically maintains her schema in terms of female spectators.

5   Todd McGowan, "Looking for the Gaze: Lacanian Film Theory and Its Vicissitudes," *Cinema Journal* 42.3 (2003): 27–47.

6   See Sarah Stanbury, "The Lover's Gaze in *Troilus and Criseyde*," *CTC*, pp. 224–38, in which Stanbury explores the intersubjectivity of the gazes of both Troilus and Criseyde and their connection to Western ideas of love, but maintains Troilus's active position. See also Sarah Stanbury, "Feminist Film Theory: Seeing Chrétien's Enide," *Literature and Psychology* 36.4 (1990): 47–66, as well as her "Space and Visual Hermeneutics in the *Gawain*-Poet," *ChauR* 21.4 (1987): 476–89; *Seeing the Gawain-Poet: Description and the Act of Perception* (Philadelphia: University of Pennsylvania Press, 1991); "The Virgin's Gaze: Spectacle and Transgression in Middle English Lyrics of the Passion," *PMLA* 106.5 (1991): 1083–93; and "The Voyeur and the Private Life in *Troilus and Criseyde*," *SAC* 13 (1991): 141–58.

disintegration of power. In an examination of the act of looking at a painting, Lacan, whose discussion of optics significantly informs Mulvey's idea of the gaze, theorizes a removal of power from the gazer by locating it with the image or painter.[7] An inability to seize power through the gaze becomes tangled in a "failure" of masculinity because, as Lacan argues, viewing moves one into a passive position as the viewer is forced

> to lay down his gaze there as one lays down one's weapons. This is the paci-fying, Apollonian effect of painting. Something is given not so much to the gaze as to the eye, something that involves the abandonment, the *laying down*, of the gaze.[8]

The gaze does not here actively project itself upon the image; rather, the image projects itself upon the eye and thus affects the viewer. The painting pacifies as well as passive-izes the (male) viewer. Lacan emphasizes this loss of power by comparing it to the laying down of weapons; it is the abandonment of active male power. Roland Barthes extends this discussion and restructures gender dichotomies through "ravishment," the result of a gaze in love-at-first-sight scenarios. Barthes destabilizes the notion of male superiority through the gaze by showing a "turnabout" at the moment of gazing.[9] The image becomes the ravisher, and the ravished subject of the gaze is made passive and feminine. As we will see, Troilus experiences this very reversal of gender and power.

This collapse of the gaze particularly suits both the Middle Ages and the romance genre. This redefined psychoanalytic theory dovetails with both the state of medieval optics and the conception of what was later termed "courtly love." Indeed, the notion of bilateral vision materializes physically in the field of optics. Out-of-favor extramission theories hypothesize that the eye emits rays moving toward and then perceiving visible objects; the eye is both the subject and the absolute agent of vision. The popularity of this theory waned in conjunction with the increasing access to translations of Arabic scientific works that opposed extramissionary theories. Replacing this theory in academic and popular thought was intromissive optics, which reverses the movement of sight. At its most basic, the theory of intromission states that the image enters the eye, thus making the image work toward the eye, as in Lacanian theory. The viewer becomes an object of the image. Alhazen, in his *Book of Optics* (*De aspectibus*), offers a theory of intromission, partially derived from Aristotle's work and debunking extramission. According to Alhazen, with the help of light, rays from a body (the image) are emitted and make an impression on the eye;

---

7   Jacqueline Rose argues that film theorists in general, and Christian Metz in particular, have consider-ably misused Lacanian psychoanalysis, in *Sexuality and the Field of Vision* (London: Verso, 1986), pp. 167–213.

8   Jacques Lacan, *The Seminar of Jacques Lacan, Book XI: The Four Fundamental Concepts of Psychoanalysis*, ed. Jacques-Alain Miller, trans. Alan Sheridan (New York: Norton, 1978), p. 101. See also Richard Wollheim, "What the Spectator Sees," *Visual Theory: Painting and Interpretation*, eds. Norman Bryson, Michael Ann Holly, and Keith Moxey (New York: Harper Collins, 1991), pp. 101–50. Wollheim discusses the power of the painter, who controls the viewing experience.

9   Roland Barthes, *A Lover's Discourse*, trans. Richard Howard (New York: Hill & Wang, 1978), pp. 188–89.

they enter the eye and are then perceived by the brain.[10] No movement occurs from the eye to the object, which consequently wields power over the viewer.[11] In this transfer of power, intromissive optical theory coincides with Lacan's "laying down of the gaze." Furthermore, the image contacts the eye, replicating the proximity of touch and resulting in a theoretical fusion of eye and object. Space between subject and object collapses, rendering a completely voyeuristic visual experience impossible. Because the eye is contacted by the image, Metz's prerequisite of separation does not exist for the viewer.

The bilateral nature of vision depicted in the work of both modern critics and medieval optical scientists becomes particularly manifest in medieval romances, in which characters participate in a gendered matrix of gazes. The courtly tradition demands attention to vision's role in love. Andreas Capellanus, for example, begins his treatise on love with vision, defining love as

> a certain inborn suffering derived from the sight of and excessive meditation upon the beauty of the opposite sex, which causes each one to wish above all things the embraces of the other and by common desire to carry out all of love's precepts in the other's embrace.[12]

Andreas highlights the importance of sight in this literary tradition by placing it at the head of the text. Gazing produces desire and leaves the male suffering and bereft of agency. Andreas integrates this visual theme throughout his treatise, repeating the sentiments of the definition and noting physiological responses to the sight of the beloved.[13] Growing out of the same tradition in which Andreas writes, romance is rife with these critical visual moments.

In *Troilus and Criseyde*, Chaucer struggles with this visual gender/genre trope. The conjunctive nature of vision and gender victimizes Troilus and endangers male hierarchy. *Troilus and Criseyde*, intimately engaging romance in its early books, endeavors to maintain a masculinist scheme through generic fluidity and generic labeling. The poem's conceptualization of vision moves from the

---

[10] David Lindberg, *Theories of Vision from Al-Kindi to Kepler* (Chicago, IL: University of Chicago Press, 1981), pp. 71–86. On Alhazen and others, see also A. C. Crombie, *Science, Optics, and Music in Medieval and Early Modern Thought* (London: Hambledon Press, 1990), pp. 175–205; Mark Smith, "Getting the Big Picture in Perspectivist Optics," *Isis* 72 (1981): 568–88, at pp. 568–69. European scholars such as Bacon, Witelo, and Pecham synthesized, expanded, and publicized the theories of Alhazen and others. See Lindberg, *Theories of Vision*, pp. 107–16. Bacon even says "visus est virtus passiva," in his *Opus Maius* 5.1.5.1, quoted in Gareth Matthews, "A Medieval Theory of Vision," *Studies in Perception*, eds. Peter Machamer and Robert Turnbull (Columbus: Ohio State University Press, 1978), 186–99, at p. 191. Note that Geoffrey Chaucer, in the *Squire's Tale*, mentions Alhazen, Witelo, and Aristotle (*CT*, 5.231–34). In the essay that follows in this collection, Richard Zeikowitz further discusses the interplay of extramission and intromission in medieval optical thought.

[11] See Suzanne Conklin Akbari, *Seeing through the Veil: Optical Theory and Medieval Allegory* (Toronto: University of Toronto Press, 2004), pp. 23–24.

[12] Andreas Capellanus, *The Art of Courtly Love*, trans. John Jay Parry (New York: Columbia University Press, 1960), p. 28. For a connection between love and physiology, see Paolo Cherchi, *Andreas and the Ambiguity of Courtly Love* (Toronto: University of Toronto Press, 1994), p. 28.

[13] Andreas Capellanus, *The Art of Courtly Love*, pp. 29, 185. See also Mary Wack, *Lovesickness in the Middle Ages* (Philadelphia: University of Pennsylvania Press, 1990) and Vern Bullough, "On Being Male in the Middle Ages," *MM*, pp. 31–45.

problematic romance mode into broader and less reflexive patterns. Chaucer produces a story that blends aspects of several genres; he affirms masculinity by narrating centrifugally into realms of epic, tragedy, history, and comedy, which are not as problematized by this crucial reversal of the gaze. The genres tend either to minimize the narrow, intromissive vision of romance love or to project expansive, outward gazes from the subject to a larger landscape.

Chaucer shows an acute awareness of genre over the course of the poem, paying considerable attention to the motifs of romance, particularly early in the text. Transforming Boccaccio's text into a more concentrated study of sight lines – and their effects on Troilus in particular – is one of several romance tropes which Chaucer emphasizes.[14] The narrator also intimates a romance inclination within the opening lines, which are often cited as signs of tragedy:

> The double sorwe of Troilus to tellen,
> That was kyng Priamus sone of Troye,
> In lovynge, how his aventures fellen
> Fro wo to wele, and after out of joie,
> My purpos is, er that I parte fro ye. (1.1–5)

Within the typically tragic language is couched a hint of love. Indeed, the first sorrow that Troilus encounters is the lover's sorrow, incited upon seeing Criseyde. The narrator and his characters also invoke Venus and Cupid repeatedly throughout the poem, calling Venus by name fourteen times and Cupid six.[15] Chaucer also laces the exchanges between the lovers with romance terminology (e.g., 3.1485–91). The poem further aligns itself with romance through its repeated allusions to a need for privacy in love, a trope highlighted in Andreas's text. Chaucer's narrator and Troilus focus on this tenet of secrecy repeatedly. Troilus is careful to hide his desire early, as the narrator explains:

> Thus took he purpos loves craft to suwe,
> And thoughte he wolde werken pryvely,
> First to hiden his desir in muwe
> From every wight yborn, al outrely,
> But he myghte ought recovered be therby,
> Remembryng hym that love to wide yblowe
> Yelt bittre fruyt, though swete seed be sowe. (1.379–85)[16]

Moreover, Troilus regularly retreats to his chamber to keep private his emotional reaction to love. As the narrator peels away layers of privacy, the romance

---

[14] See C. S. Lewis, "What Chaucer Really Did to *Il Filostrato*," *CTEC*, pp. 37–54; Thomas Kirby, *Chaucer's Troilus: A Study in Courtly Love* (Gloucester, MA: Peter Smith, 1958); and Barry Windeatt, "*Troilus* and the Disenchantment of Romance," *Studies in Medieval English Romances*, ed. Derek Brewer (Cambridge: D. S. Brewer, 1988), pp. 129–47.

[15] Venus is named at 1.1014, 2.234, 2.680, 2.972, 2.1524, 3.48, 3.187, 3.705, 3.712, 3.715, 3.951, 3.1257, 4.1661, 5.1016; her epithets Cipris/Cipride (at 3.725, 4.1216, 5.208) and Citheria (at 3.1255) also appear. Cupid is mentioned at 3.186, 3.461, 3.1808, 5.207, 5.582, 5.1590. The frequency, particularly of Venus's name, drops off significantly as the text progresses away from romance motifs.

[16] The need for secrecy crops up at various other points in the text, beyond what Boccaccio offers. See also 1.743–49, 3.309–15, 3.753.

unravels as a plotline and as a genre. Chaucer enacts this shift of genres through the visual narrative.

Despite Chaucer's indebtedness to the romance tradition, his text is not classified completely, or even primarily, as a romance. The play of genres within *Troilus and Criseyde* perhaps precludes a singular or traditional generic classification. Chaucer's text exhibits genre fluidity, showing patterns of generic movement in the poem.[17] Many critics discuss the text as a blend of genres. It can be seen, as Andrea Clough argues, as a threefold tragedy, using themes of the *de casibus*, Ovidian, and romance tragedy traditions.[18] Others argue that tragedy is used variably in conjunction with other genres. Gerry Brenner and Monica McAlpine both see its tragic elements bleeding into or combining with comedy. Brenner sees a tragic structure, which is, however, used in a manner more akin to comedy, with Troilus's "effeminate courtship" and "comic self-indulgence" resulting in a text that "disassociat[es] the reader from full participation in Troilus's decline," his tragedy.[19] McAlpine claims that the *de casibus* elements of *Troilus and Criseyde* function "as a foil or 'contrarie' as a means of presenting his own alternative Boethian genres more effectively."[20] In her view, the text combines a Boethian tragedy of Criseyde, who suffers an earthly fall, and a Boethian comedy of Troilus, who gains spiritual understanding.

Nevertheless, the romance mode governs the early stages of the text. The first three books exaggerate greatly the genre's tropes and themes to subvert them later. The narrator even dissuades the reader from the notion that this poem is a romance. In contrast to the close attention to romance tropes in the first three books (particularly in comparison to his source text), Chaucer uses metanarrative labeling and allusion to scatter genre categorization and ultimately to create a text that is decidedly antiromantic. In this effort, the narrator makes significant use of tokens of other genres. Book 1 opens with a "double sorwe" and invokes the "cruwel Furie," connecting the tale with tragedy (1.1, 9). The second book calls upon "Cleo," the muse of history (2.8). While Book 2 is initially addressed to Venus, the narrator tempers this romance/love association with the muse of epic "Caliope," drawing attention to the war storyline in the background and the epic foundations of the tale (3.3–5, 45). The narrator returns to the tragic "Herynes," or Furies, in the proem to Book 4 (4.22–24). The final book invokes the classically tragic "Parcas," or Fates (5.3). These invocations, among which one cannot find Erato, the muse of love poetry, overlay a generic reading on the text not found in Boccaccio. Chaucer further disperses genre unity by naming ancient poets of nonromance genres. Early in the poem, he connects his Trojan tale with Homer, Dares, Dictys, Vergil, Ovid, Lucan, and Statius, associating his story with their texts and ancient genres (1.146, 4.1771, 5.1792). Moreover,

---

[17] See James Wimsatt, "Medieval and Modern in Chaucer's *Troilus and Criseyde*," *PMLA* 92.2 (1977): 203–16; Windeatt, "*Troilus* and the Disenchantment of Romance."

[18] Andrea Clough, "Medieval Tragedy and the Genre of *Troilus and Criseyde*," *MH* 11 (1982): 211–27.

[19] Gerry Brenner, "Narrative Structure in Chaucer's *Troilus and Criseyde*," *CTEC*, 131–44, at p. 132.

[20] Monica McAlpine, *The Genre of* Troilus and Criseyde (Ithaca, NY: Cornell University Press, 1978), p. 45.

Chaucer twice asserts that his authority is the fictional Lollius (1.394, 5.1653), also mentioned in *The House of Fame* (1464–72), associated with the great epicist Homer and several historians of the Trojan War. Claiming this "historian" as his source aligns the work more closely with history than with romance. This generic immersion allows latitude toward the end of the piece when romance's threat to gender becomes insurmountable. For this reason the narrator calls the text "litel myn tragedye," and talks about wanting "som comedye" (5.1786, 1788). This external imposition of nonromantic genres dilutes the gendered narrative. Chaucer's unwillingness to align the text overtly with a genre that governs it in terms of plot, structure, and theme coincides with the gender crisis that Troilus's vision generates. As he closes the visual narrative, Chaucer shifts the nature of vision along genre lines. Troilus's own gaze shifts away from Criseyde and onto the broader landscapes of epic, tragedy, and comedy.

Vision in *Troilus and Criseyde* occupies a broad generic spectrum; the text exhibits an intricate pattern of gazes. Sight functions to and from the lovers, Pandarus, the narrator, and the reader. The text's visual matrix includes several instances of an active and powerful gaze.[21] However, Chaucer and his narrator lavish constant attention on the intromissive visual experience and its consequences. Troilus's gaze collapses and reverses, resulting in a marked loss of gendered agency and effecting a pull-chain of vision, gender, and genre. The romantic visual experience begins with Chaucer's introduction of Criseyde to both audience and hero. Criseyde's physical appearance becomes known immediately (1.99–105). Criseyde is presented to the reader in a highly favorable visual manner, more beautiful than all other ladies; her fairness is "forpassynge every wight" (1.101). These elements show a departure from and expansion of Boccaccio's first presentation of Criseida (1.11).[22] Chaucer reiterates Criseyde's superlative beauty shortly thereafter: "Right as oure firste lettre is now an A, / In beaute first so stood she, makeles. / Hire goodly lokyng gladed al the prees" (1.171–73). Again Chaucer employs a superlative to describe the lady, ranking her first, like the letter "A"; indeed, she is without match. This insistence on her beauty indicates a heightened interest in visuality, which continues throughout the text. The next depiction of Criseyde visually closes in on her body, person, and gender. The narrator mentions her "stature" and "lymes," which exude "wommanhod" so that "creature / Was nevere lasse mannyssh," before discussing her virtues, "[h]onour, estat, and wommanly noblesse" (1.281–87). Her limbs answer to womanhood and never was one less manly; even her social standing is bound up in her gender. The insistence on her incomparable femininity indicates

---

21 For example, at 1.325, one can see love's fatal glance. See Ruth Cline, "Heart and Eyes," *Romance Philology* 25 (1972): 263–97. Moreover, Pandarus, the reader, and the sun (at 3.1435) publicize the private narrative. See Sarah Stanbury, "The Voyeur and Private Life in *Troilus and Criseyde*"; Linda Tarte Holley, "Medieval Optics and the Framed Narrative in Chaucer's *Troilus and Criseyde*," *ChauR* 21 (1986): 26–44; Louise Fradenburg, "'Oure owen wo to drynke': Loss, Gender and Chivalry in *Troilus and Criseyde*," CTC, pp. 88–106; and A. C. Spearing, *The Medieval Poet as Voyeur* (Cambridge: Cambridge University Press, 1993), esp. pp. 120–39.

22 Giovanni Boccaccio, *Il Filostrato*, ed. Vincenzo Pernicone, trans. Robert apRoberts and Anna Bruni Seldis (New York: Garland, 1986); cited parenthetically by book and stanza number.

a powerful object of any gaze, and this attention reflects the poet's conjoined interest in vision and gender concerns.

Descriptions of Criseyde continue to focus on her unrivaled beauty. This image entrances the narrator, the reader, and later Troilus, whose association with Criseyde is initially voyeuristic. Before seeing Criseyde, Troilus maintains a disinterested and objectifying gaze:

> This Troilus as he was wont to gide
> His yonge knyghtes, lad hem up and down
> In thilke large temple on every side,
> Byholdyng ay the ladies of the town,
> Now here, now there; for no devocioun
> Hadde he to non, to reven hym his reste,
> But gan to preise and lakken whom hym leste. (1.183–89)

Troilus exudes manliness in this passage, leading troops and looking variously and dispassionately at women. He possesses a firm hold on his masculine agency, as he directs his eyes here and there at will, a "distant evaluation" which, Stephanie Dietrich argues, marks him as masculine.[23] This distance allows for a very masculine objectification of women, which Troilus punctuates with comments on men who lack control of their gaze:

> And in his walk ful faste he gan to wayten
> If knyght or squyer of his compaignie
> Gan for to syke, or lete his eighen baiten
> On any womman that he koude espye.
> He wolde smyle and holden it folye,
> And seye him thus, "God woot, she slepeth softe
> For the love of the, whan thow turnest ful ofte!" (1.190–96)

Troilus, known to scorn love, comments on the romance mode of vision. He finds humor in the entranced man. He engenders this typical relationship against the patriarchal hierarchy that assigns control to the male: in this reversal, the man will toss and turn while the woman sleeps securely. The woman will "reven," or deprive, the male of his sleep (1.188). There is a sense that love necessarily shifts the locus of agency away from the male.

The irony of Troilus's words and actions quickly becomes apparent. The hero spies Criseyde in a voyeuristic (and implicitly powerful) fashion, out of her sight and physically removed. Criseyde embodies romance and the feminine, and Troilus soon figuratively enters that space.[24] In Chaucer's conception, romance reflexively engenders a threat to the genre itself, because romance demands a visual experience that adversely affects masculinity as the gaze breaks down, and masculine identity provides a core structure to the romance genre. The

---

23 Stephanie Dietrich, "'Slydyng' Masculinity in the Four Portraits of Troilus," *MC*, 205–20, at p. 207.
24 Angela Weisl, *Conquering the Reign of Femeny: Gender and Genre in Chaucer's Romance* (Cambridge: D. S. Brewer, 1995), p. 21.

outward movement of the gaze ceases and the romance mode of vision guides the narrative. The effect of the visual experience manifests itself as Troilus's gaze falls upon Criseyde:

> This Troilus, of every wight aboute,
> On this lady, and now on that, lokynge,
> Wher so she were of town or of withoute;
> And upon cas bifel that thorugh a route
> His eye percede, and so depe it wente,
> Til on Criseyde it smot, and ther it stente.
> And sodeynly he wax therwith astoned,
> And gan hir bet biholde in thrifty wise.   (1.268–75)

While Troilus scans the crowd, his gaze pierces and smites until it falls upon her. Robert Edwards considers this exemplary of the typical male gaze.[25] However, having fixed his eyes upon Criseyde, Troilus cannot objectify her with his male gaze. The movement from eye to image literally stops on Criseyde. By visually interrupting Criseyde's romance space, Troilus initiates his own feminization: his look becomes inactive ("stente"), and he is made passive physically and grammatically ("astoned"), which is a noted change from the Italian (1.26, 28). This instantaneous shift of Troilus's gendered identity betrays Chaucer's heightened attention to the romance vision motif. This visual experience initially reflects the goals of a voyeuristic act. As Spearing explains, a powerful aspect of voyeurism is that it publicizes the private.[26] Troilus looks without being seen, but he quickly interiorizes the image. There is no visual or optical space between him and Criseyde, because voyeuristic power is absent in the romance mode. As Stanbury notes, Troilus exerts control over his gaze until he is "victimized … by the mechanics of his own look."[27] Criseyde's image "gladed" everyone except Troilus, whose masculinity is diminished (1.173).

Troilus's resultant lack of agency (and by extrapolation his lack of masculine presence) manifests itself in several manners. It first stirs up his passion:

> And of hire look in him ther gan to quyken
> So gret desir and such affeccioun,
> That in his herte botme gan to stiken
> Of hir his fixe and depe impressioun.
> And though he erst hadde poured up and down,
> He was tho glad his hornes in to shrinke:
> Unnethes wiste he how to loke or wynke.   (1.295–301)

Because of the power of the image that is optically entering him, he is left with a "depe impressioun." Perhaps more importantly, Troilus involuntarily releases power over vision. In his rewriting of *Il Filostrato*, Chaucer plays with visuality

[25] Robert Edwards, "Pandarus's 'Unthrift' and the Problem of Desire in *Troilus and Criseyde*," *CTC*, 74–87, at p. 80.
[26] A. C. Spearing, *The Medieval Poet as Voyeur*, p. 19.
[27] Sarah Stanbury, "The Voyeur and the Private Life," p. 144.

and its relationship to the romance tradition. Again emphasizing the power of the image, Chaucer reproduces Troilus's lack of visual agency:

> She, this in blak, likynge to Troilus
> Over alle thing, he stood for to biholde;
> Ne his desir, ne wherfor he stood thus,
> He neither chere made, ne word tolde;
> But from afer, his manere for to holde,
> On other thing his look som tyme he caste,
> And eft on hire, whil that servyse laste. (1.309–15)

Although Troilus tries to maintain a casualness of vision, he cannot help but "caste" his eyes "eft on hire." Troilus does not control himself but replicates and continues the visual experience; he does not move but rather looks from afar. Again this potentially voyeuristic moment does not empower Troilus.

This vision of Criseyde, which has left such a deep impression on Troilus's faculty of sight, his heart, and his soul, soon invades Troilus physically and psychologically. The love-at-first-sight moment produces in him symptoms of lovesickness, which come to fruition once he is in the privacy of his bedchamber (1.360–64). Chaucer pathologizes this lovesickness more immediately in his version than does Boccaccio (1.33). Both texts show the move to a woeful behavioral pattern on Troilus's part, but Chaucer diverges significantly from his source in eliminating the sense of pleasure that the Italian Troilo receives from this visual meditation. Troilus's emasculation and sickness are perpetuated as he is forced to visualize the beauty that has entranced him. The gazing repeats itself as Troilus begins "it newe avise" (1.364). It pervades Troilus's visual imagination:

> Thus gan he make a mirour of his mynde
> In which he saugh al holly hire figure,
> And that he wel koude in his herte fynde.
> It was to hym a right good aventure
> To love swich oon, and if he dede his cure
> To serven hir, yet myghte he falle in grace,
> Or ellis for oon of hire servantz pace. (1.365–71)

The visual fantasy, the mirror in his mind, leads directly to the romance genre, as Troilus contemplates adventures of love. Chaucer connects the visual imagination with its romance origins and pays close attention to the visual image: "His herte, which that is his brestez yë, / Was ay on hire, that fairer was to sene / Than evere were Eleyne or Polixene" (1.453–55). He again underscores the power the visual impression bears on Troilus, as he contemplates Criseyde with the heart, "his brestez yë." The symptoms of this pathological and feminizing lovesickness persist throughout the narrative.[28] Troilus is often driven to sighs, woe, madness, and sleeplessness because of Criseyde's image. In both her pres-

---

[28] See 1.499 and 1.546. This trope is repeated and emphasized throughout the poem.

ence and her absence, Troilus suffers heavily. This lovesickness and its comprehensive impotence, as Mary Wack argues, occur at key points in Troilus's love narrative, creating a "fatalistic passivity."[29] In a patriarchal society, his inability to participate in essentially masculine acts represents a fissured gender identity.

From the moment Troilus publicizes his love, Pandarus plots and literally oversees Troilus's deeds in relation to Criseyde. Troilus asks Pandarus, " 'Allas! What is me best to do?'" (1.828), at which point Pandarus assumes Troilus's agency. Troilus even finds a level of comfort in this transference of power. As Pandarus departs, Troilus's woeful spirits are lifted (1.1086–92). Troilus's passivity characterizes him for the rest of the poem, and he remains bereft of any agency to invest in wooing his beloved. He depends upon the machinations of Pandarus, who encourages Criseyde to love, meet, and embrace Troilus. Indeed, after Criseyde is traded away, Troilus needs the "stage manager" Pandarus to tell him, " 'Why nylt thiselven helpen don redresse / And with thy manhod letten al this grame? / Go ravysshe here!'" (4.528–30). Troilus cannot even invoke his own manhood. Because of his visual experience, he is neither agent nor subject.

Even as Troilus verges on the defeminizing (and, more importantly, the remasculinizing) sexual act, the "cure" for lovesickness and the ultimate signifier of male activity and female passivity, he betrays an utter lack of agency. He loses both composure and consciousness (3.1086–92). In the fullness of Criseyde's presence, both visually and physically, Troilus cannot maintain a semblance of agency. He falls "a-swowne" before her and becomes "no litel sorwe for to se" (3.1093). While on the brink of returning to masculinity through physical penetration, Troilus becomes the hyperbolic courtly lover, leaving his masculine identity again at risk. Like many of Pandarus's machinations that maneuver Troilus and Criseyde into the same room, this scene does not derive from the source text.

Even after the "blissful nyght" (3.1317), Troilus remains powerless over his own looking.[30] The seemingly ultimate male act – sexual penetration – does not return to Troilus power over his gaze:

> And Lord! So he gan goodly on hire se
> That nevere his look ne bleynte from hire face,
> And seyde, "O deere herte, may it be
> That it be soth, that ye ben in this place?"
> "Yee, herte myn, God thank I of his grace,"
> Quod tho Criseyde, and therwithal hym kiste,
> That where his spirit was, for joie he nyste. (3.1345–51)

Troilus does not control his vision. The image captures him such that he does not turn away; again he is in a visual trap. He even questions the reality of the

29 Mary Wack, "Lovesickness in *Troilus*," *Pacific Coast Philology* 19.1–2 (1984): 55–61, at p. 57.
30 See Charlotte Otten, "The Love-Sickness of Troilus," *Chaucer and the Craft of Fiction*, ed. Leigh A. Arathoon (Rochester, MI: Solaris, 1986), 23–33, at p. 27.

vision, the reality of Criseyde's presence. The gendered curative powers of sex are negated as Troilus is once again subservient to the visual. Chaucer adds this attention to the crisis of masculinity, which is enacted both by and through vision, indicating a heightened attention to the trope (cf. Boccaccio, 3.35). While Boccaccio shows a mutuality, Chaucer situates all of the uncontrolled looking on the male. Criseyde is active; she kisses Troilus. She maintains her agency while his lapses.

At this middle point in the text, the narrative reaches its peak. For a brief span, vision should not present a danger. But *Troilus and Criseyde* is a romance of failure, because of the inherited story, because of the intromissive sightlines, because of the genre that the author will not let succeed; the failure must be enacted. To this end, vision maintains its prominence after the narrative's downward spiral begins. While the text begins to escape from the genre, romance visual motifs are not entirely discarded. Troilus wants to perpetuate the visual experience that marks romance and bemoans the end of his participation in visual encounters with Criseyde:

> "O woful eyen two, syn youre disport
> Was al to sen Criseydes eyen brighte,
> What shal ye don but, for my discomfort,
> Stonden for naught, and wepen out youre sighte,
> Syn she is queynt that wont was yow to lighte?
> In vayn fro this forth have ich eyen tweye
> Ifourmed, syn youre vertu is aweye." (4.309–15)

For Troilus, Criseyde has become the *only* vision. He wants and needs the ability to perceive only so that he can see his beloved. Without her image, he believes that his eyes are "in vayn" and that sight is only a discomfort.

Romance vision forces Troilus and the text into the precarious position of feminization. This departure from the norm troubles gender and genre alike. In the romance mode of love, no "male" gaze objectifies the woman because the romance writer is not able to perpetuate a split between the viewing male and the viewed female. The gender confusion impels the author to reconsider the structural model, namely romance. Consequently, Chaucer embarks upon an overlaying of genres to assuage the gender difficulty that a romance almost necessarily encounters. While he has already established this technique, averting attention from the romance from the opening line of the poem, Chaucer intensifies this approach in the final two books. In the prohemium to Book 4, he invokes Fortune, emblematic of tragedy, as well as the Furies. Whereas Boccaccio specifically connects Fortune to love, Chaucer eliminates the source text's continued attention to romance themes (3.94). Unlike his pattern throughout the first three books, Chaucer here reverses the generic movement of his translation, disconnecting the story from love. In many ways, the tragic and the romantic oppose each other ideologically, and this poem is on the threshold of conjoining them so as to reduce the influence of romance gendering. Chaucer's blending of genres moves across a spectrum from a highly romantic text to one that combines elements of genres, and finally to one that rejects the mode.

The trend of commingling the tragedy and romance genres continues throughout Book 4. Chaucer again combines the two as Troilus exhibits symptoms of extreme lovesickness and a desire for death (4.1086–92). The intimacy of the genres here attempts the release of gender pressure. The narrator provides a quick escape, a tragic ending, as Criseyde faints and appears to be dead:

> This Troilus, that on hire gan biholde,
> Clepyng hire name – and she lay as for ded –
> Without answere, and felte hire lymes colde,
> Hire eyen throwen upward to hire hed,
> This sorwful man kan now noon other red,
> But ofte tyme hire colde mowth he kiste.
> Wher hym was wo, God and hymself it wiste! (4.1156–62)

This gaze falls not upon the bright and fresh Criseyde of the previous books, but rather one with "lymes colde" and "colde mowth." She appears dead; she appears to suffer a tragic end. Her eyes, the locus of vision, and of romance itself, are "throwen upward to hir hed," indicating her removal from the matrix of gazes. Even as the tragic begins to conquer romance, the narrator constantly reminds the reader about the elements of the foundational genre.

Chaucer also cross-pollinates elements of history and epic with the romantic to the same general effect. The private image of Criseyde competes with the public locus of the law, "parlement," the English idea of a governing body (4.659–65). This ties the poem into a national history for Chaucer's immediate audience. Chaucer does, however, cling to a visual image, reminiscent of the romance mode. Expanding on the Italian text, he speaks of Criseyde's "brighte hewe," connecting with the visuality of the romance (4.663). The poet juxtaposes these two points of contrary generic origin (both added to Boccaccio) to continue his movement out of the restrictive and gendered limits of romance.

As Book 5 begins, the narration moves fervently against the romance current. As Criseyde leaves the walls of Troy, Troilus "caste[s] his eye upon hire pitously" (5.79). Here is the last moment of shared sentiment, visual, physical, and emotional, between Troilus and Criseyde.[31] In the next stanza, Diomede, the new suitor literally and figuratively, takes Troilus's position. The Diomede plotline works against Troilus in two ways: Diomede, in control of his masculine agency and working under his own command, represents the anti-Troilus; simultaneously his wooing and winning of Criseyde represents an antiromance, following only briefly and with questionable sincerity the pattern laid out by that genre. He too reacts to Criseyde:

> And with that word he gan to waxen red,
> And in his speche a litel wight he quok,
> And caste asyde a litel wight his hed,
> And stynte a while; and afterward he wok,

---

[31] Angela Weisl considers Criseyde (like Troy), "a locus amoena of private emotion, love, and female control," in *Conquering the Reign of Femeny*, p. 21.

> And sobreliche on hire he threw his lok,
> And seyde, "I am, al be it yow no joie,
> As gentil man as any wight in Troie." (5.925–31)

This scene reminds the reader of Troilus's narrative, on a much smaller scale. The scaling downplays the romance motifs while employing them. Like Troilus, Diomede "gan to waxen red," "quok," and "stynte a while." These tropes are all in line with the lovesickness expected in the romance narrative, but Diomede's reaction lacks the sincerity that marked Troilus's romance and is, moreover, short-lived, for it is but a half line later that he "wok," and more tellingly, "on hire threw his lok." His command over his own gaze provides a startling contrast to Troilus's lengthy suffering. The use of Diomede to reject the romance mode of vision is shown earlier as he claims, "'For I have herd er this of many a wight, / Hath loved thyng he nevere saigh his lyve'" (5.164–65). Diomede's rejection of sight as the basis for love contrasts with Troilus's story and with the romance tradition. The narrator dilutes the romance to exchange that genre for others, and also to counter the story of Troilus.

The fifth book greatly expands both the visual presentation of the narrative and the generic categorization of the text. The private sphere plays a smaller and smaller role in the story as Troilus is forced into the public realm. In conjunction with the hero's outward move is the imposition of public affairs (the war) on the tale. While for much of the text the Trojan War serves only as backdrop and as a vehicle for testing and proving Troilus's knighthood, it now becomes an integral part of the narrative. Troilus pushes himself out into this world with a wish for death and an end to the misery that love, that romance, has heaped upon him. With this shift in narrative space comes a change in the type of vision that dominates the text. As the narrator lists the ancient authors, he barely pauses to tell that "hym slough the fierse Achille" (5.1806). The narrative vision has backed away from the intricacies of the story and provides now only sweeping views of the epic and tragic action below.

This shift from the private, for which the opening books exploit enclosed spaces and images of the individual, expands Troilus's own spectrum of vision. Whereas before he was content only to look upon Criseyde's face, at this juncture he tries to take solace in the sight of her home, his only recourse. He says to Pandarus: "'As go we sen the palais of Criesyde; / For syn we yet may have namore feste, / So lat us sen hire paleys atte leeste'" (5.523–25). The desired vision has expanded outside the body to a more public image. Indeed, the barred-up house that Troilus sees becomes a reminder that the private sphere no longer belongs to him visually. This too sends him into a swoon, as Criseyde's actual image has throughout the love story (5.532). It also sets up an apostrophe to the palace, one that mocks the romance tradition by focusing on the image of the house rather than the female face and body. For the vision of Criseyde herself, Troilus can rely only on his memory.[32] His desire to see her is so great that as

---

[32] See 5.218–45 for Troilus's visual memory and his wondering who sees her now. At 5.565–81, he recounts the visual (and aural) memories that he has of Criseyde in various locations in Troy.

he and Pandarus look for her from atop the walls of Troy, Troilus thinks, in an optical or psychological illusion, that each passerby is Criseyde, his emotions vacillating all the while (5.1114–20).[33] His visual capacity is reduced as the romance slips away from his personal narrative. In his letter to her, shortly after seeing the brooch that she has given to Diomede, he claims that his eyes have become useless to him: " 'Myn eyen two, in veyn with which I se' " (5.1373). This shift in space, and the concomitant one in genre, renders Troilus's vision useless to him, because it is so rooted, trapped even, in the romance mode and in replicating the visual experience of seeing Criseyde.

This acute move from the visuality and the gendering that marked the first three books affords Chaucer the opportunity to force a nonromance genre reading on the text. In hopes that the tale can be read as anything but a romance, the narrator apostrophizes the poem in generic terms:

> Go, litel bok, go, litel myn tragedye,
> Ther God thi makere yet, er that he dye,
> So sende mygth to make in som comedye!
> But litel book, no makyng thow n'envie,
> But subgit be to all poesye;
> And kis the steppes where as thow seest pace
> Virgile, Ovide, Omer, Lucan, and Stace. (5.1786–92)

He applies the generic monikers and invokes these writers in an effort to effect a reflexive back-reading of the poem in nonromantic terms. However, Chaucer's inclusion of them betrays a conviction that perhaps the text will not be read as such. Elaine Hansen argues that this digression reveals clashes of love and literature, of gender and authorship.[34] For Chaucer, the strain on gender that romance vision causes cannot be corrected within the genre. Therefore, this quick and unconvincing scattering occurs as the poem reaches its final lines.

The final motion in what becomes this antiromantic treatise is Troilus's elevation to the heavens. Chaucer, departing from his Italian source, depicts his hero transcending worldly and romantic cares (5.1808–13). This indicates, according to McAlpine, that Troilus's narrative is a Boethian comedy.[35] This shift in plot, genre, and vision is Chaucer's effort to make a "fyn … for love" and a "fyn" for the gendered problems that love and romance yield (5.1828). Carolyn Dinshaw considers this a "turn away at last from the disruptive feminine toward orderly, hierarchical visions of divine love in which desire is finally put to rest."[36] Indeed, it seems an attempted negation of gender, romance, and vision, but the first thing

---

[33] For a discussion of this scene as a sign of movement outward to the public sphere, see Sarah Stanbury, "The Voyeur and the Private Life," pp. 141–58. For a discussion of this as a worldliness that compares to the final vision from the spheres, see Roy Pearcy, " 'And Nysus doughter song with fressh entente': Tragedy and Romance in *Troilus and Criseyde*," *SAC* 24 (2000): 269–97.

[34] Elaine Hansen, *Chaucer and the Fictions of Gender* (Berkeley: University of California Press, 1992), p. 177.

[35] Monica McAlpine, *The Genre of* Troilus and Criseyde, pp. 148–81.

[36] Carolyn Dinshaw, *Chaucer's Sexual Poetics* (Madison: University of Wisconsin Press, 1989), p. 39.

that Troilus does when he reaches his ultimate destination is to see ("saugh").[37]
What he sees, however, is a broad landscape of the world, whose genders and
genres no longer concern him. He sees himself and is not affected. The image
no longer wields power over him. His gaze does not actively project, but neither
does it passively react. The text does not here elaborate on the intricacies of
sightlines as the romance mode demands. Chaucer has thus extricated his hero
and his text from the gendered dangers of romance and vision. This addendum
to the text becomes the final blow to romance: its tropes and themes, and the
threats to masculinity which they produce, are finally negated by the conclusion to the text. The attentions of the characters, the narrator, the author, and
the audience have been refocused on other genres and consequently other, less
problematic, constructions of masculinity.

---

[37] Hansen considers this a point of gender redemption for Troilus (*Chaucer and the Fictions of Gender*,
p. 182).

10

Sutured Looks and Homoeroticism: Reading Troilus and Pandarus Cinematically

RICHARD E. ZEIKOWITZ

Over the years, scholars have commented on the close friendship between Troilus and Pandarus, some suggesting that there is something more or less "erotic" about their relationship.[1] In articulating the implied homoeroticism of this relationship, scholars have left one methodological resource largely untapped: namely, film theory. Key interactions between Troilus and Pandarus in Book 1 can be read cinematically to elucidate the link between homoerotically charged visual dynamics and masculinity. By delineating unnarrated visual acts, one not only highlights the homoeroticism underlying the protracted encounter in Troilus's bedchamber, but also finds the unstable power relations between the two friends. This problematizes the concept of the gazer as active / "masculine" and the object of the gaze as passive / "feminine."[2] I am using "homoeroticism" here to refer to moments of heightened sensual (not necessarily sexual or recip-rocal) attraction between intimate friends.[3] In Chaucer's text, these homoerotic

---

[1] Recent works that consider homoerotic elements in this relationship include Tison Pugh, "Queer Pandarus? Silence and Sexual Ambiguity in Chaucer's *Troilus and Criseyde*," *PQ* 80.1 (2001): 17–35 and Richard Zeikowitz, *Homoeroticism and Chivalry: Discourses of Male Same-Sex Desire in the Fourteenth Century* (New York: Palgrave, 2003). For studies on Troilus and Pandarus's friend-ship in terms of classical ideals of male friendship, see Timothy O'Brien, "Brother as Problem in the *Troilus*," *PQ* 82.2 (2003): 125–48; John Hill, "Aristocratic Friendship in *Troilus and Criseyde*: Pandarus, Courtly Love and Ciceronian Brotherhood in Troy," *New Readings of Chaucer's Poetry*, eds. Robert Benson and Susan Ridyard (Cambridge: D. S. Brewer, 2003), pp. 165–82; Robert Cook, "Chaucer's Pandarus and the Medieval Ideal of Friendship," *JEGP* 69 (1970): 407–24; and Alan Gaylord, "Friendship in Chaucer's *Troilus*," *ChauR* 3 (1968–69): 239–64.

[2] This bifurcation is most famously expressed by Laura Mulvey in her classic film theory text, "Visual Pleasure and Narrative Cinema": "In a world ordered by sexual imbalance, pleasure in looking has been split between active/male and passive/female. The determining male gaze projects its phantasm on to the female figure which is styled accordingly" (reprinted in *The Sexual Subject: A Screen Reader in Sexuality* [London: Routledge, 1992], 22–34, at p. 27). Many theorists have responded to Mulvey's claim. Studies on the objectified male figure in films include Earl Jackson, Jr., *Strategies of Deviance: Studies in Gay Male Representation* (Bloomington: Indiana University Press, 1995); Kaja Silverman, *Male Subjectivity at the Margins* (New York: Routledge, 1992); and Steven Cohan and Ina Rae Hark, eds. *Screening the Male: Exploring Masculinities in Hollywood Cinema* (London: Routledge, 1993). I draw on film theory to examine the objectified male in medieval chivalric texts in chapter 5 of *Homoeroticism and Chivalry*.

[3] The intimacy of this friendship is illustrated by Pandarus's sleeping in close proximity to Troilus in Troilus's bedchamber in Books 2 and 3, as well as Troilus's exuberant and affectionate display of gratitude to Pandarus for his help in courting Criseyde.

moments are inextricably linked with a disparity in the power one friend wields over the other. James Schultz rightly points out that "[t]he Middle Ages had no notion of sexual orientation,"[4] and thus I make no claim that either Pandarus or Troilus is "homosexual," "bisexual," or "heterosexual." However, these moments can be referred to, following Schultz's useful formulation, as "historical particulars," against which we can set a binary arbitration such as active/passive.[5] The sociohistorical particularity of homoeroticism, informed by fourteenth-century courtly society, is illustrated in specific scenes of intimate interactions between Troilus and Pandarus.

Alain Renoir was perhaps the first literary scholar to draw attention to the cinematic properties of a medieval text. In his reading of the challenge to Arthur's knights in *Sir Gawain and the Green Knight*, Renoir observes that

> [t]he technique of our poet is to draw a single detail out of a uniformly illuminated scene which is then allowed to fade out in obscurity and of which we may be given an occasional dim glimpse at psychologically appropriate moments.[6]

He draws a parallel with cinematic filming, "where the camera may at will focus either upon the whole scene or upon a single detail, while illumination may be used so as to keep the audience aware of the background against which the action takes place," and he notes that in the famous beheading scene, "[e]xactly as if the action were taking place on a screen before us, the field of vision is progressively narrowed from the entire Green Knight, to his head, and eventually to his neck alone."[7] G. W. Turner notes that

> [t]he camera has brought flexibility of point of view in modern works, but it revives a mobility that had once been part of the expectation of medieval listeners to stories. It can sometimes be a useful metaphor, therefore, to think of a medieval "camera."[8]

Ralph Elliott finds an example of this "medieval camera" in the "rapid transition from one episode to another" in the Old English poem *The Battle of Maldon*, which is analogous to that found in modern films:

> In *Maldon*, the technique is often that of the ... [movie]-camera, close-up one moment, long shot the next. Immediately after Byrhtnoth's dismounting among his *heor-werod* (body of household retainers) ... the camera points across the river where the Viking messenger stands ready to deliver his terms.[9]

---

4   James Schultz, "Heterosexuality as a Threat to Medieval Studies," *Journal of the History of Sexuality* 15.1 (2006): 14–29, at p. 21. See also his book, *Courtly Love, the Love of Courtliness, and the History of Sexuality* (Chicago, IL: University of Chicago Press, 2006).
5   James Schultz, "Heterosexuality as a Threat," p. 26.
6   Alain Renoir, "Descriptive Technique in *Sir Gawain and the Green Knight*," *Orbis litterarum* 13.1 (1958): 126–32, at p. 127.
7   Alain Renoir, "Descriptive Technique," pp. 127 and 129.
8   G. W. Turner, "Cinematic Effects in Medieval and Modern Narrative," *Southern Review* 27 (1994): 196–206, at p. 196.
9   Quoted in G. W. Turner, "Cinematic Effects," p. 196.

While these scholars draw parallels between film technique and medieval narrative, they do not examine how a cinematic reading of a scene illuminates interactions of characters. Sarah Stanbury, in a number of engaging studies, draws on film theory for articulating visual dynamics in medieval texts. She maintains that film theory "allow[s] us to examine the sight lines of visual desire within medieval culture and medieval texts."[10] In her study of the twelfth-century romance *Erec and Enide*, Stanbury describes how the two main characters' mutual gazing is aligned "with conventional social and literary practices." She argues that twentieth-century film theory can be applied to medieval courtly texts "to explore what we might call its sociology of vision."[11] Elsewhere, she refers to the "ocular logic" of spectators in a given scene, what they would see – even if their acts of vision are not narrated.[12] In the instance of Chaucer's *Troilus and Criseyde*, the narrator does not generally describe each character's line of vision during pivotal verbal interactions. Articulating the largely unnarrated "ocular logic" of the exchanges between Troilus and Pandarus in Book 1 not only affords a fuller reading of the scene but also teases out the subtle homoeroticism underlying their interaction.

A useful methodological tool for articulating the protracted encounter between the two friends is the film theory concept of *suture*. While suture is not a new concept for film theorists, it is a largely untapped resource for reading medieval texts rich in visual encounters between characters. Elizabeth Cowie notes that in film theory, suture, a term first proposed by Jacques-Alain Miller, describes "a process in which the viewer is stitched into, takes her or his place in the cinematic discourse."[13] Daniel Dayan, drawing on Jean-Pierre Oudart's seminal work, articulates the concept of suture in film. Dayan observes that in the single frame shot, "an image [is] designed and organized not merely as an object that is seen, but as the glance of a subject." He points out that "cinema regularly and systematically raises the question … 'Who is watching this?'"[14] While this question momentarily unsettles the spectator, the shot/reverse shot resolves this situation. Dayan delineates this mechanism as follows:

> The spectator's pleasure, dependent upon his identification with the visual field [in shot one], is interrupted when he perceives the frame. From this perception he infers the presence of the absent-one [i.e. the unseen being/ apparatus looking at what is before our eyes on the screen] and that other field from which the absent-one is looking [which we cannot see]. Shot two

10 Sarah Stanbury, "Feminist Film Theory: Seeing Chrétien's Enide," *Literature and Psychology* 36.4 (1990): 47–66, at p. 49. In addition to the works cited here, see Stanbury, "The Virgin's Gaze: Spectacle and Transgression in Middle English Lyrics of the Passion," *PMLA* 106 (1991): 1083–93 and "The Voyeur and the Private Life in *Troilus and Criseyde*," *SAC* 13 (1991): 141–58.

11 Sarah Stanbury, "Feminist Film Theory," pp. 57 and 53.

12 Sarah Stanbury, *Seeing the* Gawain-*Poet: Description and the Act of Perception* (Philadelphia: University of Pennsylvania Press, 1991), p. 99.

13 Elizabeth Cowie, *Representing the Woman: Cinema and Psychoanalysis* (Minneapolis: University of Minnesota Press, 1997), p. 115.

14 Daniel Dayan, "The Tutor-Code of Classical Cinema," *Film Theory and Criticism: Introductory Readings*, 5th edn., eds. Leo Braudy and Marshall Cohen (New York: Oxford University Press, 1999), 118–29, at p. 125.

reveals a character who is presented as the owner of the glance corresponding to shot one. That is, the character in shot two occupies the place of the absent-one corresponding to shot one. This character retrospectively transforms the absence emanating from shot one's other stage into a presence. ... The reverse shot has "sutured" the hole opened in the spectator's imaginary relationship with the filmic field by his perception of the absent-one.[15]

Suture thus links two halves of a visual interaction, whereby the observed in shot one is joined after the fact with the observer. Suture constrains the spectator to adopt the point of view of the camera apparatus (disguised as a character). Kaja Silverman describes the ideology of the system of the 180-degree rule: "[it] derives from the imperative that the camera deny its own existence as much as possible, fostering the illusion that what is shown has an autonomous exist-ence, independent of ... any coercive gaze."[16] She points out that the system of suture "link[s] ... [a spectator] to the gaze of a fictional character. Thus, a gaze within the fiction serves to conceal the controlling gaze outside the fiction."[17]

As we shall see in the interactions between Troilus and Pandarus in Book 1, the narrator does not indicate that he is reporting a character's visual point-of-view. The impression is that of a bodyless camera – an unseen observer outside the room – viewing and recording the scene. We are afforded a fuller and more accurate visual interaction, however, by suturing either Pandarus or Troilus in the position of the bodyless camera/narrator. By situating the gazer and the object of the gaze within the scene – reading a visual act as occurring between two characters – we can articulate better the erotically informed visual dynamics unfolding before us. As Valerie Traub points out, "[e]rotic arousal is always imbricated with power differences – it functions by means of exchanges, withholdings, struggles, negotiations."[18] We can examine shifting power rela-tions between Pandarus and Troilus by constructing and connecting shot/reverse shot, thus suturing looks.

A cinematic reading of Chaucer's text builds on medieval optical theory, which recognizes that the object of the gaze exerts itself on the observing eye. In theorizing the act of vision, ancient and medieval writers favored either intromission, whereby the observed object was thought to be a source of light that travels to the eye, or extromission, where the eye was said to emit a ray or power that reaches the light object, seizes it, and then returns to the eye.[19] Augustine describes the process as a combination of both:

---

15   Daniel Dayan, "The Tutor-Code," pp. 127–28.
16   Kaja Silverman, "On Suture," *Film Theory and Criticism: Introductory Readings*, 5th edn., eds. Leo Braudy and Marshall Cohen, 137–47, at p. 138. The "180-degree rule" means that the cinema viewer does not normally see the camera and thus never has a full 360-degree view of a scene.
17   Kaja Silverman, "On Suture," p. 140.
18   Valerie Traub, *Desire and Anxiety: Circulations of Sexuality in Shakespearean Drama* (London: Routledge, 1992), p. 104.
19   For an in-depth study of ancient and medieval theories of vision, see David Lindberg, *Theories of Vision from Al-Kindi to Kepler* (Chicago, IL: University of Chicago Press, 1976). See also Katherine Tachau, *Vision and Certitude in the Age of Ockham: Optics, Epistemology, and the Foundation of Semantics 1250–1345* (Leiden: Brill, 1988). For brief discussions, see N. Klassen, "Optical Allusions and Chaucerian Realism: Aspects of Sight in Late Medieval Thought and *Troilus and Criseyde,*"

The vision, therefore, is produced by the visible thing, but not by it alone, unless the one who sees is also present. Wherefore, vision is produced both by the visible thing and the one who sees, but in such a way that the sense of sight as well as the intention of seeing and beholding come from the one who sees, while that informing of the sense, which is called vision, is imprinted [on the seer] by the body alone that is seen, namely, by some visible thing.[20]

While delineating the active role both observer and observed play in a visual act, Augustine seems to privilege the visible object. He describes the content of sight – the "information" – touching the seeing subject, making an imprint. The object may thus affect or stimulate the observer, whereas the observer, although controlling the gaze, has no effect on the observed object.

Carolyn Collette points out that late medieval optical theory, while not discounting the effect of the observer on the observed object, also describes the viewed object as exerting power or influence on the viewer of the object. Thus, the visual act is articulated as "a dynamic interchange between viewer and viewed."[21] Roger Bacon, one of the major writers on optics in the thirteenth century, explains his theory of vision in some detail in his *Opus maius*. Central to Bacon's theory is the understanding that rays or "species" are emitted from the visible object in the form of a pyramid reaching the observer's eye as the apex of the pyramid.[22] The object and the viewing eye are thus linked together through the species emanating from the object. While Bacon subscribes to the theory of intromission, he identifies activity on the part of the observer. In fact, the observing eye exerts itself on the species emitted from the object:

The species of the things of the world are not suited to act immediately and fully in sight because of the nobility of the latter (i.e. the observing eye). Therefore these species (coming from the observed object) must be aided and excited by the species of the eye, which proceeds through the locale of the visual pyramid, altering and ennobling the medium and rendering it commensurate with sight; and thus it prepares for the approach of the species of the visible object (itself), so that it is altogether conformable and commensurate with the nobility of the animated body, i.e. the eye.[23]

There is thus a union of sorts between the species of the observing eye and the species reaching the eye from the observed object. This is also implied by John Pecham, an influential late medieval optical theorist, who notes that "the visible

---

Stanford Humanities Review 2.2–3 (1992): 129–46; and Carolyn Collette, *Species, Phantasms, and Images: Vision and Medieval Psychology in the* Canterbury Tales (Ann Arbor: University of Michigan Press, 2001).

20   Augustine, *The Trinity*, trans. Stephen McKenna (Washington, DC: Catholic University of America Press, 1963), p. 318. For an excellent discussion of Augustine's theory of vision, see Margaret Miles, "Vision: The Eye of the Body and the Eye of the Mind in Saint Augustine's *De trinitate* and *Confessions*," *Journal of Religion* 63 (1983): 125–42.

21   Carolyn Collette, *Species, Phantasms, and Images*, p. 14.

22   David Lindberg, *Theories of Vision*, p. 113.

23   Quoted and translated in David Lindberg, *Theories of Vision*, p. 115.

object is certified by a turning of the eye (all about) over the object."[24] Since the eye excites the incoming species, according to Bacon, the object eventually registered in the viewer's senses is presumably altered in some way by the viewer's eye. I pose the possibility that this alteration could be linked to the emotional state of the viewer or the viewer's attitude toward the object. Although a recording camera was unknown to medieval optical theorists, it is, in effect, an extension of the human eye: a camera cannot gaze without the eye behind it. Thus, by suturing the shot and reverse shot of a visual interaction between two characters in a text, the reader, like a camera, records and sees from the focal point of one of the characters at a particular moment and fills in what is not narrated.

In Chaucer's text, Pandarus becomes progressively excited – and desperate – as the object of his gaze resists him. In Bacon's terms, the species emitted from Troilus's reclining and resistant body that reaches Pandarus's eye elicits an emotionally charged response from Pandarus (which can be interpreted as an action by the observer on the observed in that Pandarus's emotional response is not inherent in the incoming species). This in turn generates another gaze from Pandarus to Troilus. Pandarus, the observer, is thus both active and passive in the visual scenario, affecting and effected by the object. Moreover, both Bacon and Pecham articulate the interaction – one can say a momentary commingling – of the observer and observed. Likewise, the film theory concept of "suture" links the camera/viewing character with the observed. Both theories maintain that the act of looking must involve contact between the viewing eye and the viewed object. The two parts of this interlinking relationship, however, do not necessarily exert equal influence in a visual act. As is evident in the interactions of Troilus and Pandarus, at alternate times the observer or the observed dominate. Within the unstable power dynamics between the two friends, one can perceive the homoeroticism underlying their encounter.

In Book 1, Troilus, who has fallen in love with Criseyde at first sight, laments his lovesick condition in the privacy of his bedchamber when Pandarus quietly enters the room:

> Bywayling in his chambre thus allone,
> A frend of his that called was Pandare
> Com oones in unwar, and herde hym groone,
> And say his frend in swich destresse and care. (1.547–50)

The absent-one/narrator, who is shooting Pandarus as he enters the room, merges with Pandarus at the end of the passage. Once Pandarus is in the room, the camera shoots over his shoulder, allowing the reader to see both Pandarus (his back at least) and his field of vision, namely, Troilus lying in bed, lamenting his misfortune. Pandarus's ocular logic – what he can see from his vantage point – in the interaction about to take place is established: he has an apparently unob-

---

[24] Quoted in David Lindberg, ed. and trans., *John Pecham and the Science of Optics: Perspectiva communis* (Madison: University of Wisconsin Press, 1970), pp. 30–31.

structed view of Troilus in bed. While it is not clear whether Troilus looks at his intruding friend, Pandarus is affected and, as we shall see, becomes increasingly stimulated by the object of his gaze. In fact, the camera/narrator focuses not on the object of Pandarus's gaze but rather on Pandarus's response to what he sees. Initially, Pandarus teases his friend, suggesting that Troilus is wallowing in self-pity because he is afraid of the Greeks. At the same time the narrator describes Pandarus musing over Troilus's reputation: "as fer as tonges spaken, / Ther nas a man of gretter hardinesse / Thanne he, ne more desired worthinesse" (1.565–67). Looking at Troilus prompts Pandarus to taunt playfully yet at the same time to admire his friend. Both acts may be read as expressing affection and desire for Troilus. The text thus illustrates a complete visual act and the effects of that act on the gazer without indicating whether the object of the gaze looks back.

The scene playing out in Troilus's bedchamber can be fleshed out more fully by articulating the ocular logic of the characters. Who is watching Pandarus's response to the object of his gaze? Since Troilus is established in Pandarus's field of vision, he has replaced the absent-one/narrator. If Pandarus faces Troilus as he addresses him, then it is visually logical that the reverse shot is from Troilus's vantage point, whether or not Troilus actually looks at Pandarus. In keeping the lines of sight vague, the narrative underplays the visual dynamics of the scene. The attentive reader, however, rather than aligning with the narrator/absent-one outside the room, in effect repositions the camera, placing it inside the room, viewing only what each character sees. Troilus's response to Pandarus, "'What cas ... or what aventure / Hath gided the to sen me langwisshinge'" (1.568–69), confirms that he is both the object of Pandarus's gaze and the vantage point for the camera's previous and further study of Pandarus's reaction to seeing Troilus.

The narrative camera/eye continues to focus on Pandarus's response to Troilus and not on Troilus himself.[25] Pandarus becomes increasingly motivated to know Troilus's secret. We can examine the emotional dynamics of the scene by maintaining Troilus as the recording eye's vantage point: two friends in a bedchamber, one withholding intimate information, the other determined to extract that information. We can capture the intimacy of the scene by studying Pandarus's following speech from Troilus's position in the room:

> "Allas, what may this be?
> Now frend ... if evere love or trouthe
> Hath ben, or is, bitwixen the and me,
> Ne do thow nevere swich a crueltee
> To hiden fro thi frend so gret a care!
> Wostow naught wel that it am I, Pandare?" (1.583–88).

---

[25] Molly Martin notes that Troilus's active gaze is made passive by the object of his gaze, Criseyde, in Book 1 ("Troilus's Gaze," this volume, pp. 135–39). Similarly, Pandarus's active, probing gaze here is temporarily "de-masculinized" and rendered ineffective because of the resistance of the object of his gaze, Troilus.

Pandarus continues to use his love for Troilus as a persuasive ploy: "'I have, and shal, for trewe or fals report, / In wrong and right iloved the al my lyve: / Hid nat thi wo fro me, but telle it blyve'" (1.593–95). Although the object pronoun in each line ("the," "thow," "thi," "wostow," etc.) suggests that Pandarus addresses Troilus/the camera, Troilus's response confirms, after the fact, that the camera was shooting Pandarus from Troilus's position. And Troilus's response to Pandarus, telling him that he has fallen victim to love but withholding the name of the lady, is a result of Pandarus's emotionally charged rhetoric. By following the ostensible narrative rather than the ocular logic of the scene – that is, keeping the narrator/camera outside of the room and thus separate from Troilus – one cannot capture the heightened intimacy of the scene, which continues to build until Pandarus wrests all of Troilus's secret from him.

Pandarus relentlessly pursues this information, badgering, cajoling, and begging Troilus to reveal to him the identity of the lady with whom he has fallen in love; however, for sixty-two lines, Troilus remains silent. One can perhaps forget that he is still in the room and that he is the object of Pandarus's investigative gaze. Yet the text offers clues periodically that Troilus is indeed the object Pandarus addresses and thus we repeatedly perform an act of suture, stitching up the hole, the absent-object between clues. "[W]ithin the system of suture," Dayan points out, "the absent-one represents the fact that no shot can constitute by itself a complete statement. The absent-one stands for that which any shot necessarily lacks in order to attain meaning: another shot."[26] This aspect of the mechanism of suture is well illustrated in Chaucer's text. The following lines prompt the reader to complete the visual interaction:

> "And yet, peraunter, kan I reden the" (1.668)
> "... I shal nevere mo discoveren the" (1.675)
> "... as frend, fullich in me assure,
> And tel me plat what is th'enchesoun
> And final cause of wo that ye endure" (1.680–82)
> "... tel me, if the liste" (1.693)
> "Lat be thy wepyng and thi drerynesse
> And lat us lissen wo with oother speche" (1.701–2)
> "For bothe thow and I of love we pleyne" (1.711)
> And sith I am he that thow trustest moost,
> Tel me somwhat, syn al my wo thow woost" (1.720–21)

These prompts are not merely a litany of object pronouns without reference to a body. Rather, they represent someone who holds power over the speaker, denying him the information he seeks, someone who insists on enduring his "wo" privately and needs to be convinced that his secret will be safe once the speaker knows it. Moreover, he is someone very close to the speaker – a friend who apparently trusts him more than anyone else. Finally, the narrative clears up the ambiguity by indicating that Troilus is the object of Pandarus's speech: "Troilus for al this no word seyde, / But longe he ley as stylle as he

[26] Daniel Dayan, "The Tutor-Code," p. 128.

ded were" (1.722–23). Thus, two processes occur: during Pandarus's sixty-two-line address, the reader uses periodic prompts to suture tentatively the absent-object who is being addressed; at the end of the monologue, the reader then definitively sutures the absent-object who heard "al this." Suturing Troilus as the absent-object here establishes a continuum of intimacy between the two men that begins with Pandarus's entering Troilus's bedchamber and concludes 500 lines later. Because the text periodically calls to mind that Pandarus is not wresting a secret from a narrative void but rather from his prostrate and hence vulnerable friend, one is enabled to appreciate how the interaction builds towards an erotically charged climax.

While this scene ostensibly positions Pandarus as an aggressive, "masculine" interrogator, manipulator, or, as some have argued, an extremely sympathetic and caring "physician," and Troilus as a helpless, passive, "feminine" victim of both lovesickness and Pandarus's relentless badgering, I suggest the power relations are not so clearly drawn.[27] Troilus's responses and criticism of Pandarus not only remind us that he is after all a valorous prince who is highly regarded for his prowess but also the *active* object of Pandarus's gaze. Particularly in the context of medieval chivalry, the object of the gaze is not necessarily passive. Stanbury's rebuke of some film theorists' bifurcation of spectatorship into active/male and passive/female positions is relevant here. She asks:

> Since the very concept of a "phallic gaze" emerges from a regime of the visual that splits vision as male and the object of the gaze as paradigmatically female, can we speak of a "phallic gaze" in medieval representations – if the central body in that system of representation is not female at all?[28]

The power relations in the visual act described above are even more complicated because Troilus is both recipient and recorder of Pandarus's words, whether or not he actually looks at Pandarus. He is the camera through which the reader observes Pandarus. Troilus/camera thus objectifies Pandarus – who, unlike Troilus, is not celebrated as a knight of great prowess – rendering him less controlling, less masculine/active. Yet in this scene Pandarus also wields power and influence over Troilus through his relentless badgering and coaxing. By paying attention to the unnarrated lines of sight and suturing a character into the recording eye's position, readers can glean the unstable, shifting positions of control between the two friends. Within this alternating power differential, one can glean the homoeroticism at play.

After Pandarus's cry, "'Awake!'" (1.729), Troilus dismisses his friend's efforts, exclaiming that Pandarus is powerless to "save" him. Analyzing this interaction from both vantage points highlights each friend's competing desire

---

[27] For studies of Pandarus's role as healer, see Martin Camargo, "The Consolation of Pandarus," *ChauR* 25 (1991): 214–28 and Mary Wack, "Pandarus, Poetry, and Healing," *SAC, Proceedings* 2 (1986): 127–33.

[28] Sarah Stanbury, "Regimes of the Visual in Premodern England: Gaze, Body, and Chaucer's *Clerk's Tale*," *New Literary History* 28 (1997): 261–89, at p. 261.

to dominate the other. Troilus first reminds Pandarus that, although lying still, he is alive, alert, and comprehending:

> "Frend, though that I stylle lye,
> I am nat deef. Now pees, and crye namore,
> For I have herd thi wordes and thi lore;
> But suffre me my meschief to bywaille,
> For thy proverbes may me naught availle." (1.752–56).

He goes on to order Pandarus: "'Lat be thyne olde ensaumples'" (1.760). Pandarus counters with a defiant "No" and proceeds to reprimand Troilus for his foolishness in disregarding his (Pandarus's) demands to reveal the source of his pain: "'Swych is delit of foles to bywepe / Hire wo, but seken bote they ne kepe'" (1.762–63). Troilus nevertheless attempts to maintain control over his secret, telling Pandarus that he would never succeed in solving Troilus's dilemma (1.773–74). Pandarus's frustration with Troilus is evidenced in his further denigration of Troilus's resistance: "'But oones nyltow, for thy coward herte, / And for thyn ire and folissh wilfulnesse, / For wantrust, tellen of thy sorwes smerte'" (1.792–94). Viewing this scene cinematically in alternating shots, suturing Pandarus and Troilus sequentially as the absent-one/camera gazing at the other, highlights the power struggle between the two. Pandarus/camera sees Troilus's defiant, stubborn resistance and lack of confidence in Pandarus's abilities; Troilus/camera registers Pandarus's increasing frustration and anger at his friend's stubborn resistance. Despite the fact that there are no explicit narrative descriptions of each character's facial expression or line of sight, Chaucer's text nevertheless provides a cinematic scenario of an emotionally charged dialogue playing out in a confined space. The reader needs only to connect the looks.

After trying different tactics, Pandarus ultimately uses soothing words of promised requited love to wear down Troilus's resistance and bring him closer to his grasp. He persuades Troilus of the need to make his love known to the lady in question, offering a tempting picture of a lover who pleasurably serves his "deere hertes queene" (1.817). At last, Troilus succumbs: "Of that word took hede Troilus, / And thoughte anon what folie he was inne, / And how that soth hym seyde Pandarus" (1.820–22). Pandarus's tactic reveals a key component of seduction, namely, the promise of pleasure cloaked in the formal language of chivalric oaths, and he offers this pleasure to Troilus: "'And have my trouthe, but thow it fynde so / I be thi boote, er that it be ful longe'" (1.831–32). The seduction is, however, not yet successful. Pandarus needs to take a more physical approach.

Pandarus insists that Troilus reveal his "wownde" (1.858), by which act Troilus would not only expose his carefully guarded secret but also leave himself vulnerable to Pandarus's "healing" technique. Given their respective active and passive roles throughout this scene, Pandarus's positioning himself as a healer about to take some action on Troilus's body has homoerotic associations. Pandarus badgers Troilus into letting him see his wound: "'Look up, I seye, and telle me [who] she is / Anon, that I may gon about thy nede'" (1.862–63). He persists:

"'Knowe ich hire?'" (1.864). His words elicit a physical response from Troilus: "Tho gan the veyne of Troilus to blede, / For he was hit, and wax al reed for shame" (1.866–67). This brief passage offers a step-by-step illustration of a seduction about to be successfully performed. Pandarus begins by insisting that Troilus look at him. With the eyes of his "patient" focused on him, he makes a tempting offer to take care of his "nede." Given that Troilus's "nedes" are sexually informed, Pandarus's promise eroticizes the moment. Having secured Troilus's gaze, Pandarus pushes further, adding the incentive of offering his love if Troilus reveals the lady's identity. Troilus's blush is certainly in part a reaction to Pandarus's stumbling so near the truth (for the lady in question is his niece, Criseyde); however, it is also an indication of the heightened eroticism between the seducer and his object. Troilus's eyes are evidently focused on Pandarus as he closes in on his secret. Pandarus's excited reaction to Troilus's blush, "'A ha! ... Here bygynneth game'" (1.868), paves the way for his final maneuver. He does not wait for Troilus to reveal his "wownde"; instead, "with that word he gan hym for to shake, / And seyde, 'Thef, thow shalt hyre name telle'" (1.869–70). Pandarus's seductive power building up over the last 240 lines – many of which are addressed to an ostensibly absent-object – reaches its climax in an expression of physical force, and Troilus at last succumbs, trembling, as he reveals Criseyde's name (1.871–74).

Pandarus's seduction involves manipulating Troilus into confessing an erotically charged secret. Foucault's observations on the play of desire in the act of confession are useful for examining the underlying homoeroticism in this scene. In the first volume of his *History of Sexuality*, Foucault notes that "[o]ne confesses – or is forced to confess. When it is not spontaneous or dictated by some internal imperative, the confession is wrung from a person by violence or threat." He then describes the intermingling of pleasure and power:

> Pleasure . . . comes of exercising a power that questions, monitors, watches, spies, searches out, palpates, brings to light; and on the other hand, pleasure ... kindles at having to evade this power, flee from it, fool it, or travesty it. ... [P]ower ... lets itself be invaded by the pleasure it is pursuing; and opposite it, power assert[s] ... itself in the pleasure of showing off, scandalizing, or resisting.[29]

Like Foucault's inquisitor, Pandarus questions, "searches out" the truth of Troilus's secret love. His excited exclamation, "'A ha! ... Here bygynneth game'" (1.868), illustrates that he derives pleasure from wringing out Troilus's sexually related confession. After Troilus gives in enough to ask Pandarus what he should do (1.828), might his continued resistance (he does not name Criseyde until 1.874) be informed by pleasure – pleasure in keeping his friend/examiner in the dark? While Troilus is indeed the passive partner in this homoerotically inflected confession scenario – Pandarus is invading Troilus's private space – we see suggestions that Troilus might enjoy his position. For as long as he with-

---

[29] Michel Foucault, *The History of Sexuality, Vol. 1: An Introduction*, trans. Robert Hurley (1978; New York: Vintage, 1990), pp. 59 and 45.

holds information that Pandarus seeks, Troilus, from his prostrate position in bed, wields power over his friend. By fleshing out the ocular logic of the scene, we can be attentive to Troilus's active role in the interaction. He would "logically" see Pandarus becoming increasingly desperate to have the pleasure of this knowledge. Even if Troilus does not look at Pandarus, "species" would be emitted from him, reaching Pandarus's inquisitive eye. Medieval optical theory recognizes the union between the incoming species and the observing eye. As reflected in Bacon's and Pecham's terminology, Pandarus's eye attempts to render the viewed object "commensurate with sight," "turning the eye all over the object." Yet, the object – knowledge of Troilus's secret – resists the efforts of Pandarus's eye to *see* it. In this act of visual intimacy, might Troilus's resistance, wittingly or not, be in part playful and teasing?

After Pandarus makes his exaggerated oath to be Troilus's "'boote, er that it be ful longe, / To pieces do me drawe and sithen honge!'" (1.832–33), Troilus nevertheless is not convinced Pandarus can actually help: "'Ful hard were it to helpen in this cas'" (1.836). The text suggests that Troilus is not looking at Pandarus, but the camera, shooting "over the shoulder" from Troilus's vantage point, records Pandarus's final campaign to wrest Troilus's secret. That Troilus asks for Pandarus's advice (1.828) yet continues to resist him highlights Troilus's teasingly resistant hold over Pandarus. Pandarus becomes so desperate that he orders Troilus to look at him (1.862), and having secured Troilus's gaze, observes Troilus's blush and ultimately physically shakes the secret out of him.

Troilus's capitulation stabilizes the masculinity of the two friends in respect to each other. Troilus no longer exerts power over his friend by resisting him from a weak position in bed. Pandarus dictates to Troilus the actions he must now take, and he no longer needs to convince Troilus to accept his advice. One may forget that during Pandarus's subsequent long speech to Troilus of his plans to help, Troilus is being addressed, and he is the point of view through which the reader hears/sees Pandarus. The text sutures this interaction after the fact:

> Whan Troilus hadde herd Pandare assented
> To ben his help in lovyng of Cryseyde
> Weex of his wo, as who seith, untormented,
> But hotter weex his love, and thus he seyde,
> With sobre chere, although his herte pleyde:
> "Now blisful Venus helpe, er that I sterve,
> Of the, Pandare, I mowe som thank deserve." (1.1009–15)

By making this visual connection, Troilus's homoerotically inflected gratitude becomes evident. Charged with his "hotly" growing love, Troilus turns not to an image of Criseyde but rather to Pandarus, wishing to bring him into a similar erotically blissful state. This places Troilus again in a position of power. He is not merely the malleable love-victim whom Pandarus will help, but also someone who might be capable of providing Pandarus with the same pleasure. They thus both prove to be masculine in the intimacy of Troilus's bedchamber. Yet Troilus's pronouncement is focused on a vague future action while Pandarus's accomplishment has actually occurred.

Applying the film theory concept of suture to a reading of Chaucer's *Troilus and Criseyde* and, more specifically, to the articulation of homoerotically charged currents underlying the protracted encounter between Troilus and Pandarus in Book 1, enriches the narrative. Connecting the gazes of the two friends in the scene played out in Troilus's bedchamber, keeping the lines of vision exclusively in the room, builds on medieval concepts of visual acts. Every look has two components – even when not explicitly narrated. While suture, when operating within film, according to Silverman, "serves to conceal the controlling gaze outside the fiction,"[30] thus suggesting the imposing of restrictions on meaning, it has the opposite effect in Chaucer's text. Positioning one of the characters as the unnarrated gazer or object of the gaze allows for a reading more complete than that ostensibly offered yet one still remaining true to the text. The struggle waged between Pandarus and Troilus, each one asserting his will on the other – one resisting, the other persuading – is clearly laid out, but without connecting the lines of sight one can at times forget that they are not being addressed to open space. Moreover, recognizing both parts of these visual encounters highlights the interrelationship of looking, dominance, and (homo)eroticism with neither the gazer nor the object of the gaze occupying a stable active or passive position. Pandarus's ultimate, erotically charged domination of Troilus is best appreciated through examining the series of visual interactions that lead up to Troilus's capitulation.

Continuing this method of reading through Books 2 and 3 highlights the homosocial love story between Pandarus and Troilus that is developing parallel to the love story of Troilus and Criseyde. By articulating the unnarrated optical logic and suturing looks in regard to Troilus and Pandarus in the scenes of intimacy occurring in the dark seclusion of Troilus's bedchamber as well as in the scene prior to Troilus and Criseyde's consummation, one can discern the homoeroticism underlying Pandarus's contact with Troilus. One thus needs to keep the recording eye within the room and in the hands of the characters.

---

[30]   Kaja Silverman, "On Suture," p. 140.

11

Being a Man in *Piers Plowman*
and *Troilus and Criseyde*

Critics are increasingly studying Chaucer and Langland together, since, as textual scholarship reveals ever more comprehensively, the poets were sometimes copied by the same scribes and in the same workshops and manuscripts.[2] A critical separation between the *Canterbury Tales* and *Piers Plowman* is ever being bridged, and Chaucer and Langland are coming to be seen as London poets deeply engaged in the religious and social issues of their day. However, less work has been done to bridge the larger divide between *Troilus and Criseyde* and *Piers Plowman*.[3] Why is there such a critical chasm between these two poems, despite the cultural and textual evidence of their connections? For one, the poems, as presented to modern eyes in modern editions, are very different in genre, aesthetics, and poetics and seem to emerge from distinct sensibilities. *Troilus and Criseyde*, for example, coming from a definitive Continental source, is very Italian, a descriptor seldom applied to *Piers Plowman*. The poems also

---

[1] This essay is dedicated to Melissa Fu.
[2] On the two poets see George Kane, *Chaucer and Langland: Historical and Textual Approaches* (London: Athlone Press, 1989); David Aers, *Chaucer, Langland and the Creative Imagination* (London: Routledge, 1980); John Bowers, "Two Professional Readers of Chaucer and Langland," *SAC* 26 (2004): 113–46; and George Economou, "Chaucer and Langland: A Fellowship of Makers," *Reading Medieval Culture*, eds. Robert Stein and Sandra Prior (Notre Dame, IN: University of Notre Dame Press, 2005), pp. 290–301. Lynn Staley's chapter "Chaucer and the Postures of Sanctity," in David Aers and Lynn Staley, *The Powers of the Holy: Religion, Politics, and Gender in Late Medieval English Culture* (University Park: Pennsylvania State University Press, 1996), pp. 179–259, associates the *Canterbury Tales* and *Piers Plowman*: "The struggle Langland's work reveals between a Pentacostal utopian vision and the sight of actual institutions compromised by a mercantilist ethic and a punitive conception of justice may well have set the terms for Chaucer's lifelong exploration of the components of community" (p. 180). Central to the recent work is Simon Horobin and Linne Mooney, "A *Piers Plowman* Manuscript by the Hengwrt/Ellesmere Scribe and Its Implications for London Standard English," *SAC* 26 (2004): 65–112, attributing MS Trinity College Cambridge B 15.17 to the scribe elsewhere identified by Mooney as Adam Pinkhurst ("Chaucer's Scribe," *Speculum* 81.1 [2006]: 97–138). A major study of the two authors, John Bowers, *Chaucer and Langland: The Antagonistic Tradition* (Notre Dame, IN: University of Notre Dame Press), 2007, was published after this essay went to press.
[3] A prominent exception is Marion Turner, "*Troilus and Criseyde* and the 'Treacherous Alderman' of 1382," *SAC* 25 (2003): 225–57, which, although it does not address *Piers Plowman* specifically, relates the history of the "treacherous aldermen" accused falsely of admitting rebels into the city during the Revolt of 1381 to the instances of treachery in *Troilus and Criseyde*.

engage with different types of love, and *fin amour* or even basic gender issues, which dominate studies of *Troilus and Criseyde*, were, until recently, only obliquely addressed by students of *Piers Plowman*, so much so that a *Yearbook of Langland Studies* special section was convened to encourage feminist scholarship on the poem.[4]

I would like to contribute to the burgeoning criticism on Chaucer and Langland by considering their poems together as strangely parallel stories of men, Troilus and Will, journeying, questing, and suffering as men in search of truth. Masculinity studies can help us relate the experiences of two characters who have dominated our attention in these colossal texts of English medieval fiction but whose names are seldom heard in the same sentence. Both poets knew that every role, every desire, and all the pressures and obligations of public manhood cannot be divorced from simply "being" male. They therefore use the male bodies of their heroes to explore, through loss and renewal, the nature of Christian civic and personal life.

We are accustomed to lavishing gendered attention on Troilus, who has often been studied as a body, sighing, swooning, stripped, and otherwise dragged into the first night of sexual bliss with his lady.[5] But Langland too tells the story of a male body and its place in the larger civic and spiritual communities it looks to for guidance and salvation.[6] Men are often in a double bind: Nature tells the body what to want and what to do, while performance pressures dominate both private and public relationships and responsibilities. Performance demands an erection, and erections play important roles in both poems.[7] Troilus struggles to achieve one, and yet when his prowess in the bedroom is no longer of use to Criseyde, he dies. When Will can perform no longer, his wife wants him dead

---

4   See the "Special Section: Gender in *Piers Plowman*," *YLS* 12 (1998): 1–152. In regard to *Piers Plowman* and gender, Colette Murphy, "Lady Holy Church and Meed the Maid: Re-envisioning Female Personifications in *Piers Plowman*," *Feminist Readings in Middle English Literature*, eds. Ruth Evans and Lesley Johnson (London: Routledge, 1994), pp. 140–64, notes that it is "high time for issues of sexual politics and gender representation to be incorporated into the field of Langland criticism" (p. 141).

5   On Troilus's fainting, see Gretchen Mieszkowski's essay in this volume, pp. 43ff.

6   That Langland is interested in the realities of the body has recently been explored by Jill Mann, "The Nature of Need Revisited," *YLS* 18: (2004): 3–30. Ralph Hanna also traces one of Will's distinctly gendered biographies, "germane to the issue of being constructed as a Real Man, an antifeminist" (p. 213), exploring how various episodes about schooling and encounters with teachers (often female) in the poem reflect the historical process in elementary education of "get[ting] your book-tools only by giving up your anatomical 'tool,' your maleness" (p. 215); see his "School and Scorn: Gender in *Piers Plowman*," *New Medieval Literatures* 3 (1999): 213–27. Masha Raskolnikov traces how the poem "struggle[s] with its own desire to exclude the feminine," as Langland "gradually disentangles himself from ... female personifications" to explore the "silence of the soul in communion with itself, a silence broken only by the monologue of man communing his own male self" ("Promising the Female, Delivering the Male: Transformations of Gender in *Piers Plowman*," *YLS* 19 [2005]: 81–105, at p. 105).

7   While I study the sexual demands that define performance and usefulness, John Bowers, in this collection, examines the culturally situated dynastic imperatives that lie behind that performance in the text: "The Trojan hero's neglect for begetting heirs, shadowed by the specter of male impotence, haunts Chaucer's *Troilus and Criseyde*" (p. 12).

as well.[8] In both poems, when the mortal body fails, the metasexual humanity of Christ provides grace and spiritual comfort – for the reader if not for the dead pagan Troilus or the alienated Will. Christ offers not only relief from temporal objects of love but also liberation from the flawed male body in favor of His own, which is, *in deitate Patris*, however battle-worn from jousting in Piers's arms, the only hope for a man rejected and dejected for his earthly impotencies.[9]

How else may we link Will and Troilus? Both men are committed to "truth," but as they seek it, they encounter figures whose conception of that treasure is situational. Troilus is undone by a woman who has mastered the sexual economy better than he has and by an expedient councilor who does not share or understand his sense of truth, best understood as fidelity and loyalty.[10] "'This town is ful of ladys all aboute'" (4.401), says Pandarus, who cannot understand why Troilus will not just go out and get another girl. Will's search for the truth embodied in Piers, in Holy Church, and in the redemption of Christ is undone by the intrusive friars, and by Lady Meed and her minions among the vices and the field of folk; she is the grand mistress of all economies and the enemy of truth in all forms. Will's trust in truth as a reflection of fidelity and civic integrity profits him meagerly in the experiential world of Meed, a world of profiteering and trade that reduces all social and spiritual relationships to forms of "winning" and advantage. It may be akin to the game of "racket to and fro" that Troilus says he will not play with truth and love: he cannot employ a

---

8   Although we tend not to think about sex in *Piers Plowman*, Teresa Tavormina, *Kindly Similitude: Marriage and Family in* Piers Plowman (Cambridge: D. S. Brewer, 1995), underlines its importance in the poem: "The sexual and procreative dimension of human life is not as central to Langland's poem as, say, truth or faith or the reformation of the will, but its nearly universal influence, its affective force, and its potential for good or evil all combine to make it a significant factor in the well-lived life of ordinary Christians" (p. 185).

9   Consider the imagery in *Piers Plowman* at B.1.148–58 when Holy Church describes the Incarnation as a divinely natural act of love, the plant of peace that grows heavy and dips down to earth, as studied by J. V. Crewe, "Langland's Vision of Society," *Theoria* 39 (1973): 1–16. This image of redemptive procreativity establishes in the poem an idealized standard that looms over Will's bodily and sexual biography. The movement here is also akin to the dynamic tension identified throughout the poem recently by Nicolette Zeeman (Piers Plowman *and the Medieval Discourse of Desire* [Cambridge: Cambridge University Press, 2006, p. 18]), as the "reiterative experiences of failure, rebuke and loss" that inspire new desires and move the narrative and the dreamer ever forward to spiritual renewal.

10   The *MED*, s.v. *Treuth*, prefaces its definitions with the following statement: "Freq[uently] a specific gloss entails or implies yet another; it would be misleading to suggest that the assignment of a quot[ation] to a sense excludes other glosses. The complex meanings of 'treuth' in such texts as *Piers Plowman* are more a matter of literary than lexicographical analysis; for this, the reader is referred to specific commentaries on these texts." In this spirit, I list here but a few of the various interlocking meanings operative in *Troilus and Criseyde* and *Piers Plowman*: 1(a) Fidelity to one's country, kin, friends, etc.; loyalty; allegiance; also, genuine friendship; also, faithfulness; (b) fidelity or constancy in love; 2(a) A promise; an undertaking; a commitment; a pledge of loyalty; 4(a) Honesty in the conduct of one's business, work, etc.; the practice of honesty in one's occupation; 6(a) Divine righteousness, esp. as reified as that which governs creation; also, the righteousness attributed to God's actions; (b) character or behavior that conforms to religious or divine standards, righteousness, holiness; goodness; purity. See Richard Green, *A Crisis of Truth: Literature and Law in Ricardian England* (Philadelphia: University of Pennsylvania Press, 1999). On Troilus's allegiance to truth in a world of rhetoric and deception, see my *Chaucer's Ovidian Arts of Love* (Gainesville: University Press of Florida, 1994), pp. 33–80, passim.

doctrine of exchange when it comes to love, and he accepts no substitute, no replacement of equal value. And yet it is "exchange" that devastates Troilus while profiting Criseyde, who attains her survival through an exchange and by mastering that game of "to and fro." A prisoner exchange, a change of heart, an exchange of lovers, a change from "weel to wo": this economy serves Criseyde well, while Troilus lies spent and bankrupt. Our two heroes thus are both loners, locked in rhetorical and philosophical battle with all they meet and out of step with the values around them. And however different the armies, in each poem's finale, both men are besieged by violent forces. When Achilles kills Troilus, he relocates his fruitless stewardship of truth, in death, to a plane where it can flourish, at least for a moment of insight.[11] In *Piers Plowman*, Pride so corrupts Holy Church that Will, if we can equate his hope with the pilgrimage begun by Conscience, must relocate as well, searching for Truth somewhere away from the field of folk, Langland's version of that "litel spot of erthe," where fidelity is profaned. Chaucer and Langland have constructed quests, social and philo-sophical journeys toward truth, where each man, beset by various forms of moral corruption, strives while his city, Troy or London, weighs heavily about him and his hopes.

As a Trojan, Troilus is an "ancestor" of the English Will, if we take the English foundation myths seriously. The quests of these distant brothers, and the fates of Old and New Troy, separated by hundreds of years (or rather by around a dozen), are mired in disillusionment and alienation. Marion Turner associates the two cities in her discussion of the 1381 Peasants' Revolt, seeing *Troilus and Criseyde* as "another text of the 1380s concerned with a city destroyed through internal corruption and betrayal."[12] Josephine Bloomfield connects Chaucer's setting to his historical reality in arguing that "Troy's goals are as wrongheaded and destructive to its people as were those of the rulers of Chaucer's fourteenth-century England," made apparent in a "war that by the time of the composi-tion of the *Troilus* had lasted four times as long as the Trojan war."[13] In these connections between Troy and London, Troilus becomes a microcosm for his city. Sealy Gilles reads him as a diseased body, that, "like the body of Troy, is invaded and overcome."[14] "The microcosm," continue Gilles, "takes on a new extended valence. It expands to embrace the agonistic dynamics of the larger world." Gilles's analysis of "troubled bodies in a besieged town" can apply as well to Will and thus helps us associate the two men, however differently dressed in historical time, as exemplars of the same microcosmic but no less physically real manhood.[15] As Vance Smith puts it, what sets that male body

---

[11] Tison Pugh, "Christian Revelation and the Cruel Game of Courtly Love in *Troilus and Criseyde*," *ChauR* 39 (2005): 379–401, notes that Troilus's death brings only "momentary Christian revelation to a pagan afterlife;" "the play of Christianity," he continues, "asserts hope yet does not fully deliver it in this ultimately pagan setting" (p. 397).

[12] Marion Turner, "Treacherous Alderman," p. 234.

[13] Josephine Bloomfield, "Chaucer and the Polis: Piety and Desire in the *Troilus and Criseyde*," *MP* 94.3 (1997): 291–304, at p. 291.

[14] Sealy Gilles, "Love and Disease in Chaucer's *Troilus and Criseyde*," *SAC* 25 (2003): 157–97, at p. 168.

[15] Sealy Gilles, "Love and Disease," pp. 170 and 171.

"apart from the female body is its involvement in the productivity of the world," a result of which is that "its labor is never finished."[16] Troilus may emblemize restless human "desire," seeking truth in *amor falsa*, while Will keeps one foot in allegory as he pursues truth in societal "commune profit." But allegory and universality cannot protect the men from living, desiring, and suffering as men, in both public and private regimes of manhood.[17]

Being a Man in Piers Plowman

This becomes apparent in the autobiographical C-text additions, when Reason interrogates Will about his work and social usefulness. Will must make a case for himself that his labors, though not physical and agricultural (he is no Piers Plowman), are of value. Reason lets him off with a warning as long as he will shape a "lyif that is louable and leele to thy soule" (C.5.103).[18] The episode reveals that Langland could not keep the issue of public masculinity out of the poem and that every Christian man, subject to rigorous testing and endless judgment, must justify his function in society:

> "Can thow seruen," he sayde, "or syngen in a churche,
> Or koke for my cokeres or to the cart piche,
> Mowen or mywen or make bond to sheues,
> Repe or been a rypereue and aryse erly,
> Or haue a horn and be hayward and lygge theroute nyhtes
> And kepe my corn in my croft fro pykares and theues?"
>
> (C.5.11–16)

The exhaustive and exhausting list continues with other "kynes craft that to the comune nedeth" (C.5.20), and the gangly Will finally defends himself against the charge of idleness by describing his service as a clerk at large. While acknowledging that he has also "ytynt tyme and tyme myspened" (C.5.93) (we presume with his life's work, the poems themselves), he promises to turn all of

---

16 Vance Smith, "Body Doubles: Producing the Masculine *Corpus*," *BMMA*, 3–19, at p. 5. "Like the world," Smith continues, "the male body is a *discordia concors* that resists resolution, and that requires continual exertion" (p. 6).

17 On allegory and gender in *Piers Plowman*, see Helen Cooper, "Gender and Personification in *Piers Plowman*," *YLS* 5 (1991): 31–48; James Paxson, "Gender Personified, Personification Gendered, and the Body Figuralized in *Piers Plowman*," *YLS* 12 (1998): 65–96, and his "Inventing the Subject and the Personification of Will in *Piers Plowman*: Rhetorical, Erotic, and Ideological Origins and Limits in Langland's Allegorical Poetics," *William Langland's* Piers Plowman: *A Book of Essays*, ed. Kathleen Hewett-Smith (New York: Routledge, 2001), pp. 195–231. Paxson's essays respond to Cooper's study of the "maleness" of Will and of Langland himself.

18 William Langland, *Piers Plowman: The C-text*, ed. Derek Pearsall (Exeter: Exeter University Press, 1978). All references to the C-text are to Pearsall's edition; references to the B-text are to William Langland, *The Vision of Piers Plowman: A Critical Edition of the B-Text Based on Trinity College Cambridge MS B.15.17*, ed. A. V. C. Schmidt (London: Everyman, 1978). For the purposes of this essay, I consider both texts to be *Piers Plowman* and draw from them freely.

his time now to "profit" in hopes to have a "gobet of [God's] grace." (C.5.100).[19] Contributing to society expends time for the social good, and this "expense," however nonsexual, is yet another manifestation of male duty, akin to the physical expenditure demanded by Wit when he enjoins Will to "wive" and to work "in time" and not "in untyme" to ensure healthy, socially acceptable offspring (B.9.184, 6). Will's series of interludes, which are really forms of self-confrontation and introspection, reveal that in all aspects of his life, a man must "spend" his body and his time wisely if he is to attain public approval, a sense of personal worth, and God's grace.

Therefore, to his labors here in crafting a spiritually legitimate social function and a contribution to common profit, we must add his duties as husband, culminating in his ultimate failure to please his wife. That famous scene seems lighthearted, even fabliau-esque, but it forms part of the story of Will's body that defines his manhood and allows Langland to tell the larger story of societal degeneration and pride. Let us look specifically at a sequence of images involving Will's body running throughout the second half of *Piers Plowman*, culminating at the poem's end when Unity is overrun and Will, beset by fear and failure, sees Conscience begin a new quest for Piers, as the poet wakes and the poem ends.

In passus 9, Wit tells the story of Lady Anima, secured in the Castle of Flesh that Nature has made for her – in other words, as the poem tells us, "man with a soule" (B.9.50). A discussion of marriage follows logically from care of the body and soul, leading to one of the poem's famous, if provisional definitions: "Trewe wedded libbynge folk in this world is Dowel" (B.9.108). Stay away from prostitutes, who bring death, says Wit, and if you cannot be chaste, get married:

> "And every maner seculer that may noght continue,
> Wisely go wedde, and ware hym fro synne;
> For lecherie in likynge is lymeyerd of helle.
> Whiles thow art yong, and thi wepene kene,
> Wreke thee with wyvyng, if thow wolt ben excused."
>
> (B.9.179–83)[20]

(The C-text revision is significant, reading, in part, "And whil thou art yong and yep and thy wepene kene / Awreke the therwith on wyfyng, for godes werk y holde hit" [C.10.284–85]).[21] An injunction to controlled and timely marital sex

---

[19] This episode is the subject of a collection of essays, *Written Work: Langland, Labor, and Authorship*, eds. Steven Justice and Kathryn Kerby-Fulton (Philadelphia: University of Pennsylvania Press, 1997); although the essays do not address masculinity per se, they explore the religious, social, economic, and authorial pressures that Langland faced, as reflected in the experiences of Will.

[20] On prostitutes in the poem, see my "Prostitutes in the C-Text of *Piers Plowman*," *JEGP* 105.2 (2006): 275–311.

[21] Teresa Tavormina, *Kindly Similitude*, notes this addition as well, in discussing Wit's doctrine of marriage as a conventional "*remedium*" for desire; she declares that this does not indicate that "the poet looks at marriage in a negative or condescending way," and further that "he doesn't seem to have worried very much about the too-ardent loving of one's spouse that Chaucer's Parson mentions" (pp. 180–81).

then follows in both B and C, based on fear that the fruit of improper sex will be "gedelynges" and "fals folk, fondlynges, faitours, and lieres, / Ungracious to gete good or love of the peple; / Wandren and wasten what thei cacche mowe" (B.9.193–96). Will's weapon thus has a social function: used rightly it creates offspring pleasing to God, but used wrongly it creates the criminality that marks the sinners in the field of folk – the false, the liars, the wasters.[22] Wit's excursus is thus a genealogy of the wayward people we met in the *Prologue*, who will return en masse with Antichrist and Pride to besiege Unity. The phallus in marriage is a natural tool for building a society pledged to truth and to Dowel. This societal obligation, located in Will's body, complements the communal, labor-related obligations outlined by Reason in the C-text's autobiography. Will may be a clerk and a poet, but he cannot escape his role as a man, and no one, it seems, nominates him as a candidate for chastity. The chivalric conceit with which Langland begins the passus dissipates quickly, but the act of "wivyng" substantiates the protection of the damsel in the castle of Caro, since good marriage is Dowel and Dowel is the courtly lover of Anima. Wit's injunctions to Will and his weapon, therefore, represent the best possible function for male desire, channeling it into a divinely sanctioned, communally healthy enterprise that serves the most important courtly lady of all, the human soul.

This is not the last that we hear of the issue, for Will later violates these dicta for the healthy use of the body when he follows the reckless encouragements of Fortune and her minions, Concupiscentia Carnis and Coveitise of Eighes. Will is easily convinced by their appealing arguments, and the former becomes his new best friend. Her tone and diction echo those of Wit, but she suggests a very different function for the male body:

> Thanne hadde Fortune folwynge hire two faire damyseles:
> *Concupiscencia Carnis* men called the elder mayde,
> And Coveitise of Eighes ycalled was that oother.
> Pride of Parfit Lyvynge pursued hem bothe,
> And bad me for my contenaunce acounten Clergie lighte.
>
> *Concupiscentia Carnis* colled me aboute the nekke
> And seide, "Thow art yong and yeep and hast yeres ynowe
> For to lyve longe and ladies to lovye;
> And in this mirour thow mighte se myrthes ful manye
> That leden thee wole to likynge al thi lif tyme."
> The secounde seide the same: "I shal sewe thi wille;
> Til thow be a lord and have lond, leten thee I nelle
> That I ne shal folwe thi felawship, if Fortune it like."
> "He shal fynde me his frend," quod Fortune therafter;
> "The freke that folweth my wille failled nevere blisse."
>
> (B.11.12–26)

---

22 *MED* s.v. *wepene* 2.(b) "male genitalia" "penis" lists this instance in *Piers Plowman* as the sole example; def. 2.(a) provides an interesting biological context, in reference to the hedgehog: "part of an animal's body serving as a natural defense."

Once Recklessness adds his encouragement to the plan, Will is on board, and for the next forty years "*Concupiscentia Carnis* acorded til alle [his] werkes" (B.11.43).

Both Wit (in C) and Concupiscentia Carnis use the word "yep." But do they intend the same meaning? In his discussion of manhood in *Troilus and Criseyde*, Derek Brewer refers to lines in praise of young Edward the Black Prince from the early alliterative poem, *Wynnere and Wastour*, describing how the boy distinguished himself in battle at the age of sixteen when "he was yongest of yeres and yapest of all."[23] Langland's use of this vocabulary may indicate that Wit summons Will to a heroic, marital sexuality that is akin, aided by the metaphor "wepene," to military valor and achievement; Concupiscentia Carnis, however, invokes not heroism but the excesses and abuses of an unrestrained carnal appetite. Brewer glosses "yapest" in *Wynnere and Wastour* as "liveliest," corresponding to *MED* "yep(e)" 2.(a). The *MED* however, lists this verse under 1.(a) "mentally agile," "sharp-witted," "astute," and both definitions likely apply to the Black Prince. The two instances of this term in *Piers Plowman* (in the C-text addition to Wit's speech and in the words of Concupiscentia Carnis from B) are listed under 2.(a) "physically alive, active, quick, vigorous," "youthful in appearance or manner." *In bono*, this definition fits well with Wit's injunction, indicating the proper use of male vitality. But in Concupiscentia Carnis's injunction, spoken with her comforting arm around Will's neck, "yeep," while certainly meaning something like "vigorous," can also connote *MED* 1.(b). "wily," "crafty," "cunning," indicating not just the animal power of youth but also the distinctly human *craft* of desire, the practice of male seduction we see, for example, in the *Miller's Tale*, in ballads, and throughout vernacular narrative. Thus when Concupiscentia Carnis echoes Wit's injunction, she perverts its divinely sanctioned, and potentially heroic, conception of youthful virility. But being young and "yepe," Will prefers her advice to that of Wit. His compressed forty-year party ends abruptly when Fortune becomes Will's foe and he runs into Elde, igniting complex discussions of grace and, finally, Trajan's intervention, as the question of one's worthiness for salvation arises – a logical next topic for a man who wasted forty years in serving his body without considering his soul.

The story of Will's male body goes underground until passus 20, when the dreamer again meets Elde, who makes good on his threats from passus 11, rendering him bald, toothless, and sexually dysfunctional. The scene unfolds during the dénouement of the poem, the siege of Unity, as Lyf, in a fit of reckless despair, flees from Elde and runs to Revel; Elde chases him and takes a shortcut over Will's head:

> "Sire yvele ytaught Elde" quod I, "unhende go with the!
> Sith whanne was the wey over menne heddes?
> Haddestow be hende," quod I "thow woldest have asked leeve!"
>   "Ye – leve, lurdeyn?" quod he, and leyde on me with age,
> And hitte me under the ere – unnethe may Ich here.

---

23   Derek Brewer, "Troilus's 'Gentil' Manhood," *MC*, 237–52, at p. 240.

He buffettted me about the mouth and bette out my wangteeth,
And gyved me in goutes – I may noght goon at large.
And of the wo that I was inne my wif hadde ruthe,
And wisshed wel witterly that I were in hevene.
For the lyme that she loved me fore, and leef was to feele –
On nyghtes, namely, whan we naked weere –
I ne myghte in no manere maken it at hir wille,
So Elde and he[o] it hadden forbeten.   (B.20.186–98)

Exhausted by what Paxson calls an "amusing *ménage à trois*,"[24] Will is not so "yepe" any more, and now that he can no longer function, his wife wants him dead.[25] Starkly, at this moment in the poem, the erection is the defining mark not only of manhood but of life itself; without it, Will has no utility. Medieval narrative often depicts men rejected in favor of Christ by women whose spiritual needs cannot be fulfilled by an earthly partner. We see this in the *Second Nun's Tale* and in the story of Margery and John Kempe, whose manhood, however fruitful in procreation, becomes useless to Margery when her need for love and security evolves beyond what he can provide. Although not sexually dysfunctional, John is nonetheless rejected specifically as a man, as a body. Ironically, notes Margery, she must care for that body when it falls into complete dysfunction. Further enriching this complex web of associations, when Margery rejects her husband as a man, she nonetheless pays his debts, for he, like Will, will not be allowed to pay his own "debt," in any sense, any more.[26] Despite these parallels, Tavormina is right to maintain that this episode between husband and wife in *Piers Plowman* is a "difficult passage to interpret" because of its tone and register: is lechery involved or is this a morally neutral, "human" moment? She concludes that it depicts "the past sexual bond between Will and his wife with affection, wistful nostalgia, and a certain element of comic self-deprecation."[27]

But as domestic as the episode may be, it also occurs as the epic battle rages between Unity and the assembled forces of Pride and Antichrist, with the other Vices joining the fray. Conscience, defending Unity, hopes that Elde will dampen the pride of the populace, as it has Will's in passus 11. As Langland returns specifically to Will's body, the epic struggle gets both personified and personalized. The sense of social promise inherent in Wit's injunction to use his "wepene" well in B.9 evolved in passus 11 into his misuse of that tool in reckless

---

24 James Paxson, "Personification of Will," p. 200.
25 Ralph Hanna, "Will's Work," in Steven Justice and Kathryn Kerby-Fulton, *Written Work*, pp. 23–66, exploring Will's identity as a hermit, wonders whether "Kytte," elsewhere apparently Will's wife, is really only a generic reference to "female companionship" such as that of a concubine (p. 33). Since she is not mentioned by name in this passage about what Will's "wife" has done, Langland may not be shaping an entirely consistent personal biography for Will. James Paxson, "Gender Personified," offers a queering of this scene in that Kit and Elde are both agents in Will's sexual exhaustion, rendering Elde therefore a "sodomist" (pp. 89–92).
26 See, in particular, chapter 11, for the couple's negotiated chastity and her paying of his debts, and 76 for her care for him in his infirmity, in the *Book of Margery Kempe*, EETS 212, ed. Sanford Brown Meech (Oxford: Oxford University Press, 1940).
27 Teresa Tavormina, *Kindly Similitude*, pp. 209, 210.

carnality, and now it resolves into the failure of Will's male body to perform. Society's failure, its sickliness and impotence in defeating Pride, are enacted in Will's body, which thus becomes the locus of the degeneration and frailty that bring the poem to an end. Along with Concupiscentia Carnis and Coveitise of Eighes, Will was joined in passus 11 by "Pride of Parfit Lyvynge." His life of proud desire now devolves into a languishing detumescence, which here in passus 20 marks the spiritual state of his people, as their careless, wasteful, and sterile pride rages against Conscience, Contrition, Holy Church, and ultimately against Truth Himself.

Accordingly, a moment before Elde runs over Will and robs him of his functionality, we witness a bizarre sexual encounter in an extended chivalric conceit. Pride (a version of Pride of Parfit Lyvynge) comes pricking against Lyfe, who (before he flees to Revel) takes up a lover, Heele, and the two "geten in hir glorie a gadelyng" named "Sleuthe," who spreads despair with his sling (B.20.157). This parodic procreation, recapitulating Will's reckless sexual life, directly fulfills Wit's warning that untimely sex will breed "gedelynges," among other "fals folk" (B.9.193). At this point Conscience summons Elde, who runs over Will, as Langland intertwines the Dreamer's sexual biography with the larger social history of spiritual decay. Lyfe, pricking forth with Pride in fear of Deeth and Elde (B.20.147–48), uses his weapon in reckless and desperate sex that only breeds a sin that spreads more sin with his sling of despair. The fear of Elde and Deeth is all that Kynde can arouse to dampen Lyfe's pride and curb the sexual urges, either literal or metaphorical, that bear false fruit, be it in bastards, as Wit warns, or in moral despair, as we see here in the poem's grim finale.

If the failure of the male body plays a role in this spiritual failure at the poem's end, we must wonder how the humanity of Christ, the infallible, ageless, deathless, virgin manhood of Christ, figures in the fray. However much his body is ravaged by violence, Christ's exemplary manhood should emerge as the solution, the redemptive remedy to Will's failed body and to the sickly body politic.[28] As Tavormina notes, "Langland has Will come completely to the end of his natural capacities for physical love and fruitfulness" to emphasize that "those capacities are necessarily finite" in relation to the "craft of heavenly love."[29] Christ practices that craft, as Faith describes in an extended military conceit, by fighting *in Piers's arms*, that is, with human flesh as his battle gear. Inviolable God *as man* defeats death:[30]

> "This Jesus of his gentries wol juste in Piers armes,
> In his helm and his haubergeon, *humana natura*.
> That Christ be noght biknowe here for *consummatus Deus*,

---

[28] On the role of Christ's humanity in medieval spiritual writings, see Aers, "Humanity of Christ" in Aers and Staley, *Powers of the Holy*, pp. 43–76, arguing that Langland's and also Wycliffite texts see the body of Christ and the *imitatio Christi* differently from the orthodox, often feminizing conception of Christ as the locus of suffering.

[29] Teresa Tavormina, *Kindly Similitude*, p. 210.

[30] On the depiction of Christ as victorious knight, see R. A. Waldron, "Langland's Originality: The Christ-Knight and the Harrowing of Hell," *Medieval English Religious Literature*, eds. Gregory Kratzman and James Simpson (Cambridge: Boydell & Brewer, 1986), pp. 66–81.

> In Piers paltok the Plowman this prikiere shal ryde;
> For no dynt shal hym dere as *in deitate Patris.*" (B.18.22–26)

Accordingly, no "boy," a word well-rendered by Economou as "punk,"[31] is bold enough to break his legs. And even when dead, the body of Christ, when pierced by the keen "wepene" of Longinus (C.20.101), displays a salutary, ejaculatory power in healing and converting him, and the C-text addition of the term "wepene" recalls the image of Will's phallus as a tool of healthy procreation, while also anticipating his impending impotence. In contrast to that human degeneration, after this triumphant story of Christ as the son of God, the next passus provides a very human biography of Jesus from infancy to knight, king, and conqueror, culminating in his victory over death: *Christus resurgens.*

But in the narrative of *Piers Plowman,* by passus 20 that battle and its victory celebration are over. Langland is not writing a clearly heroic narrative that marches toward justice or revelation, as we see, variously manifested, in *Pearl,* the *Siege of Jerusalem,* or *Cleanness.* Will and the whole populace inside Unity, embodied in the character Lyf itself, falter after Satan is foiled and after the daughters of God have kissed. Will's battle with Elde is thus a mock version of Jesus' jousting in Piers's arms, a Shakespearean "low" episode, and his battle with Death an absurd parody of Jesus' victory: "deeth drogh neigh me – for drede gan I quake, / And cryde to Kynde, 'Out of care me brynge!'" (B.20.200–1). Christ defeats death, while Will cries and runs from him; Christ rebuilds the temple in three days, while Will remains trapped in an aging, toothless body, with no hope but to run to the "unity" that the manhood of Christ has wrought. Christ fought in Piers's arms, the flesh itself, but Will's fleshly "wepene" fails, and the poem ends in restless chaos, with Unity nearly falling, much as that "old London" falls while King Priam girds himself in impotent arms, as his wife too mocks him for his efforts.[32]

Comprehending Will's impotence in relation to medieval marital law, we can read it as an inability to "pay his debt" for he cannot render the required *debitum.* The theme of paying "what one owes," not in sexual but in spiritual and social realms, runs throughout *Piers Plowman* and returns here powerfully at the end in Conscience's demands that the debt of sin be paid as the only healing salve for those wounded by vice: "redde quod debes." Will's condition metonymically reflects the nonfunctioning, impotent spirit, the Pauline aging, and the paralyzing selfishness that prevents the folk from paying their debts, both literally within the community and also figuratively as rigorous contrition for sin. Ironically this moral impotence and spiritual sloth, represented by Sire Leef-to-lyve-in-lecherie, finds healing ministration in the lusty potency of Sir Penetrans-domus and his request for an "pryvee paiement." While an impotent Will hobbles into Unity for protection, a man more active and vital than he uses

---

31 *William Langland's* Piers Plowman: *The C Version,* trans. George Economou (Philadelphia: University of Pennsylvania Press, 1996), p. 184.
32 *The Aeneid of Virgil,* ed. R. D. Williams (Basingstoke: Macmillan, 1972), 2.506–25.

his profane virility to penetrate that same structure. Peace knows his kind, tries to keep him out, recounting his history of scandalous impregnation:

> "I knew swich oon ones, noght eighte wynter passed,
> Coom in thus ycoped at a court there I dwelde,
> And was my lordes leche – and my ladies bothe.
> And at the laste this lymytour, tho my lorde was oute,
> He salvede so oure wommen til some were with childe."
>
> (B.20.344–48)

He can so "enchant" the sick folk in Unity with his easy penance that they fear no sin. However obliquely, in a bizarre nexus of male competition, the success of the lusty Penetrans reflects Kytte's rejection of her impotent husband, for Will is here metaphorically cuckolded by the power of this glib friar. In a fallen world, virility sells and wins.

These various male bodies map the moral plane of the commune, and the story of Will's "privitee" functions throughout this drama as a measure of the folk's spiritual health. His failing, fragile male body, friend of Concupiscentia Carnis, has not paid its spiritual debts. As James Dean writes about this aging, "Will, too, is implicated in the decay of society; his hands are by no means clean, his conscience not entirely clear."[33] Will's body, ransacked by Elde, is beyond the pleasures of hypocrisy and Lechery, and one only hopes that after waking he will not, like Chaucer's Reeve, doom himself to live in bitter nostalgia for sexual sin, thriving on as much filthy talk and vice as his ailing body can muster, trapped in "wanhope," and waiting for death.

Being a Man in Troilus and Criseyde

The young hero of Chaucer's poem, by contrast, keeps his hair and teeth and never runs into old age. His dysfunction and failure, his encounters with "impotence," despair, and death take different forms from those of Will. But before examining Troilus's love scenes and their fateful consequence, that is, those scenes closest to the episodes examined in *Piers Plowman*, I want to survey the general environment of masculinity and manhood at Troy while it, like Langland's Unity, is besieged. As we enter the doomed city of Troy in the opening verses of Chaucer's poem, its men are in shambles. One, Criseyde's husband, is dead. Another, her father, lives in infamy, having failed in his paternal obligations and betrayed his people. The rest are doomed to die, for although the poet says he will not tell the fall of Troy, in fact he will – one doomed man at a time. While men live in *Troilus and Criseyde*, civic duties, fighting war, and protecting the weak, including Criseyde, dominate their lives. Emblematic of manhood in the poem, Troilus, as he vows to protect Criseyde in every way, becomes a wall: "wel she felte he was to hire a wal / Of stiel, and sheld from

---

[33] James Dean, *The World Grown Old in Later Medieval Literature* (Cambridge: Medieval Academy, 1997), p. 222.

every displesaunce" (3.479–80). The image seems flattering, but being a wall has its costs and points to the objectification and depersonalization of male obligation. A wall protects, keeps safe, holds up a structure or a city, but when a man is a wall he bears a heavy burden and suffers pressures and stress. For example, to help protect Criseyde and meet her high standard of discretion, Troilus, in an act called "manhood," must restrain his emotions publicly throughout the poem, dissimulating so that no one will discern the love that privately guides his life:

> But in hymself with manhod gan restreyne
> Ech racle dede and ech unbridled cheere,
> That alle tho that lyven, soth to seyne,
> Ne sholde han wist, by word or by manere,
> What that he mente, as touchyng this matere.
> From every wight as fer as is the cloude
> He was, so wel dissimilen he koude.
>
> And al the while which that I yow devyse,
> This was his lif: with all his fulle myght,
> By day, he was in Martes heigh servyse –
> This is to seyn, in armes as a knyght;
> And for the more part, the longe nyght
> He lay and thoughte how that he myghte serve
> His lady best, hire thonk for to deserve. (3.428–41)

Chaucer's half line is stark: "This was his lif," a long day's work as a soldier and a hard day's night burdened with the pressures of love and serving his lady. Freighted by these two masters, Troilus practices unto death a watchful, imprisoning manhood.[34] This was his life. Accordingly, when the council decides Criseyde must be exchanged, despite being "neigh deyde," "he no word to it seyde, / Lest men sholde his affeccioun espye; / With mannes herte he gan his sorwes drye" (4.151–54). Perhaps if this control were the final word, then Troilus could endure his losses and emerge like Job, Constance, or Griselda, but his public stoicism masks an internal chaos that unmans him as his desperation increases. The deluded placement of his love prevents a comprehensive civic and spiritual masculinity. Love progressively draws him away from both duty and truth, and before he loses Criseyde, he loses his manhood.

Ironically *Piers Plowman* supplies the military imagery of "wepene" that Chaucer's war poem, ever mannered and courtly, never touches. But just as

---

34 Derek Brewer, "Troilus's 'Gentil" Manhood," explores the pressures on Troilus's manhood in relation to contemporary examples of military and political accomplishment, particularly by young men before the age of twenty. Implying the danger of a presentist approach, he cautions that "[w]e should not approach [the past] as propagandists for a new social order which the past could not know, but in the spirit of sympathetic social anthropologists" (p. 238). Shannon McSheffrey studies how men were socially defined not by sexual prowess but by restraint and self-governance: "As with women, sexual impropriety in men was seen as part of a complex of generally bad behavior; for men it was related especially to the sorts of faults associated with men who refused their responsibilities to their families and to their communities and threatened other men's rule over their dependents" (*Marriage, Sex, and Civic Culture in Late Medieval London* [Philadelphia: University of Pennsylvania Press, 2006], p. 262).

Langland's Will faces male duty and obligation, as worker, father, husband, and clerk, so too does Troilus, as a soldier, civic leader, and lover with sexual responsibilities. Critics call into question the status of Troilus's "weaponry" on the first night of love, although no one doubts that he is as "yong" and "yeep" as Will once was. Looking at the lovers' first night together, Derek Brewer confronts David Aers's interpretation of Troilus's famous swoon (3.706–7), contending that "there is simply no evidence nor any reason to suppose that Troilus may fear sexual impotence."[35] In opposition to this, Maud McInerney, employing Vern Bullough's contention that in the Middle Ages "the male was defined in terms of sexual performance, measured rather simply by his ability to get an erection," explores the episode as a scene of sexual impotence, brought on by lovesickness and requiring the intervention of Pandarus and Criseyde as masseur and masseuse to render "a sort of sexual first aid."[36] Sex is the "mannes game" that Troilus must learn to play (3.1126–27), but he is trapped, says McInerney, between the courtly ethic of restraint and the "pornographic" Ovidian imperative: "Troilus … regularly behaving like a heroine when he should be playing the hero," she continues, "remains tragically unaware of the degree to which he is out of step with the world in which he has been placed."[37] Whether Chaucer playfully encodes impotence into his courtly language or not, one cannot deny the importance of performance at this point in the poem. Pandarus and Chaucer have not brought Troilus and Criseyde together to talk politics or to become friends, and the urgency of their private moments when the lovers do "as hem liste" demands Troilus's sexual functionality, which thus fulfills Criseyde's estimation of him and completes her picture of his manhood.

With love physically attained, Troilus is not only the best soldier, brother, son, and friend, but also the greatest benefactor and public exemplar of nobility and virtue. Chaucer leaves little doubt, however, that the soldier enjoys only a false paradise, and no Christian medieval poet could have written the following lines without irony: "'Thou hast,'" Troilus tells Pandarus, "'in hevene ybrought my soule at reste / Fro Flegitoun, the fery flood of helle'" (3.1599–600). As a reader of Dante, Chaucer knows that the way from hell to heaven involves more than falling, as a dead body falls, at the feet of Paulo and Francesca, where Dido is, and Paris, and "more than a thousand" whom love "separated from our life."[38]

Troilus's period of bliss, however magnificently adorned in the trappings of romance and classical grandeur, corresponds to Will's long friendship with Coveitise of Eighes and Concupiscentia Carnis, a period when Fortune smiles on Troilus, as she had on Will, and when a little recklessness seems harmless

---

35 David Aers, as quoted by Brewer, "Troilus's 'Gentil' Manhood," p. 239.

36 Maud McInerney, "'Is this a mannes herte?' Unmanning Troilus through Ovidian Allusion," *MC*, 221–35, at p. 223.

37 Maud McInerney, "'Is this a mannes herte?'" pp. 225, 234. On the issue of this Ovidianism, see my *Chaucer's Ovidian Arts of Love* and Jamie Fumo, "'Little Troilus': *Heroides* 5 and Its Ovidian Contexts in Chaucer's *Troilus and Criseyde*," *SP* 100.3 (2003): 278–314.

38 Dante Alighieri, *La Commedia*, vol. 2 *Inferno*, ed. Giorgio Petrocchi (Florence: Casa Editrice Le Lettere, 1966–67), 5.61ff.

enough and even appropriate for the "yong and yepe." But Troilus, like Will a fledging clerk, tries to understand his good Fortune philosophically and to integrate it with Love and Truth, forces that Will seeks constantly throughout *Piers Plowman*. Troilus's Boethian *canticus* ends with the hope that this love, the cosmic force that binds the universe, may encircle the hearts of others who are "true":

> "So wolde God, that auctour is of kynde,
> That with his bond Love of his vertu liste
> To cerclen hertes alle and faste bynde,
> That from his bond no wight the wey out wiste
> And hertes colde, hem wolde I that he twiste;
> To make hem love, and that hem liste ay rewe
> On hertes sore, and kepe hem that ben trewe!" (3.1765–71)

The Trojan fully believes that when all treasures are tried, truth is the best. "'[T]routh and diligence,'" he tells her, "'shal ye fynden in me al my lif'" (3.1297–98), and for this reason above all other "treasures," Criseyde loves him:

> "For trusteth wel that youre estat roial,
> Ne veyn delit, nor only worthinesse
> Of yow in werre or torney marcial,
> Ne pompe, array, nobleye, or ek richesse
> Ne made me to rewe on youre destresse,
> But moral vertu, grounded upon trouthe –
> That was the cause I first hadde on yow routhe!" (4.1667–73)

Riches? We never thought of Troilus's wealth as a draw, but the inclusion of these temporal attributes marks this passage as a Boethian winnowing of false goods from true, and however individualized Criseyde's own conception of "good" is, she correctly identifies Troilus's moral and philosophical core. Kynde instructs Will to "learn to love" (B.20.208), and Troilus is himself in constant training, even considering lost whoever does not share his new-found vision: "For soth to seyne, he lost held every wyght, / But if he were in Loves heigh servise" (3.1793–94), while he follows eagerly the fortunes of others in love, rooting them on, as it were, to find the transcendent joy that he has found.

Practicing the zeal of the converted, he also makes love the ground for civic virtue. It creates military might and has altered his "spirit so withinne" that love, prowess, and virtue become one in him, opposing every vice: "And moost of love and vertu was his speche" (3.1778ff., 1786). As Troilus's logic goes, if each man learned to love, the body politic and all of society would benefit. Langland would not dispute this, but the folk in the final passus abandon love and truth in favor of, if we may borrow Criseyde's terms, "pomp" and "richess," and other false goods as the vices besiege Unity. Despite the different settings of these poems, *truth* and *love* cannot mean inherently different things for Chaucer and Langland. Both poems distinguish desire for gain from desire for grace, as they value forms of truth that develop the personal integrity, justness, and loyalty that serve commune profit. Both poets express this conflict in one hopeful, loving man who struggles with "mede" and "exchange" while never losing his particularity as a man, whose obligations are rooted in the needs, desires, and natural functions of the body.

We are not really used to thinking of Will as a sexual being, and although Lechery takes a back seat to Covetousness throughout *Piers Plowman*, he comes on strong in the assault on Unity as a combatant and also in the characters Lyfe to Live in Lecherie, Spille-love, and Sir Penetrans, as we have seen. If Will, both as man and as allegory, misunderstands the quest for love, then his delusion resembles that of Troilus who theorizes love as a binding force of order but mistakenly locates that treasure in a lover who is committed to "casual plesaunce," activity with an immediate cause but no long- term ambition. The immediate causes for Criseyde are not only delight and emotional love but also protection, survival – clearly her needs from the start of the poem when she, isolated and alienated, appeals to Hector for security. When her needs change, or rather, when forces "cause" her needs to relocate, she adjusts her love, "exchanges" it for better. Despite occasional tears, she is perfectly content to do so, and, as Laura Howes refreshingly puts it, "what … is so bad about that?"[39]

Let us explore Criseyde a bit more, specifically in relation to her Langlandian counterpart, Lady Meed. To see her as Meed credits her with a power and agency that defies the main thrust of the critical tradition, which insists on her powerlessness and her commodification by patriarchy. Monica McAlpine opposes this tradition by examining Criseyde as a type of the "prudent woman" offering wise wifely counsel, as a number of characters in the *Canterbury Tales* do.[40] Meed herself, particularly in the C-text additions in which two types of Meed are outlined – one treacherous and the other true and crucial to society – is prudent, wise, efficient, and rational. She is constrained neither by patriarchy nor by a romantic allegiance to "Truth" whom, accordingly, she refuses to marry. She can be either ally or enemy, depending on what calculation she makes and what precise problem she attempts to solve. Sheila Delany says as much about Criseyde, noting that her very femininity "includes conscious and manipulative self-presentation, coyness, calculation, egocentricity, self pity, self deception, fear, and passivity."[41] Most of this list correlates well with Langland's flamboyant lady in red.

How may we further associate the two women, one so rich psychologically and emotionally and the other, supposedly, so allegorical and flat? Both women make grand, "ravishing" first appearances, and concerning lineage, both their fathers, Calkas and Favel, embody treachery and falsehood. When Troilus fears that Calkas is too artful and manipulative to allow her to escape, Criseyde tells

---

[39] Laura Howes, "Chaucer's Criseyde: The Betrayer Betrayed," *Reading Medieval Culture*, eds. Stein and Prior, 324–43, at p. 339. Howes reconsiders Criseyde's actions and finds them to be sensible and, in the context of her struggles as a woman, perfectly acceptable. For a powerful exploration of Criseyde's agency and control over gender, see Angela Jane Weisl's essay in this volume, exploring how Criseyde, "within a feminized context, plays a 'mannes game' with a 'mannes herte'" (p. 130).

[40] Monica McAlpine, "Criseyde's Prudence," *SAC* 25 (2003): 199–224.

[41] Sheila Delany, "Techniques of Alienation in *Troilus and Criseyde*," *CTC*, 29–46, at p. 36.

him not to worry because she can "calculate" better than the old man. She plans to win him over with money, for she knows his appetite and greed: "'I right now have founden al the gise, / Withouten net, wherewith I shal hym hente'" (4.1370–71). "'Desir of gold,'" she continues, "'shal so his soule blende / That, as me lyst, I shal wel make an ende.'" If he suspects through his arts that she is lying about the offer, she will defeat all his "calkullynge" by bearing "hym on honde" (4.1399–400, 1404), finally converting him, she says, to "don my red" (4.1413). In this rich and under-discussed passage, Criseyde performs the role of Lady Meed, confident in her gifts and her persuasive, calculating power. How ironic it is, therefore, when Troilus miscalculates, as he waits fruitlessly for her return and "thought he misacounted hadde his day" (5.1185).

Criseyde's first action in her poem is to go to the highest male authority in the town, Hector, to ask for protection; Meed does the same, though less conclusively, with the King in the early passus of *Piers Plowman*. Both women worry about reputations: Meed mourns that everyone called her a "queynte comune hore" (C.4.161), and Criseyde fears the judgment of history, now that she has "falsed Troilus" and lost her "name of trouthe in love, for evermore!" (5.1054ff.). Criseyde is called by Marcia Marzec and Cindy Vitto "co-dependent," and although this reading may sound anachronistic, if we were to understand codependence in the premodern, prepsychological sense, we could see both Criseyde and Meed as forces of exchange who exist always in dependent, measured, and calculated relation to others and who, through "exchanges" of various sorts, seek their own survival at the cost of truth.[42] As Vance Smith describes it, "unless meed is preceded by a willingness to honor bonds that have already been established, it rapidly gives rise to guile."[43] Meed is not a "woman" because she is irrational and flighty but because she is practical and efficient, however guileful, and knows, like Criseyde, how to keep her accounts in order. As John Fleming shows, far from displaying "passivity," a chestnut of victimological criticism, Criseyde, rather, engages in "a rampage or perhaps orgy of efficacious agency."[44] In fact her ultimate triumph and survival make us question the critical fixation on her suffering, well displayed in Fradenburg's focus on "the profound role of loss and violence in the construction of the feminine chivalric subject."[45] We might want to point out that while Criseyde suffers the trauma of being constructed into the "symbolic order," Troilus experiences a different kind of cultural work as he is butchered in battle by Achilles, the masculine hero who exceeds all comparable male power in combat.

Adding insult to injury, Criseyde, aptly called Troilus's "sweete foe" (1.874), berates him for his impractical and unmanly plan to run away with her:

---

[42] Cindy Vitto and Marcia Smith Marzec, "Criseyde as Codependent: A New Approach to an Old Enigma," *NPC*, pp. 181–206.

[43] Vance Smith, *The Book of the Incipit: Beginnings in the Fourteenth Century* (Minneapolis: University of Minnesota Press, 2001), p. 156.

[44] John Fleming, "Criseyde's Poem: The Anxieties of the Classical Tradition," *NPC*, 277–98, at p. 278.

[45] Louise Fradenburg, "'Our owen wo to drynke': Loss, Gender, and Chivalry in *Troilus and Criseyde*," *CTC*, 88–106, at p. 105.

> "But that ye speke, awey thus for to go
> And leten alle youre frendes, God forbede
> For any womman that ye sholden so,
> And namely syn Troie hath now swich nede
> Of help. And ek of o thing taketh hede:
> If this were wist, my lif lay in balaunce,
> And youre honour; God shilde us fro meschaunce." (4.1555–61)

Her rational, disciplinary tone, particularly in the depersonalizing "for any woman," indicates her lost respect for him. Criseyde wants to "sle with resoun al this hete" (4.1583), and does so to chilling and emasculating effect. Despite the conventions of medieval scriptural exegesis, men seldom display "reason" in vernacular narrative, and Troilus shows almost none at all. Here a woman's survival instinct puts an end to his dream and exposes the deficiencies of a love that he thought would bring comprehensive private and public virtue but that actually shatters his manhood in both spheres.

The episode converts Criseyde emotionally; she sees her lover as desperate and reckless, and as his manhood and utility collapse, she herself must become a wall. Who is Troilus at this point? As his love unravels, he becomes ever more implicated in Classical allusion and parallel, as McInerney, Stephanie Dietrich, and Suzanne Hagedorn observe.[46] Jamie Fumo argues that Troilus is not only a type of Paris (who orchestrates a *raptus*) but also of Paris's rejected lover Oenone.[47] In sum, he becomes a woman, the scorned and doomed Heroidean lover, no longer the wall, no longer of use. That his manhood has been fragile all along is evidenced early in the poem when lovesick Troilus vows to kill himself. This audition for the *Heroides* clearly feminizes him, for in this, says Pandarus, he would be committing both "unmanhod and a synne" (1.824), reducing him to a Dido, who killed herself for love. Desperation has never been attractive or efficient in retaining or regaining love, and as Troilus pledges to befriend recklessness and "ravish her," he only solidifies Criseyde's departure. Highlighting Criseyde's status as "polytropos," Fumo also connects her ingeniously to Ovid's Ulysses, the "rhetorician and manipulative liar,"[48] the partner and compeer of Diomedes, to whom he is linked in Dante's *Inferno* in twin fires eternally punished for their treacherous counsel. The end of the poem thus brings these two strategic rhetoricians together, when Criseyde, as the saying goes, finds herself a new flame.

---

[46] Maud McInerney, "'Is this a mannes herte?'" notes specifically Troilus's feminization, observing that he "regularly behave[es] like a heroine when he should be playing the hero" (p. 234). Stephanie Dietrich studies how Chaucer's descriptive vocabulary sometimes undermines rather than bolsters Troilus's manhood ("'Slydyng' Masculinity in the Four Portraits of Troilus," *MC*, pp. 205–19). Suzanne Hagedorn explores detailed parallels, concluding that "through its network of allusions to the *Heroides*, Chaucer's *Troilus and Criseyde* keeps figures of abandoned women in the background of a narrative that eventually upsets the gendered pattern – Troilus rather than Criseyde metamorphoses into a forlorn letter writer begging for the return of the beloved" (*Abandoned Women: Rewriting the Classics in Dante, Boccaccio, and Chaucer* [Ann Arbor: University of Michigan Press, 2004], p. 157).

[47] Jamie Fumo, "Little Troilus," p. 300.

[48] Jamie Fumo, "Little Troilus," p. 304.

In this swirl of allusion and implication, one thing is particularly clear: Troilus's alleged bedroom impotence, if it even occurs, is irrelevant compared to this impotent display of unmanliness. At no time in Christian medieval culture were men defined positively by kidnapping. Hector is the shining star of the tradition, not Paris, and even the suggestion of a *Paris redux* spells the effective end of Troilus's manhood.[49] Criseyde, understandably, is going through the mental processes of planning to "exchange" this enfeebled man for another of greater utility and effective protection; as a woman, she does this "suddenly," with resolve and a healthy lack of sentimental regret. This is not to say that Criseyde falls into the role of Langland's Kyte and rejects Troilus because of age and impotence. But leave him she does, when he can no longer perform any of the functions central to her survival, and so he dies, as an abandoned woman dies.

Where does Pandarus, the sole interlocutor and guiding force in Troilus's life, fit into these parallels? He is Wit, Imagination, Scripture, Study, Holy Church and the rest combined. Most apparently he can be seen as a type of Recklessness, who, in turn, can be seen as a kind of "pander" for Will. His contention that Troilus's love puts him in a "worthy place" and that he ought "not to clepe it hap, but grace" to have found such a lover (1.895–96) recalls Recklessness's exhortation to Will to follow Coveitise of Eighes and Fortune, forces that offer only the illusion of surety. Pandarus shares his surprise that Troilus, who always scorned love, now prospers:

> "But wel is me that ever that I was born
> That thou biset art in so good a place;
> For by my trouthe, in love I dorste have sworn
> The sholde nevere han tid thus fayr a grace." (1.904–7)

"Som grace," he knows, they will find in Criseyde since Troilus has now been "converted out of wickednesse" (1.980, 999). He then celebrates the traditional zeal of the converted that he detects in his pupil:

> "Ensample why, se now thise wise clerkes,
> That erren aldermost ayeyn a lawe,
> And ben converted from hire wikked werkes
> Thorugh grace of God that list hem to hym drawe,
> Thanne arn thise folk that han moost God in awe." (1.1002–6)

This registers as conventional "religion of love" doctrine, but the verses are more Langlandian than one would think, for a Christian vocabulary drives the irony and exposes the recklessness of the notion that carnal desire pleases "God" and brings "grace."

Although, as Pearsall notes, "much remains unclear" in Langland's expansion of the character of Recklessness from B to C (see C.11.196 note), it is

---

[49] In this vein, Monica McAlpine, "Criseyde's Prudence," explains that Criseyde's argument against elopement is prudent and "ethically necessary" and that Troilus, in taking her advice, guarantees that he "is no Calkas, no Antenor – and no Paris" (p. 214).

clear that his doctrine strikes a similar note to Pandarus's. He too argues that grace is important but contends that what Clergy and Scripture teach is worthless in regard to salvation. But more than simply underlining the supremacy of grace over knowledge, Recklessness tells Will to seize the day and to live a life according to Concupiscentia Carnis and Coveitise of Eighes as Fortune dictates: "'Folowe forth that Fortune wole, thou hast ful fer to elde; / A man may stoupe tyme ynowe when he shal tyne the croune!'" These two females, he later tells Will in conclusion, "'Ne shal nat greue the grettly, ne bigyle the, but yf thow wolle'" (C.11.197–98, 311). Like Pandarus, he believes his charge has found himself in a "good place," one that is (in Pandarus's terms) "digne" unto his "worthinesse" (1.968). In both poems false friends encourage reckless behavior (called in *Piers Plowman* "Pride of Parfit Lyvynge") under the illusion of "grace" and leave their friends alone and helpless when Fortune rescinds the imaginary favor and offers more mere "hap." Pandarus is not allegorical, but he winds up as useless as Will's good-time buddies and just as insensitive to Troilus's misfortune as they are to Will's. Pandarus knows that Troilus is doomed and cannot understand why he took it all so seriously. "You wanted a girl, you got one; you lost her, get another." He can do nothing outside these parameters.

If Pandarus roughly corresponds to Recklessness and Criseyde to Lady Meed, we can continue these parallels with Criseyde's new lover and the other major character in the poem, Diomede, also an amalgam of various figures in *Piers Plowman*. He is Lechery, for one, whom Langland depicts "with laughynge chiere / And with pryvee speche" (B.20.114–15) and also, certainly, Sir Penetrans and Hende Speech, all forces that rout Truth and Unity at the end of the poem. Diomede succeeds in this economy because, with his own form of "hende speche," he understands love as Meed would, as expenditure and investment, but really with very little risk, as he tells himself when he is about to make his first assay with Criseyde: "'I shal namore lesen but my speche'" (5.798). He seeks advantage, noting that one who misses an opportunity, one that "wol foryete hymselve" (5.98), is a fool. He speaks to Criseyde deceptively, so that "'she naught wite as yet shal what I mene'" (5.105). Armed, like Meed, with a seemingly unlimited reserve, not of coin but of Ovidian "words" [*dare verba*], he is appropriately called "of tonge large" (5.804). Reflecting parodically the heroic vocabulary Langland applies to Christ, Diomede says that in winning Criseyde a man might call himself a "conquerour." We know already that Diomede is a "knight," and, accordingly, he completes the tripartite identity of Christ when he calls himself nearly a "king," if only his father had not been slain (5.932ff). Christ, for his part, as knight, king, and conqueror, was not so inhibited (see the depiction at B.19.1–62), and thus in *Troilus and Criseyde* these terms remain earthly, pagan, and unredeemed, however seductive to Criseyde.

When Diomede meets Criseyde, she is beset with "Peyne, torment, pleynte, wo, distresse!" along with "Anoy, smert, drede, fury, and ek siknesse" (4.842, 845).[50] So charmed by Diomede's speech and the promise of healing it might

---

[50] Sealy Gilles, "Love and Disease," begins with these lines, focusing on the body of Criseyde as the

bring to one "in swich disese" (5.109), Criseyde later "Welcomed hym and down hym by hire sette" (5.849) much as, in *Piers Plowman,* "Hende-Speche" compels Peace to welcome Sir Penetrans-domus: "'Opene the yates. / Lat in the frere and his felawe, and make hem fair cheere'" (B.20.349–50). In both poems a sickly person is consoled and healed through infiltration and rhetorical conquest.[51] The Church on earth is falling, just as love and truth fall at Troy, as sweet-talking, large-tongued men penetrate and perpetuate processes of exchange. The Friar's easy confession puts an end to the tears of Contrition, who has now "clene foryeten to crye and to wepe" for "comfort of his confessour" (B.20.370, 372). And we observe, as well, an end to Criseyde's tears and to her contrition once she is comforted by her new advocate. Diomede, like Penetrans, insinuates and charms, assessing his patient's needs and offering himself as the sole provider of care. The results for Troilus, for Will, for Troy, and for Holy Church are disastrous, although tempered in each case with hope, embodied in both poems in Christ, the friend who will not "falsen" young lovers and the savior who remains eternally ready, in Piers's arms, to guide the "will" to truth.

Afterword

As I have intimated, central to both poems' dénouements are sickness and healing. Addressing disease in the relations between man and city in Chaucer's poem, Fumo argues that "in the Christian perspective, Troilus's [love] sickness becomes, in a sense, unredeemed humanity's diseased state, remedied by *Christus Medicus* (who took on the sickness of humanity so as to effect a cure)."[52] This notion of Christian medical remedy also arises in *Troilus and Criseyde,* as Gilles reveals, in the "sacrificial lexicon of the crucifixion," referenced when Troilus attempts to cure his sickness with "ful bitter drink," evoking "Christ's drink of gall as well as the salutary bitterness of medicine."[53] That Henryson saw fit to inflict Criseyde with leprosy as a natural punishment for her untruth testifies to the power of the medical conceits implicit in the poem. However artfully Chaucer implies these themes in *Troilus and Criseyde,* Langland makes them explicit in *Piers Plowman* by casting its final battle as an extended medical allegory.

With Antichrist, Pride and Lechery leading the siege against Unity, Conscience encourages Kynde and Elde to humble the people, to make them "Leve Pride pryvely and be parfite Cristene" (B.20.108). But the people resist reform as Fortune flatters them and Lechery, armed much like the pagan god of love, shoots them with his bow. As long as Life and Health stick together, they do not fear Death or Age or sin. Life goes to Physic with little real result and

bringer of both disease and cure: "The beloved infects, then cures, only to prove by her willful absence and fickleness that earthly salve is illusory" (p. 162).
51 Sealy Gilles, "Love and Disease," p. 187, provocatively connects the notion of penetrating disease to the ultimate fate of Troy, breeched by the Trojan Horse.
52 Jamie Fumo, "Little Troilus," p. 312.
53 Sealy Gilles, "Love and Disease," p. 192.

then decides to seek Revel for comfort. Elde nonetheless stalks him and at this point runs over Will's head, involving him in the action of the final passus, as we have examined. Soon after, to heal Contrition and the others sick with hypocrisy, Confession mixes the salve of "redde quod debes." With Contrition so sick, strong medicines are needed, but he refuses to pay what is owed, to suffer for sin and labor for proper spiritual health. Enter Sir Penetrans-domus, the false healer and sexual predator, offering an alternative both to Will's failed phallic manhood and to the bitter payment of Contrition's debt, although his confectionary plasters provide no real healing. This imagery of the physician with the healing salve further connects this climactic scene in *Piers Plowman* to *Troilus and Criseyde* when we note that among the medieval medical remedies for lovesickness discussed in the commentary on Constantine's *De coitu* is the application of "plasters or women" "to the testicles."[54] Chaucer's lovesickness and Langland's sickly sinful hypocrisy both require healing plasters, as both poets explore the dangers of adopting deceptive sources of wellness – what we might call, adapting Pandarus, "casual" healing.

Of Chaucer's lovers, both variously "dis-eased," Criseyde fares better with her cures than does the doomed Troilus. Like Langland's "Contrition," once comforted by her own glib knight, she weeps no more. Will is rejected for dead because he no longer has what his wife wants, and Troilus is exchanged by Criseyde for Diomede, because he no longer provides what she wants – the environment of protection and safety, her own version of *Piers*'s stalwart Unity. If Criseyde were not only contrite but Contrition, she would pay Troilus what she owes him, fulfilling his loyal truth. But the price is simply too high, and she gains more, so she calculates, from her own large-tongued "flatterer," her knight, king, and conqueror. Just as in *Piers Plowman*, when "contrition" finds comfort, "truth" is doomed. For the rejected, dejected men in each poem, nothing is left but personal awakenings, for Troilus to his absurdity as a steward of truth in a false world, and for Will to composition of all he has seen with covetousness of eyes, with desire of the flesh, but also with P/patience and with C/conscience, his only hopes for reuniting with Piers and all he embodies. In these complex sexual biographies, Langland and Chaucer have interrogated the trials, functions, and obligations of the male body as it finds its dutiful place in love and in the world. In doing so, they have explored what it means for a worker, a lover, a husband, a citizen, and a Christian simply to be a man.

---

[54] I am indebted to Sealy Gilles, "Love and Disease," p. 163, who cites this remedy from Peter of Spain's *Questiones super Viaticum* in Mary Wack's *Lovesickness in the Middle Ages* (Philadelphia: University of Pennsylvania Press, 1990), pp. 218–19.

12

"The Monstruosity in Love":
Sexual Division in Chaucer and Shakespeare

R. ALLEN SHOAF

This will not have been an historicizing essay.[1]

But it will be historical. It is mired in history. It is min(e)d in history. It recognizes that unity is a delusion – this is why there is history, history is always two or more. Where there is history, there is no unity.

Separation is the psychogenetic crisis most particular to human males.[2] In over a century of heroic thinking (often opposed by unspeakable, inexcusable petty-mindedness), psychoanalysis (and the artists who have followed it[3]) have demonstrated in many ways that the male's separation from the mother, from the different body that is hers and yet that is also the source of his nature and

---

[1] Although I acknowledge the importance of Foucauldian interventions in contemporary thought, I have grave doubts about many leftist appropriations of "historicism." "Tantum religio potuit suadere malorum" – "Such great evils can religion compel" (Lucretius, *De natura rerum / On the nature of things*, trans. W. H. D. Rouse [Cambridge, MA: Harvard University Press, 1992], 1.101); and I have seen "historicism" at work when it was just another religion.

[2] See, especially, Lacan's rich meditation on separation in "Position de l'inconscient," in *Écrits* (Paris: Éditions du Seuil, 1966), p. 843. For accessibility and simplicity, I quote the translation of Bruce Fink, *Jacques Lacan, Écrits: The First Complete Edition in English* (New York: Norton, 2006):

> *Separare*, separating, ends here in *se parere*, engendering oneself. ... this slippage is grounded in the fact that they are both paired with the function of the *pars*.
>
> The part is not the whole, as they say, though usually without thinking. For it should be emphasized that the part has nothing to do with the whole. One has to come to terms with it [*en prendre son parti*]; it plays its game [*sa partie*] all by itself. Here the subject proceeds from his partition to his parturition. This does not imply the grotesque metaphor of giving birth to himself anew. Indeed, language would be hard pressed to express that with an original term, at least in Indo-European climes where all the words used for this purpose are of juridical or social origin.
>
> "*Parere*" was first of all to procure (a child for one's husband). This is why the subject can procure for himself what interests him here – a status I will qualify as "civil." Nothing in anyone's life unleashes more determination to succeed in obtaining it. In order to be *pars*, he would easily sacrifice the better part of his interests. ...
>
> But what he thus fills is not the lack [*faille*] he encounters in the Other, but rather, first of all, the lack that results from the constitutive loss of one of his parts, by which he turns out to be made of two parts. Therein lies the twist whereby separation represents the return of alienation. For the subject operates with his own loss, which brings him back to his point of departure. (pp. 715–16)

[3] Of whom among the most significant for me is Salvador Dalí, especially in his *Metamorphosis of Narcissus*, one of the most moving interpretations of separation anxiety in the visual arts that I have ever seen. Reprints of the painting can be accessed on numerous websites – e.g., http://www.usc.edu/schools/annenberg/asc/projects/comm544/library/images/742bg.jpg (last accessed 12.21.2006).

nurture, leaves indelible artifacts of angst and hostility in his unconscious mind. The Oedipus is but one such artifact. Its resolution is only one step. In my dreams since my boyhood, I have met many monsters more horrible than the Sphinx. Even if I lived in a body without organs, if my libido were not subject to organization, I imagine I would meet monsters ineffable but insistent still that I let them speak.[4]

And I acknowledge, unapologetically, that I believe Chaucer and Shakespeare encountered their own monsters of sexual division as well.

I begin with Shakespeare. In a scene important for modern literary criticism and theory,[5] Troilus exclaims,

> "This, she? No, this is Diomed's Cressida.
> … … … … … … … …
> If there be rule in unity itself,
> This is not she. O madness of discourse,
> That cause sets up with and against thyself!
> Bifold authority, where reason can revolt
> Without perdition, and loss assume all reason
> Without revolt! This is and is not Cressid.
> Within my soul there doth conduce a fight
> Of this strange nature, that a thing inseparate
> Divides more wider than the sky and earth,
> And yet the spacious breadth of this division
> Admits no orifex for a point as subtle
> As Ariachne's broken woof to enter." (*Tro.* 5.2.140; 144–55)[6]

Many commentaries are possible. But mine is the simplest, perhaps. The "thing inseparate / Divides more wider than the sky and earth." One male sees another male claim the sex of a female, and division heaves up "madness of discourse." Eve after all is a division of Adam's body, excised rib. And the division of my syntax from "heave" to "Eve" is rigorously logical, "logic" itself a word of things divided (< *leg*[1] : "to collect or gather together") – I but gather together what lies in the language.[7] As, with far greater (di)vision, did Milton:

> "Hast thou not made me here thy substitute,
> And these inferiour farr beneath me set?
> Among unequals what societie
> *Can sort*, what harmonie or true delight?
> Which must be mutual, in proportion due

---

4   It is important, I believe, that I acknowledge Deleuze and Guattari's *Anti-Oedipus*, which has had a profound effect on me since I first read it in my youth, even though I quarrel with and struggle to understand its covert utopianism (body without organs?). See Gilles Deleuze and Félix Guattari, *Anti-Oedipus: Capitalism and Schizophrenia*, trans. Robert Hurley, Mark Seem, Helen Lane (reprinted Minneapolis: University of Minnesota Press, 1983).

5   See J. Hillis Miller, "Ariachne's Broken Woof," *Georgia Review* 31 (1977): 44–60.

6   My text is the second edition of *The Oxford Shakespeare*, eds. John Jowett, William Montgomery, Gary Taylor, and Stanley Wells (Oxford: Clarendon Press, 2005).

7   Calvert Watkins, *The American Heritage Dictionary of Indo-European Roots*, 2nd ed. (Boston: Houghton Mifflin, 2000), *sub voce*.

> ... ...
> ... Of fellowship I speak
> Such as I seek, fit to *parti*cipate
> All rational delight, wherein the brute
> Cannot be human *consort*; ...
>
> ... Supream of things;
> Thou in thy self art perfet, and in thee
> Is no deficience found; not so is Man,
> But in degree, the cause of his desire
> By conversation with his like to help,
> Or solace his defects. No need that thou
> Shouldst propagat, already infinite;
> And through all numbers absolute, though One;
> But Man by number is to manifest
> His *single imperfection*, and *beget*
> *Like of his like*, his Image multipli'd,
> In *unitie defective*, which requires
> Collateral love, and deerest amitie."[8]

Every male laments his "single imperfection." Every male seeks a consort with whom he can sort. (So does every female, but hers is not my narrative now.) Every male is untimely ripped from his mother's womb, and, even if he forgives her, he cannot escape the consequences: he must "beget / Like of his like, his image multipli'd, / In unitie defective."

Shakespeare and Milton learned from their medieval countryman Chaucer something of their poetic understanding of *eros* (sexual desire) and *eris* (strife) – both words derive from the same root meaning "to separate, adjoin" ("Greek *erasthai*, to love [< 'be separated from']"), that condition of separated attachment and attached separation that we euphemistically call "marriage." Few poets between Virgil and Milton, including Dante, grasped, as did Chaucer, so nearly completely the pitilessness of our sexual condition, which is still just as pitiless though we grow old and cynically project it onto adolescence. As a recent *National Geographic* article reported, the brain chemistry of someone "in love" resembles nothing so much as the brain chemistry of a madman, and few of us remain "in love" for the simple reason that our chemistry cannot support it – neurotransmitters are finite, serotonin especially.[9]

There are those of us, nonetheless, who try anyway, heroically. Troilus, Chaucer says, was "Trewe as stiel in ech condicioun" (*T&C* 5.831). The famous *effictio* (literary portrait) in which this line is found conveys a great deal of crucial information for understanding Chaucer's poem, but in the context of masculinity studies, this is the line that matters the most. Here is the machismo that will not let go:

---

8   My text of *Paradise Lost* is *The Riverside Milton*, ed. Roy Flannagan (Cambridge, MA: Houghton Mifflin, 1998), 8.381–85, 389–92, and 414–26 (emphasis added).
9   Lauren Slater, "True Love," *National Geographic* 209.2 (2006): 32–49, at 38b.

> And certeynly in storye it is yfounde,
> That Troilus was nevere unto no wight,
> As in his tyme, in no degree secounde
> In durryng don that longeth to a knyght.
> Al myghte a geant passen hym of myght,
> His herte ay with the first and with the beste
> Stood paregal, to durre don that hym leste. (*T&C* 5.834–40)

Just so, Shakespeare's Troilus, at the end, will exclaim:

> "For th' love of all the gods,
> Let's leave the hermit pity with our mother,
> And, when we have our armours buckled on,
> The venomed vengeance ride upon our swords,
> Spur them to ruthful work, rein them from ruth.
> ... ...
> I do not speak of flight, of fear of death,
> But dare all imminence that gods and men
> Address their dangers in.
> ... ...
> – You vile abominable tents
> Thus proudly pitched upon our Phrygian plains,
> Let Titan rise as early as he dare,
> I'll through and through you! And, thou great-sized coward [Achilles],
> No space of earth shall sunder our two hates.
> I'll haunt thee like a wicked conscience still,
> That mouldeth goblins swift as frenzy's thoughts."
>   (*Tro.* 5.3.46–50; 5.11.12–14; 23–29)

Separation hardened to steel, pitiless "like a wicked conscience," makes the man. It also unmakes him:

> "Thorugh which I se that clene out of youre mynde
> Ye han me cast; and I ne kan nor may,
> For al this world, withinne myn herte fynde
> To unloven yow a quarter of a day!" (*T&C* 5.1695–98)

A great part of what distinguishes Chaucer as a poet echoes in the phrase "unloven yow": the very grammar teaches us the dehumanizing steel-likeness that has overtaken Troilus, as if we were watching a sci-fi scenario of molten metal consuming a man from within until it turns him into a macabre monolith, unable to *un-*.

Pandarus has no idea of what he wrought when he "fond his contenaunce / As for to looke upon an old romaunce" (*T&C* 3.979–80). He thinks that he has written a story of sexual consummation, a romance to pass a summer season. In the end, he pays for his mistake, precisely, "'I kan namore seye'" (*T&C* 5.1743), lapsing into silence as he wishes his niece dead ("'fro this world, almyghty god I preye / Delivere hire soon'" [*T&C* 5.1742–43]). Silence for him is almost the same as the death he imprecates upon her since voyeurism and vicariousness, so dependent on discourse and intercourse, are his *modi vivendi*. But his fate instructs us precisely in what Chaucer knew with which to teach Shakespeare – there is no escape in language:

PANDARUS: Why should our endeavour be so desired and the performance so loathed? What verse for it? What instance for it? Let me see,

> Full merrily the humble-bee doth sing
> Till he hath lost his honey and his sting,
> And being once subdued in armèd tail,
> Sweet honey and sweet notes together fail.
> … … … … … … …
> As many as be here of Pandar's hall,
> Your eyes, half out, weep out at Pandar's fall.
> … … … … … … …
> Brethren and sisters of the hold-door trade,
> Some two months hence my will shall here be made.
> … … … … … … …
> Till then I'll sweat and seek about for eases,
> And at that time bequeath you my diseases.[10]

To lose both honey and sting, to lose the media by which you overcome separation, manipulate it to your satisfaction, is to be left with nothing but your diseases to leave your brethren and sisters, separation now legacy as it was (and is) at birth inheritance.

PANDARUS: What a pair of spectacles is here! Let me embrace you too. "O heart," as the goodly saying is,

> "O heart, heavy heart,
> Why sigh'st thou without breaking?"
> where he answers again,
> "Because thou canst not ease thy smart
> *By friendship nor by speaking.*"

There was never a truer rhyme. Let us cast away nothing, for we may live to have need of such a verse. (*Tro.* 4.5.13–21; emphasis added)

The helplessness of speaking to reduce separation between us ("There was never a truer rhyme") is galling to us just in that our bodies, like the heart in the rhyme, are so heavy. If only words were winged and might fly like the soul to join the beloved's soul,[11] but then, that really is maudlin, we know, when we read Criseyde's letter, "Th'entente is al, and nat the lettres space" (*T&C* 5.1630) and listen to Troilus summarize Cressida's:

---

10 The text of Shakespeare's *Troilus and Cressida* is unusually vexed, even for Shakespeare, and I quote here from the Quarto's variant ending to the play (p. 776 B. [unlineated]).

11 On the importance of this Platonic and neo-Platonic image to Chaucer's *Troilus*, see my "*Troilus and Criseyde*: The Falcon in the Mew," *Typology and English Medieval Literature*, ed. Hugh Keenan, *Georgia State Literary Studies* 7 (New York: AMS, 1992), pp. 149–68.

> (*tearing the letter*)
> "Words, words, mere words, no matter from the heart.
> Th'effect doth operate another way.
> Go, wind, to wind: there turn and change together.
> My love with words and errors still she feeds,
> But edifies another with her deeds." (*Tro.* 5.3.111–15)

It is important not to ignore how shocking "edifies" is. Masculinism and patriarchalism clang together in that one word (which, note well, is also an exact anagram of "deifies"), the word of the construction of cities and dynasties, and they clang there to tell us how far down Troilus sinks into the ideology that shrouds and mystifies (masculine) separation: an*other* man wins the city and the dynasty, goddamn him.

In the film *When Harry Met Sally*, when Harry and Sally finally have sex, the scene fades to their post-coital snuggling in bed. Sally under the covers smiling all over hugs Harry and rubs against him like a contented cat. Harry lies looking straight up (the camera angle is from above), one leg out of bed, foot on the floor, ready for flight – and on his face a look of cornered disbelief sufficient to tell the story of separation almost by itself.[12] Here is Shakespeare's version of the same scene:

> TROILUS: To bed, to bed! Sleep lull those pretty eyes
> And give as soft attachment to thy senses
> As infants empty of all thought.
> … … … … … … … …
> CRESSIDA: Are you aweary of me?
> TROILUS: O Cressida! But that the busy day,
> Waked by the lark, hath roused the ribald crows,
> And dreaming night will hide our joys no longer,
> I would not from thee.
> … … … … … … … …
> CRESSIDA: Prithee, tarry. *You men will never tarry.*
> O foolish Cressid! *I might have still held off,*
> *And then you would have tarried.*
> $\qquad\qquad\qquad$ (*Tro.* 4.2.4–6; 9–13; 17–19; emphasis added)

Men will never tarry, true; cigarettes and coffee are always somewhere nearby. There are crows out there. There are Greeks. There are construction sites. In fact, let there be anything but lying here in this bed, connected.

So it goes. Damaged by separation, terrified of connection, the masculine edifies/deifies his palace, hardly unaware it is also his prison (however many remote controls he may own). Chaucer's Troilus, although he may resemble steel, is hardly without feeling of his predicament:

"But ende I wol, as Edippe, in derknesse
My sorwful lif, and dyen in distresse.

O wery goost, that errest to and fro,
Why nyltow fleen out of the wofulleste
Body that evere myghte on grounde go?
O soule, lurkynge in this wo, unneste,
Fle forth out of myn herte, and lat it breste,
And folowe alwey Criseyde, thi lady dere.
Thi righte place is now no lenger here." (*T&C* 4.300–8)

If anyone were ever to transcend *Harry*-ism, it would be, we might propose, Chaucer's Troilus; certainly, it appears that he would always follow Criseyde, his right place. But Chaucer cautions us. Troilus's self-assimilation to Oedipus, his lust for suicide, his desire to fly (above, note 11), to un-nest (notice again the fetish of the negative prefix, *un-*), unmistakably suggest the psychopathology of the automaton, the machine capable of only one task at a time. If the cure for *Harry*-ism should be automatism, then the impost with which separation taxes males is arguably insupportably heavy. Where is the right place between a life of flight and a life of robotic obsession?

In some of the most extraordinary language in English literature, Troilus explains to Cressida:

"This is the monstruosity in love, lady – that the will is infinite and the execution confined; that the desire is boundless and the act a slave to limit. ... Praise us as we are tested; allow us as we prove. Our head shall go bare till merit crown it. No perfection in reversion shall have a praise in present. We will not name desert before his birth, and being born his addition shall be humble. Few words to fair faith. Troilus shall be such to Cressid as what envy can say worst shall be a mock for his truth; and what truth can speak truest, not truer than Troilus." (*Tro.* 3.2.77–80; 87–95)

"Not truer than Troilus"; "as trewe as stiel in ech condicioun"; Chaucer and Shakespeare, equally, and the one in part as a student and reader of the other, grasp with stunning precision the monstruosity in love – its name is man. Exaggerative, boastful, macho, and, above all, insecure (is mine as long as his?), man turns love into a lair for monsters: "will ... infinite ... execution confined ... desire ... boundless ... the act a slave to limit." Whether it is Chaucer's Troilus fainting in Criseyde's bed as he lies to her about Horaste, needing help in even removing his shirt before copulating (*T&C* 3.1095–134), or whether it is Shakespeare's Troilus mewling pseudo-pity for mothers:

"Let it not be believed, for womanhood.
Think: we had mothers. Do not give advantage
To stubborn critics, apt without a theme
For depravation to square the general sex
By Cressid's rule. Rather, think this not Cressid." (*Tro.* 5.2.131–35)

– we have before us, in visions, it may be, almost too clear to see, the terrible insecurity of the divided, separate male, in (threatened) conjunction with the right place of the female genital: "vagina," it is called, Latin for "sheath," the sheath of the man's sword,[13] but what if his sword should fail? what then of his word? – "and what truth can speak truest, not truer than Troilus"?

In Book 1 of Chaucer's poem, Troilus first sees Criseyde in the temple of Minerva, the right place that is not "the right place":

> Withinne the temple he wente hym forth pleyinge,
> This Troilus,
> … … … … … … …
> And upon cas bifel that thorugh a route
> His eye percede, and so depe it wente,
> Til on Criseyde it smot, and ther it stente.
>
> And sodeynly he wax therwith astoned,
> And gan hir bet biholde in thrifty wise.
> "O mercy, God," thoughte he, "wher hastow woned,
> That art so feyr and goodly to devise?"
> Therwith his herte gan to sprede and rise,
> And softe sighed, lest men myghte hym here,
> And caught ayeyn his firste pleyinge chere.
>
> *(T&C 1.267–68; 271–80)*

The erotic violence in these lines is staggering. His eye pierces, penetrates deeply, like a sword, smites Criseyde, and he, having seen the Medusa, is petrified, "astoned,"[14] even as female sexuality causes erection in him, "gan to sprede and rise."[15] *Eris* is always close by *eros*. Chaucer understands that Minerva is no help: offspring of parthenogenesis, the illusion of androgenesis, the female without any need of femaleness, her virginity amounts to little more than provocation; she punishes Medusa when Poseidon rapes Medusa on the floor of her, Minerva's, temple since she can hardly punish her uncle, brother of Zeus (it is always the woman's fault, even when the virgin goddess of wisdom is attending).[16] The temple of Minerva is the site of rape, of erotic violence, and even as the great horse/penis will penetrate the quasi-hymeneal wall of Troy once Ulysses has stolen Minerva's Palladium from the hapless Trojans, so Troilus has already raped Criseyde with and in his imagination, although he is too naive and un-self-aware to know it.

---

[13] Watkins, 94[b], notes that the IE origin of the word *vagina* is a stem that means "to break, split, bite" and observes that the Latin word means "sheath (probably made of a split piece of wood)."

[14] On the pun in "astoned," and its importance to Chaucer, see my essay, "Chaucer and Medusa: The *Franklin's Tale*," *ChauR* 21.2 (1986): 74–90; reprinted in *New Casebooks: Chaucer*, eds. Valerie Allen and Ares Axiotis (New York: St. Martin's Press, 1997), pp. 242–52.

[15] See, further, *The Medusa Reader*, eds. Marjorie Garber and Nancy Vickers (London: Routledge, 2003), chapters 15, 16, and 18.

[16] Ovid, *Metamorphoses* 4.790–803 – "neve hoc inpune fuisset" ("that the deed might be punished as was due" – 800), trans. Frank Justus Miller (Cambridge, MA: Harvard University Press, 1916). Miller's translation is accurate, but note that Ovid's expression is in the negative.

It is Pandarus who is aware, hardly naive, "Pandarus that wel koude eche a deel / Th'olde daunce, and euery point therinne" (*T&C* 3.694–95):

> "for the am I bicomen,
> Bitwixen game and ernest, swich a meene
> As maken wommen unto men to comen;
> Al sey I nought, thow wost wel what I meene.
> For the have I my nece, of vices cleene,
> So fully maad thi gentilesse triste,
> That al shal ben right as thiselven liste." (*T&C* 3.253–59)

Pandarus does all the lubricating, and we know how much he enjoys it by the very protesting-too-much that he indulges in his apparent remorse:

> "And were it wist that I, thorugh myn engyn,
> Hadde in my nece yput this fantasie,
> To doon thi lust and holly to ben thyn,
> Whi, al the world upon it wolde crie,
> And seyn that I the werste trecherie
> Dide in this cas that evere was bigonne,
> And she forlost, and thow right nought ywonne." (*T&C* 3.274–80)

Every man loves his own "engyn" and the "fantasie" it affords him. He need not literally indulge "solitary sex,"[17] to have always to hand this potential escape from separateness. And it should hardly surprise us that Troilus becomes an exact copy of his friend Pandarus:

> "And that thow knowe I thynke nought ne wene
> That this servise a shame be or jape,
> I have my faire suster, Polixene,
> Cassandre, Eleyne, or any of the frape,
> Be she nevere so faire or wel yshape,
> Tel me which thow wilt of everychone,
> To han for thyn, and lat me thanne allone." (*T&C* 3.407–13)

Women, after all, are really only a herd ("frape") of cows, however a man may affect one of them in particular, and so "lat [him] thanne allone." That such sordidness should actually be invisible to Troilus – "'this that thow doost, calle it gentilesse, / Compassioun, and felawship, and triste'" (*T&C* 3.402–3) – so that he can deceive himself so thoroughly – "'Departe it so, for wyde-wher is wist / How that ther is diversite required / Bytwixen thynges like'" (*T&C* 3.404–6) – can only shock us if we actually take the trouble to stand outside the masculinist, patriarchal system of "trafficking in women."[18] If we remain within the pale of delusions by which insecure masculinity protects itself from

---

17 See Thomas Laqueur, *Solitary Sex: A Cultural History of Masturbation* (New York: Zone Books, 2004).
18 Gayle Rubin, "The Traffic in Women: Notes on the 'Political Economy' of Sex," *Toward an Anthropology of Women*, ed. Rayna Reiter (New York: Monthly Review, 1975), pp. 157–210.

separation and its myriad anxieties, we can hardly doubt that Troilus just loves his good buddy and wants to get him a girl the way he got him a girl.

This is to have arrived at the level of Thersites ("[a] slave whose gall coins slanders like a mint" [*Tro.* 1.3.193]), which is more or less the sewer. Just listen for a moment to the slanders fly one after the other from the sewer: "All the argument is a whore and a cuckold" (*Tro.* 2.3.71); "Sweet draught! 'Sweet,' quoth 'a? Sweet sink, sweet sewer" (*Tro.* 5.1.72–73); "How the devil Luxury with his fat rump and potato finger tickles these together! Fry, lechery, fry!" (*Tro.* 5.2.55–57); "A proof of strength she could not publish more / Unless she said, 'My mind is now turned whore'" (*Tro.* 5.2.115–16); "Lechery, lechery, still, wars and lechery! Nothing else holds fashion" (*Tro.* 5.2.196–97); "Hold thy whore, Grecian! Now for thy whore, Trojan! Now the sleeve, now the sleeve!" (*Tro.* 5.4.22–23); "lechery eats itself" (*Tro.* 5.4.32);

> That dissembling abominable varlet Diomed has got that same scurvy doting foolish young knave's sleeve of Troy there in his helm. I would fain see them meet, that that same young Trojan ass that loves the whore there might send that Greekish whoremasterly villain with the sleeve back to the dissembling luxurious drab of a sleeveless errand. (*Tro.* 5.4.2–8)

When we have caught our breaths and cleared our nostrils, we can easily see that this is not Chaucer's version of the story. To be sure, Chaucer knows how sordid the story is (so did Boccaccio), he is hardly deceived, but his examination of the anguish of separation has a different agenda, one best summarized, I think, by the conclusion he writes:

> Thow oon, and two, and thre, eterne on lyve,
> That regnest ay in thre, and two, and oon,
> Uncircumscript, and al maist circumscrive,
> Us from visible and invisible foon
> Defende, and to thy mercye, everichon,
> So make us, Jesus, for thi mercy digne,
> For love of mayde and moder thyn benigne. Amen.
>
> (*T&C* 5.1863–69)

Mercy and maternity matter much to him; and though this will not exonerate him from feminist rage (nor probably can it), he seems, at least as far as I can intuit from his words, to have had faith in the working-through of separation – it has to do with his humor (in all senses).

Of Shakespeare I am far less sure. I have for years read feminist critiques,[19] some of them withering, and often it seems that nothing he wrote is immune to feminist outrage.[20] But I may misunderstand. After all, I am masculine, too, and I am heterosexual, I know, having worked through that question in my life

---

[19] See, perhaps most moving, Janet Adelman, *Suffocating Mothers: Fantasies of Maternal Origin in Shakespeare's Plays, Hamlet to* The Tempest (New York: Routledge, 1992).

[20] See, e.g., Jean Howard's introduction to *Cymbeline* in *The Norton Shakespeare*, based on the Oxford Edition, ed. Stephen Greenblatt et al. (New York: Norton, 1997), pp. 2962–63 especially.

to a certainty that mainly now just seams my separateness. But if I do misunderstand, I finally find myself less troubled by that than I am by the understanding that I have gathered from decades of reading the Shakespeare canon and that I find illuminated best by Stanley Cavell:

> The answer I have depends on taking the existence or occurrence of the woman's satisfaction (the satisfaction of our feminine side?) as the essential object or event of the skeptical question: Is she satisfied and is the satisfaction directed to me? There is no satisfaction for me (my masculine side) apart from a favorable conclusion here; it is a conclusion that must be conferred, given, not one that I can cause or determine on the basis of my senses. My senses go out; satisfaction happens in my absence, only in it, by it. To elicit this gift, the extreme claim of male activeness, thus requires the man's acceptance of his absolute passiveness.
>
> I have already indicated that Othello is destroyed by the requirement. It was within his play that this line of thought first began for me, specifically in suggesting that the pivot of *Othello's* interpretation of skepticism is Othello's placing of a finite woman in the place made and left by Descartes for God.
>
> The next step was the conviction that Leontes' jealousy is a cover for his doubt over whether his children are his, and that this is in turn a cover for doubt whether Hermione's satisfaction is of him, whether it proves or destroys his existence. The present step in this line of thought begins with my linking of the developments of cinema and of psychoanalysis as both originating in the sufferings of women, in particular in the form of a conviction in the woman's unknownness, hence in her existence, and that these developments may therefore be said to form a late stage in the progress of skepticism in the West, that history (assuming there is such thing, or one thing) that begins no later than Descartes and Shakespeare.[21]

I consider this meditation one of the most sublime I know on the cruelty of sexual division, cruelty, all the same, that all of us, women as well as men, must acknowledge and strive to transmute into love. When Shakespeare, in his even more powerful version, writes that

> So they lov'd, as love in twain
> Had the essence but in one,
> Two distincts, division none.
> Number there in love was slain.
>
> ("The Phoenix and the Turtle," 25–28)

the impossibility of my ever knowing what she feels when I am inside her is driven home hard by the pure vision of utter fantasy – there can never be "two distincts, division none," *never*. There can never be that moment when "either was the other's mine" ("The Phoenix and the Turtle," 36). There will always come that moment, in Chaucer's simple (and simply devastating) phrase, when "'now fele I that myn herte moot a-two'" (*T&C* 4.1475).

---

21   Stanley Cavell, *Disowning Knowledge in Seven Plays of Shakespeare* (Cambridge: Cambridge University Press, 2003), pp. 34–35.

If I understand him at all, this truth hurt Shakespeare so badly, drove him so relentlessly, that he could never, the feminists are right, leave the (m)other alone. But I feel, at the same time, a humanity in the seeker not unlike that of his medieval countryman (perhaps because they both were Catholics?[22]), if a humanity defined by loss (is there any other definition for us who suffer the "kalendes of chaunge" [*T&C* 5.1634]?), loss of a flesh that might inw*o*rd itself in the unity that departs from history.

---

[22] On the issue of Shakespeare's relation to Catholicism, a topic of immense scholarly interest in recent years, there is far too much work to cite for any sort of summary. In my own reading so far, I have found helpful Richard Dutton, Alison Gail Findlay, Richard Wilson, eds., *Lancastrian Shakespeare: Region, Religion and Patronage* (Manchester: Manchester University Press, 2004), as well as their *Lancastrian Shakespeare: Theatre and Religion* (Manchester: Manchester University Press, 2004); see, too, Dennis Taylor and David Beauregard, eds., *Shakespeare and the Culture of Christianity in Early Modern England* (New York: Fordham University Press, 2003).

Index

CHAUCER STUDIES

Printed in the United States
151026LV00001B/16/P